José Ferrer de Couto

Enough of war

The question of slavery conclusively and satisfactorily solved, as regards humanity

and the permanent interests of present owners

José Ferrer de Couto

Enough of war

The question of slavery conclusively and satisfactorily solved, as regards humanity and the permanent interests of present owners

ISBN/EAN: 9783337131661

Printed in Europe, USA, Canada, Australia, Japan

Cover: Foto ©ninafisch / pixelio.de

More available books at **www.hansebooks.com**

ENOUGH OF WAR!

ENOUGH OF WAR!

THE QUESTION OF

SLAVERY

CONCLUSIVELY AND SATISFACTORILY SOLVED,

AS REGARDS

HUMANITY AT LARGE

AND THE

PERMANENT INTERESTS OF PRESENT OWNERS

BY

D. JOSE FERRER DE COUTO,

Knight of the Order of Santiago; Commander of the Royal American Order of Isabel la Católica; Knight of the Order of Charles the III · Honorary Member of the Mexican Geographical and Statistical Society· Fellow of the Commission of the History of Spanish Infantry, of the Royal Academy of Archæology and Geography of Madrid,
&c., &c., &c.

NEW YORK:
S. HALLET, PRINTER No. 107 FULTON STREET.
1864.

Entered according to Act of Congress, in the year 1863, by
DON JOSE FERRER DE COUTO,
In the Clerk's Office of the District Court of the United States,
for the Southern District of New York

PREFACE.*

On commencing the perusal of this work the reader should not be startled if he finds therein some doctrines at variance with his own opinions, nor should he be discouraged at the multiplicity of details in which it abounds.

Any subject to be properly and thoroughly comprehended requires to be studied with care and deliberation; and the question discussed in these pages is of such importance that it is well worthy of being understood. Let then the reader give his attention to this work, and peruse its pages in a spirit of investigation, and with the impartiality of justice. Let him analyze the arguments; weigh the reasons; and compare with them his own opinions, *pro* and *con*. Let him beware of being misled by his own passions and by the sophisms resulting from them, though they may appear in the garb of truth; and lastly, let him subject his deductions to the test of a thorough ratiocination, for by these means, added to the conviction that this work originated in a benevolent desire to restore the shattered interests of the country, and to re-establish therein that peace which is the basis of prosperity in all

---

(*) This "Preface" was written before the peace project had been spoken of at all as founded on probability. Circumstances have since occurred which are favorable to that idea, as will be seen in the last chapter of this work; nevertheless I have decided not to alter a single word in the Preface, for the reason that I wish to retain integral the spontaneousness of its inspiration by a generous sentiment, and, because, such as it is, it forms a code of doctrines which is applicable to any other nation under similar circumstances.

enlightened nations, he will arrive at a discriminating knowledge of the subject, which may, perhaps, be of service to him.

"Search the Scriptures," said our Saviour to those who dared to question the authority of his divine mission on earth; and I will here apply that injunction to human writings also, for I contend that, as society at large is regulated by the knowledge derived from such works, the ignorant have no right to avoid the perusal of what may enlighten their understandings by combating their narrow opinions, and the learned should not contemn a work which is the result of many years of study and experience.

This work treats of the great and momentous question which has divided the people of a great nation into two different sections and arrayed them in arms one against the other, viz: *the civil status of the Negro in America*, a question which for nearly a century has kept the minds of the most humane and preeminent men in a continual state of excitement. It treats of Humanity and of Interest: of Order and of Labor: of Slavery, and in fine, of Freedom in its truest sense.

But let not the reader imagine that I intend merely to indulge in fruitless declamation, following the ordinary routine of analysis by which every subject is handled and none decided. No! after all that has been written and said on these subjects, another book is not needed for such a purpose. My work is not to be the apotheosis of some metaphysical ideas; its purpose is to expose a very great evil and to point out the most certain remedy.

I have seen the sectarians of two opposite doctrines exert all their energies and display the most extraordinary activity in favor of their respective causes: I have listened to their speeches, read their publications, studied their works, and consulted their first statesmen personally and by letter; I have compared both systems and weighed their respective interests in the scales of justice. And by this attention, this spirit of investigation which gave the first impulse to my movements and encouraged my lucubrations, this eagerness to inquire after truth and to give the feeble support of my approval to those measures which should appear most expedient, I have become convinced that, as yet, neither of the belligerents have any idea what these measures should be.

Each party, obstinately adhering to its original creed, persists in supporting it and in endeavoring to force it upon the enemy. "*The evil exists*" say those of one party "*and it must and shall be eradicated, even though it should be necessary to destroy the people who uphold it.*" "*The evil is an institution which is absolutely necessary to our social state,*" say their opponents, "*and we know of no moral sentiment which can rightfully demand from us the sacrifice of even the smallest fraction of that necessary though calamitous institution.*"

And in the meanwhile, in numberless places which have hitherto been the centers of industry and prosperity, the shriek of the locomotive has been supplanted by the martial tones of the war-trumpet and the clashing of arms; while the cannon thunders and its death dealing messengers speed on their horrible mission of havoc and desolation; the fields with their plentiful fruits are inundated with blood and magnificent cities fall amid carnage and ruins.

And it is thus that an enlightened people consider their interests! It is thus that a domestic difficulty is being settled by a nation which has hitherto been distinguished for its respect and observance of the laws enacted by its representatives! It is thus that a question of political law is discussed by a nation which has always led the van in all the liberal ideas which belong to the spirit of modern times, and has been a model and a guide to all others! And the entire energies of that nation are directed solely to the improvement of engines of war that the contending parties may the more effectually carry on the work of mutual destruction! And no one, absolutely no one, thinks of seeking out a remedy, which should be both conciliating and effectual, against that fearful scourge which is never perpetual except among barbarians!

Oh! who can tell what divine purpose is being unfolded among the most favored of God's creatures by the desolation which now reigns in the Northern countries of the New World. For if we reflect on the habitual clearness of mind for which these people have been noted, if we take into consideration their wellknown spirit of aggrandizement, (which they sometimes carried to a dangerous extent), and the circumspection with which they almost invariably proceeded in all home questions, to a Divine purpose alone can we attribute the blindness which has fallen on their eyes, the fury which rages in their breasts, and the blood-thirsty persistency which deprives them of their reasoning faculties.

But if the downfall of this great nation has not been decreed by the infinite wisdom of the Almighty; if it be still possible, by means of a humane and considerate policy, to settle this question decisively and satisfactorily, with due respect to the interests of both parties, then let all who are interested read this work and ponder well on its contents, for perhaps the remedy proposed in these pages may be found useful.

In this work will be found the history of the negroes in Africa, before the discovery of America, and from its perusal the reader may perhaps be led to justify the practice of redeeming Africans, and to appreciate the sentiments of humanity in which it originated.

The reader will find next a full explanation of the original foundation of the trade in Africans: its progress and development: the laws which related to it, and the alterations made in those laws. In order that these facts may appear in their proper light before the tribunal of history, I take care to demonstrate the practical as well as legal state of the negroes, whether laborers or freemen, in the Spanish colonies; and in support of these statements I bring forward the testimony of all the ancient and modern laws which have existed, in those colonies, and, it may be, in others.

These details are of the utmost importance as they will enable all persons to understand properly the ideas which are now being discussed on the battle field; for which reason I dwell on them with extreme minuteness, and also comment on the effects which have resulted from the absolute freedom of the negroes in all the places where it has been unconditionally granted.

And as this subject has shaken the foundations and threatened the very existence of many countries in the Western hemisphere, it may readily be supposed that I shall not neglect to point out the real causes which have advocated the emancipation of the enslaved negroes, as well as the apparent ones which have effected this emancipation in some places and which are intended to produce similar results in all parts of the world.

If the reader does not become wearied by this time, and if the drawing up of this plan does not appear to him entirely unskillful, then let him continue to read and he will find the treaties made with England for the suppression of the redemption, and next, he will see how these treaties have been void and of no effect since they were first drawn up.

The violation of the respect due to international relations will pain the reader if it does not cause him to blush, when he considers that with regard to this question, deceit and craftiness have taken the place of truth, and an ignominious law has been substituted for the respect which is mutually due among all civilized nations.

And next will be seen how insignificant cruisers, leagued against the laws, can set at defiance the fleets of the most powerful nations, and traverse the vast expanse of the ocean without any other protection than their boldness, but incited strongly by the profit held out to them—by the violation of treaties the execution of which has proved utterly impracticable.

Having come to the end of the first part of this work, which contains the documentary history of that institution whose name is hateful to all because it recalls to mind the odious tyranny and the repugnant barbarism which reigned over the civilized nations before the light of Christianity shone upon them, and which prevails to the present time in the countries where the negroes are redeemed, the reader's attention is particularly called to the next subject, that being the exposition of a scheme which conciliates the extremes that have come into collision. The plan I propose destroys slavery, in its true acceptation, and guarantees the organized labor of negroes; it satisfies all moral exigencies and serves to consolidate property; it opens the gates of freedom, by redemption, to the victims of barbarism, and introduces Christian civilization into those lands into which it has never penetrated; it imposes silence on the philanthropic abolitionists since it deprives them of all reason to continue their clamor; it effectually removes the doubts and apprehensions of the wealthy proprietors, who have, hitherto, refused to adopt a measure which is evidently so suitable, and morally, so unobjectionable, merely because they had no practical knowledge of its workings.

I am well aware that this project will meet with opposition from two contradictory elements which have ever appeared to combat all manner of reform or progress, viz.: custom and doubt; or, in other words, prejudice and mistrust.

To attempt to perpetuate and legalize an order of things which, to all appearances, is contrary to the spirit of civilization and to the treaties existing among powerful nations, at a time when one of these nations is endeavoring to bring about the abolition and final extinction of the system of organized labor of the negroes in America, is an undertaking which certainly appears superior to the comprehension of an unknown and humble individual.

And no doubt it will be proclaimed as such, in scorn, by the majority of my readers, who still adhere to obsolete prejudices; but there are others who will undoubtedly remember that the greatest events and the most important undertakings have originated with names previously unknown to the world.

To discover if a thing or measure ought to be adopted it is only necessary to ascertain, in the first place, whether it will prove useful, and, in the next place, whether it is just; and this novel project which I desire to introduce is not only useful but of absolute necessity; and is not only remarkable for its justice, but without it a total disregard in all questions of social morality and international resspect would prevail.

The practice of offering pretexts for the purpose of misconstrueing an agreement, whenever owing to passing events one of the contracting parties wishes to cajole the other, is nothing more than a departure from truth, the infraction of the laws, and the most positive evidence that the agreement which gives rise to such pretexts is not based upon justice and true morality.

And, in this question of the negroes, who has not experienced feelings of astonishment, indignation and skeptical contempt on seeing the inconsistency with which the most accomodating concessions were made to certain international demands, at the very time when an entirely opposite course was pursued towards other nations, with regard to the identical question.

Even at this time, when the war caused by slavery in the United States has become fully developped, we have all seen in a celebrated document, two different doctrines, which, though they are entirely incompatible in their nature, could have emanated only from the same principle and the same law.

By this "Proclamation" the institution of slavery was declared totally abolished, as a punishment for rebellion, in such States as should refuse to return to the Union within a given time, while in the others, it was declared permanent, as a reward for their loyalty to the Constitution of the Republic.

It is not my purpose to enter, at present, into an analysis of these antithetical measures for the purpose of submitting their legality to the test of the express and definite provisions of the laws. But, nevertheless, I can not refrain from pointing out their inconsistencies, in order to deduce therefrom, as a positive and undeniable inference, that the cause of the abolitionists is not so indisputably just as it appears, and that the war is not so justifiable as might be desired in view of the principle in which it originated.

And, notwithstanding, slavery (if the organized labor of negroes can with truth be named thus), ought not to be tolerated among the enlightened nations of the XIX century, it being contrary to the Divine law, and also, opposed to the moral progress of mankind. While, on the other hand, humanity ought not to consent, in this era of progress, that a degraded race should continue undisturbed in the possession of vast regions, where their normal condition is a state of warfare, and where their victories are celebrated by human sacrifices and cannibalism.

Let the reader, then, direct his attention to that part of my work which treats of reformatory measures, and should these appear useful, let them not be considered impracticable. Should the obstinacy of any party prove a stumbling block in his way, then let him and all others who desire to render a just tribute to social morality and to their own interests, lift up their voices in defence of those measures.

The experiments which have been made, for the last half century, to suppress the redemption of negroes and to destroy slavery, have invariably produced results contrary to the intentions which originated them: a disastrous war in which all principles appear to be under discussion, while not one of them has been defined with sufficient clearness: the prospect of a total dissolution of that Republic which had hitherto adopted as the basis of its political existence, the famous motto *E pluribus unum:* the contradictions of the law, and the degrading pretexts which reflect equal discredit on those who apply them as on those who profit by them: all these are appealing to the public to open their eyes and look at things in their proper light; to fix their attention and devote all their faculties to the proper comprehension of the truth with its highest attributes; and to subject all these matters to a thorough ratiocination and draw thence the most positive and unanswerable conclusions.

And should the self love or the irresistible vanity of the extreme parties also rise in opposition against a new code formed on the équitable, conciliating and moral principle which inspires this work: should the people of the United States, i. e., the most violent partisans of both schools, believe that a just and reasonable adjustment of their difficulties is incompatible with the integrality of their exclusive opinions, let these fanatics divest themselves of their passions and open the history of all human strife and contentions, for therein they will learn that the appeal to arms has never solved any social problem of positive transcendency and permanent character.

The arguments of force and of arms may oppress, but they cannot convince, and when they are employed against a common idea, universal sentiment or positive interests, they cannot be of long duration. Their supremacy is almost invariably stained with blood; their fruits are devastation and misery as long as they last, and their ruinous end is an axiom which time has demonstrated and made evident.

During the first years of a civil war it is difficult, if not impossible, for either party to acquire a correct knowledge of its own strength, and to form an approximate estimate of the definite results of the strife. Each one considers itself omnipotent, or at least invincible, as it compares its power with that of the opponent; and, nevertheless, when years have rolled back into the past, and blood has flowed in torrents, and armies are being anihilated, and weariness commences to appear: when all resources are exhausted, and credit is lost through the extravagance and waste which attend war, and moral order is disturbed by the same cause, and society is losing its healthful customs and adopting others which threaten to destroy all civil liberty and material order in the future, truth ever appears, with sorrowful and remorseful aspect, amongst the shattered remains of a ruined power, and, while fanaticism flees abashed from her presence, concessions of principles and of interest are made, which are immeasurably greater than those which had formerly been considered unnecessary and humiliating.

This is the history of all litigation, whether individual or collective: political as well as civil.

At the commencement of a lawsuit no litigant consents to compromise his right for half a dollar less than the amount of his claim; but in the end there will hardly be found one who would not rather have relinquished his right were it but to secure the half of his claim free of expense.

Let then all fanatics abandon their contumacy and sophistry, and believe that this question ought to be analyzed and decided according to the practical teachings of past events and of those which common sense predicts for the future.

This is no time for conservative theories when a prudent and equitable reform is demanded by all circumstances: by the barbarism of the negro race, by the spirit of the times, by the morality of public law, by the respect due to legal property, by the duty of re-establishing peace where war now reigns with all its horrors, by the civilization which a barbarous race can acquire through labor and instruction, and, finally, by all the moral and material interests of the New World and of Africa.

The attention of the intelligent and of the lovers of justice is particularly called to this work, in which the extremes, against which said reform is directed, are fully exposed and attested by historical and legal data. They that have ears let them hear,—and they that have eyes let them see, and read with care; for the time spent in the perusal of these pages will be profitably employed in the interest of humanity.

CHAPTER I.

The origin of slavery in primitive times.—Its various characters among the heathens.—Its successive features from the first appearance of Christianity in the countries of the negroes, as those countries were successively discovered.—Causes for redeeming* in those countries, and the reasons justifying the forced labor exacted from the redeemed negroes in America.—The existence of cannibalism among the people of that race and among the greater portion of savage nations shown by abundant historical facts and other proofs as regards Asia, Africa, and America, from the most remote times down to the present day.

THE history of slavery has its origin in the history of war, and the history of war in that of the human race. For men, ever envious of one another and covetous of their neighbors' goods, have since the days of Cain, by an instinct inherent to our fallen nature, been bent upon their own destruction, warring against each other with all the fury that passion kindles in the human heart, and killing their captives either through revenge, or from their superstitious belief in a false religion.

But if the elements of a primitive civilization, in the early days of the world, did not allay the fury of the combatants in war, it at least suggested to them the advantage of sparing the lives of the conquered, in order to benefit themselves by their labor.

Thus the custom of sacrificing numerous victims captured after a bloody contest, was partially abolished in the nations which successively carried the banner of civilization in each epoch of the world; and from that time slavery was established and asserted as a right by all victors.

(*) It should be noticed that the author uses the word *redeem* when he alludes to the *purchase of negroes* in Africa, by the Spaniards.

The use which the nations of antiquity made of this right varied according to the state of their culture, or was adapted to events and circumstances.

Among the Eastern nations the blood of these unhappy victims was considered an acceptable offering to their false gods. The martial spirit of Rome invented amphitheatres where multitudes, thirsting for the sight of bloody scenes, flocked to witness, among other sanguinary exhibitions, the death struggles of a certain number of captives; whilst liberal Greece, less given to these cruel spectacles, employed her slaves in agricultural labors, mechanical and industrial occupations, and oftentimes in the cultivation of the fine arts, acquiring them in trade in such numbers, that in a single province, Attica, there were, at one time, no less than four hundred thousand slaves.[1]

And when we proceed to examine the nations which, at a later period, succeeded those famous empires, though in the dark ages, we find proofs of their influence on the customs of subsequent generations. Among the Scythians, in Italy, and also in France, on the slopes of the Alps, prisoners were enslaved, sacrificed, and sometimes eaten, as is testified to by very respectable authorities.[2] In Spain, where slavery had been imposed upon the natives by the Roman legions, eloquent historical reminiscences of which are preserved, this principle was applied in the war against the Saracens, and was continued afterwards for a very long time; fleets of galleys being manned with the Moors that were captured on the coast of the Levant.

If such was the common practice among enlightened nations, (where the sentiments of charity had been exercised for many centuries, after the preaching of the Gospel in the Christian world, as was the case until the middle of the last century, when Barbary slaves were retained in the Spanish squadron,) what would not happen among those savage nations, where not only the light of the Christian religion had never shone, but where the missionaries of civilization had never been able to penetrate a single mile into the interior of the coast where the Negro traffic was carried on? Alas! in those lands

---

(1) Aristotle's *Politics*, lib. ii, chap. vii.

(2) Pliny: Book vii. chap. ii. Oviedo: *Historia Natural y General de las Indias*: 1st Part. lib. v. chap. iii.

where in the darkness of the primitive rudeness of the world, lives a degenerate race, which of itself is incapable of the moral or material improvement to which all the other races of the human species tend, and which opposes to the social intercourse of civilized nations the insurmountable barrier of its ferocity ; in those lands, I repeat, the wild existence of the individual is subject to no other physical or moral law, than that of chance, if there exist any such laws. For as they have not the most remote notions of the social intercourse by which the other nations of the world are connected, and as, unlike other human beings, the activity of their minds and the vigor of their bodies do not incline them to exertions tending to civilization and improvement, they feel no propensity except for war, a tendency common to all barbarians; and stimulated to frenzy by the sight of blood, they are not withheld from murdering their prisoners by the feeling, unknown to them, of compassion.

For this reason, no doubt, since it was not the inherent consequences of conquest, all the Negroes who fell into the hands of the Spaniards, Catalans, Mayorquinos, Andalucians, and Portuguese, who frequented the coasts of Western Africa from the 13th century down,[1] were in the dark ages considered at once as slaves and lawful prize. And this proceeding became so frequent, and was so thoroughly sanctioned by the moral sentiment of the age, that not only at the court of Henry III., that monarch being in Seville at the time, some magnates presented themselves parading their liveries on the backs of their bondsmen,[2] but many years afterwards, and, of course, before the commencement of the American slave trade, a large number of Portuguese and Spaniards possessed black slaves, especially in the Island of Tercera, in the Canaries, in Lisbon, and in Seville.[3]

---

(1) This date will be distasteful to those who, with their claims of priority, deny what belongs to our navigators in the discovery of those African countries. But with the testimony of Raimundo Lulio, whose knowledge and veracity are admitted by all the world, we may affirm unhesitatingly what is above stated.

(2) Ortiz de Zúñiga: *Anales de Sevilla*, lib. xii. Martinez de la Fuente: *Compendio de la Historia de la India*. lib. i. chap. ii.

(3) Viera: *Historia de las Islas*. Barros: *Asia Portuguesa:* Década primera, lib. i. chap. vi.

So indisputably was this the case, and so habitually was slavery considered by the whites as the natural condition of the Negro, that in 1505, seventeen black slaves were taken to Española (now Santo Domingo) by an expedition of Spanish colonists, and five years afterwards, one hundred more were conveyed to that island in the same capacity; and be it understood that at that time, no arrangement whatever had been made for employing them in the cultivation of the colonial soil, nor had any idea been formed as to the practicability of any such arrangement. This auxiliary force was introduced into the Spanish island under no legal authority, although it is stated that for every Negro composing the second expedition of 1510 to which I allude, two ducats were exacted from the owner as a tax or import duty on each slave.[1]

Father Las Casas,—better known for his hatred of the Spaniards than for his real sympathy for the Indians—commenting with bitter censure on the fact of Columbus having enslaved some of them and brought them to Europe, to be sold, on his return from his first voyage, which Indians, be it remembered, were set free by the magnanimous Queen Isabel I—exclaimed in one of his philanthropic bursts of passion:—"As if the Indians were Africans!"[2]

This exclamation of Las Casas, coupled with his strange morality in relation to the slavery of the Indians, shows the predominant conviction of the times in regard to the justice with which forced servitude was imposed on the Negroes.

Besides, it is known that in "*Aristotle's Politics*," the enslavement of the savage by enlightened nations, is set down as a civilizing, equitable principle of sound morality,[3] and it is known, also, that in the time to which I

---

(1) La Sagra.—*Historia Politica.*—Appendix No. 18.

(2) Navarrete.—*Viajes y Descubrimientos*, &c. Vol. i. Introduction, paragraph 57; and vol. ii. page 112, 145 & 176.

(3) Oviedo, chaps. i. v. and vii., commenting on these passages of Aristotle, in his *Historia Natural y General de las Indias*, says: "It would seem as though they wished to have it understood that the barbarians are by nature slaves of rational men; and as war can be made against beasts, so also against those men who by nature are to be subjected."

As Columbus agreed to a similar philosophy, in which he was so well versed, he hesitated not to bring slaves to Spain, to the number of not less than three hundred Indians from the West Indies when he returned from

allude, and more particularly among the nations of the Latin race, it was a very common custom to study the philosophers of antiquity, and, above all, Aristotle, on account of the contrast between his philosophy and that of Plato, in deducing relative truths, as well as for his indisputable merit and the superiority of his reasoning; therefore, the proceedings of the Spaniards and Portuguese, in relation to enslaving the savages of Western Africa, must have been considered the more natural and justifiable, since the ferocity of those people in all the acts of their lives counselled the measure for the sake of humanity.

I must here observe, in order that it may be borne in mind by those who may make remarks either in public or in private respecting the contents of this work, that the greater part of the African negroes, from the beginning of the world down to the present day, in the most civilized districts, (if such a state of things may be called civilization,) have lived devouring one another in bloody, desolating wars, as have also the Indians of the new world, with the difference, however, between the two regions, that while in America (in Mexico for example) before its discovery by us, a native emperor never desired to subject or reduce to his authority, as he could have done, the hostile nations which surrounded the famous empire of Anahuac, in order that he might always have enemies at hand to fight with, and victims to immolate in the *Teocalis*, the filthy temples of their bloody gods;[1] so the negroes of

---

his first voyage; which slaves, after being sold by him in the Peninsula, were ordered to be set at liberty by her Catholic Majesty (Pizarro y Orellana: *Varones ilustres*, cap. vi. &c.) And our D. Alonzo de Ercilla, as wise as he was just in the practice of the soundest morality, not only by what is gathered from his glorious poem, but also from what is known of his public life, so agrees with what is above stated respecting the enslavement of the savages in war, that he expresses himself thus in one of his outbursts of sincerity:

> In legitimate warfare, at will
> The victor, (though t'ought not to be),
> Is allowed to wound, capture and kill,
> And make bondsmen and slaves of the free.
> For he who is Master, besides
> Of the lives he has fought for and won,
> May dispose of their persons likewise,
> Sure that none will condemn what he's done.
> *Araucana*, canto xxxvii.

(1) "The barbarous custom of the kings of Mexico is not to be forgotten; after being elected, and before their coronation, they went to

those miserable countries, where even now the traffic in their bodies and the ransom of their souls is not entirely suppressed, waged war solely for the object of destroying and eating each other like cannibals, as many of them are.

To demonstrate the facts which are here stated, I have at hand more than sufficient data, though not so many respecting Africa as relating to America, owing to the more particular attention I have paid to the study of the new world than to that of the former continent. Nevertheless, treating of other matters connected with the glories of Spain and the history of its discoveries and conquests, I have consulted many Portuguese historians, and not a few celebrated French, Dutch and English travellers, as well as some from other parts, and the result has been that they all agree with what I have said about the negro, namely, that the more warlike people of the western coast, and of the southwest down to Asia, lived in continued exterminating wars, and indulged in hideous feasts on the flesh of their prisoners. Lest from the omission of quotations it may be thought that the truths I state are interested inventions of mine, I refer the reader to the reliable authority of Juan de Barros, Faria y Sousa, Juan Felix Pereyra, Fernan Lopez, Ruiz de Pina, Damian Goes, and my illustrious and distinguished ancestor, Diego de Couto, as to the best national historians; and also to Mungo Park, Bontekoe, Bernier, Maire, Nicoli, Roberts, Cadamosto, Pyzard and de la Harpe, in the narratives of their different voyages.

All of whom agree that there were among the Africans and Ethiopians many nations of cannibals; so that one might have said of them with much justice what Pedro Martir said of the Indians of the New World, when he learned that the feasts of cannibalism were in use there, viz., " the stories of Lestrigon and Polyphemus, who fed upon human flesh, are no longer doubtful. Read! but let

---

fight with some hostile province, not for the purpose of exhibiting feats of valor in the presence of their vassals, but to secure a large number of prisoners in battle to be sacrificed in their honor on the occasion of the ceremony. So truly was this the case, that Motezuma himself confessed to Hernan Cortes, that he had abstained from subjugating the independent provinces of Mechoacan, Tlascala and Teapeaca, in order to have some place to wage war in whenever there should be a necessity for victims at a new election and coronation."—Acosta, *Historia Natural*, lib. vii., chap. xxi.

not your hair stand on end with horror!"[1] And let it not be imagined that these assertions of the fact, that Indians and Africans in their respective countries sacrifice and eat their own species, are the exaggerated fancies of travelers who impose upon the credulity of the vulgar; for though it be true that many narrators of protracted voyages and remote customs invent and state what suits their purposes without regard to the truth essential to history, it is not the less certain that not only those who have written accounts of travels, but also the gravest and most truthful historians coincide on this subject; and from these writers I will quote some passages relating to America, to insure a better understanding of what I wish to say.[2]

Dr. Chanca, the companion of Columbus on his second voyage, I know not whether by appointment of the corporation of Seville, for the purpose of giving an account of his observations, or of his own free will, wrote a letter to said corporation, in which, describing his arrival and landing in the island of Guadalupe, he makes the following statement: "The men they (the natives of the island) capture, if alive, are taken to their houses to be butchered, and those who are dead, they eat. They say that the flesh of man is so good that there is nothing equal to it in the world; and so it would seem, for from the bones which we found in these houses, everything that was eatable had been gnawed off, so nothing remained on them but what from its toughness could not be eaten. *The neck of a man in process of being cooked* was found in one of their houses."[3]

---

(1) *Letter to Pomponio Laetus.* Navarrete: *Coleccion de Viajes y descubrimientos.* &c., tomo. i.

(2) Since I have already quoted from *La Araucana*, on account of the profound learning it contains, I will not deprive my readers of the following lines with which their author corroborates, in anticipation, the narratives written by the historians of the West Indies, even when they appeared most extravagant:

    Travelers see many things on their way,
      Which as fables are received,
    And the greater the marvel, the less that they say,
      The more they'll be believed.
    And although the doubtful 'tis as well to suppress,
      So that people won't say I lie,
    I'll tell them true, I found truth on the ground,
      Though 'tis thought it has flown to the sky.
                              Canto xxxvi.

(3) Navarrete—*Viajes y descubrimientos*, tomo i.

This testimony, from so reliable and competent an authority, who was an eye witness, and not merely a narrator from hearsay, ought almost to suffice to confirm the fact, (at least in the present work, in which this question appears to be of secondary consideration), of the existence of cannibalism among the Indians.

Nevertheless, when I see the odium of the slave trade charged against us, and call to mind the innumerable insults which all nations, and especially the English, have inflicted upon our honor respecting the discovery, conquest and government of the West Indies, apostrophizing us as cowards and the oppressors of a simple, pusillanimous and innocent people, I cannot help giving some latitude to the refutation of such deniable denunciations, since I have abundant data for the purpose. With the help of these I will not only establish a doctrine on the subject of the slavery of savage people, according to ancient philosophy; but will also endeavor to dispel, by a chain of rigorous consequences, the opinions which have been gratuitously advanced, and which have attributed to a natural inhumanity of Spaniards, what is founded only in the bad faith or the imagination of our rivals.

In the *Historia natural y general de las Indias* written by Gonzalo Fernandez de Oviedo, who of all the contemporary writers of those facts, is perhaps, the most truthful and the most reliable, from his official position and superior knowledge,[1] there are many passages relating to cannibals and many more that tell of bloody human sacrifices. And as it would be tedious to recount them all, I will give at random those which will suffice to prove the truth of my statements, as follows:

"There never was a war," (says the writer), "among the Indians of this Island (Santo Domingo), but for one of three causes; either for contested boundaries and jurisdiction, or about the fisheries, or when cannibal Indians from other Islands came to rob."[2]

To this he adds in the same chapter and passage, that

---

(1) He was chronicler of the Indies by royal letters patent; he having been Inspector of the smelting of Gold in Darien; Governor of the fortress of St. Domingo; (at that time the head of our colonization in the New World), Governor and Captain General elect of the Province of Carthagena in the Indies, &c., &c., &c.

(2) Part I., Book III., Chapter VI.

the Islands of the cannibals were Boriquen (now Porto Rico), Guadalupe, Dominica, Matinino and Cibugueyra, therefore it appears that nothing further is needed to show that my testimony is supported by that of so great an authority as Oviedo. And as to the sacrifices, chapters III of book V, and IX of book VI may be consulted; and besides, the preface of book XII wherein he thus depicts the Indians in general: "Because the people of these Indies, although rational and of the same origin as the eight persons within the holy Ark and in company with Noah, have been made irrational and beastly *by their idolatry, sacrifices and infernal ceremonies*, the devil has had full possession of their souls for centuries."

Oviedo did not exaggerate on this point, nor were the Spaniards tyrants, but, on the contrary, they were commendable in reforming the customs of the Indians, whether with their consent or by constraint, forming new settlements of those who led a roving life about the country, and making ordinances of humane policy wherever they took possession. And to show with what reason I assert this opinion, let us hear the testimony of Father José de Acosta, whose historical truthfulness admits of no contradiction, seeing that his work is the result of a legal investigation made at that time in those places by order of the king; speaking of the sacrifices which were executed in Mexico, he describes them as follows:

"After the sacrificers were arranged in order, all the prisoners of war, who were to be slaughtered in this festival, were brought forth well guarded, entirely naked, and made to ascend in single file the long series of steps which lead to the place where six priests awaited them; as each one arrived in turn, four sacrificers seized him, each by one limb, and threw him on his back on a sharp-pointed stone, where the fifth of these ministers put a halter around his neck, and the sixth (the High Priest) with a long knife ripped open his breast with astonishing dexterity, tearing out the heart with his hands, and, while it was yet reeking with animal heat, held it up to the Sun, to which he offered that smoke and heat, and then turning to the idol, cast it at his face, after which the body of the victim was tossed down the steps of the temple." In this manner all the victims were disposed of one by one, and their bodies being handed over to their respective owners, by whom they had been captured, were distributed among their friends and companions, and devoured by all with great solemnity; however small the number of victims might be, there never was less than forty or fifty, for they were very expert in taking captives."[1]

These same accounts, in different words and style, were given before, and have been given since as regards Mexico, by Hernan Cortes, in his famous letters to the Emperor Charles V., by Bernal Diaz del Castillo, Lopez de Gomara, Antonio de Herrera, D. Antonio de Solís, and by many others whom I cannot now recall to mind.

But Mexico was not the only part in the New World where such abominations were practised under the influence of a civilization which partook of all the iniquities of the most odious heathenism; for the same author, speaking of the Incas of Peru, says:

"This Guaynacopa was worshipped as God by his subjects during his life—a fact affirmed by the oldest inhabitants as having never taken place with his predecessors. When he died, one thousand persons of his household were killed, that they might go to serve him in the other world; and such was their willingness to die, in order to remain in his service, that many who were not among the appointed, offered themselves for that purpose."[2]

And in another passage which precedes the foregoing description he expresses himself in these terms:

"Besides this, it was customary in Peru to sacrifice children of from four to six and ten years of age; chiefly in matters which concerned the Inca; if he were sick, that he might recover his health, and when he was going to war, that he might gain the victory. And when the Tassel, which was the insignia of kings as the sceptre or the crown is with us, was conferred on the new Inca, two hundred children, of from four to ten years of age, were sacrificed—a cruel and inhuman spectacle! The manner of sacrificing these was by strangulation, and they were then buried with some food, certain ceremonies being performed on the occasion; at other times they beheaded the victims, and smeared themselves from ear to ear with the blood. They also sacrificed the virgins who were brought

---

(1) Acosta: *Historia Moral y Natural de Indias*, lib. v., cap. xx.
(2) Acosta: *Historia Moral y Natural de Indias*, lib. vi., cap. xxii.

to the Inca from the monastries of which I have already spoken. A great and general superstition existed among them, which was, that when an Indian of either high or low degree was sick, and his disease was pronounced fatal by the augur, they sacrificed his son to the *Sun* or to the *Viracocha* (God), asking him to be satisfied with the offering, and not to require the death of the father.[1]

The reports of these murders and abominable sacrifices, as well as the conviction that cannibalism existed among those people, became so public and universal, that even the poets, with their fanciful conceptions, were considered truthful historians, so far as this subject was concerned. In fact, those who distinguished themselves the most in the poetic line, in writing on the subject of the Indies, viz.: Juan de Castellanos, in his *Elegias de Varones ilustres*, and Don Alonso Ercilla, in *La Araucana*, wrote history rather than fiction, as has been proved by comparison of their works with those of the most weighty authors, and by the assurances which both authors gave in advance, and repeated from time to time, that they would not indulge in false inventions.

In Porto Rico, says Castellanos, the war waged by the Spaniards against the natives originated in the diabolical intentions of the latter to seize a youth from Seville, named Juan Juarez, for the purpose, of course, of eating him—a game of ball being intended to decide to whose lot he should fall.[2]

Narrating afterwards the expedition of Jorge Espina, Governor of Venezuela, between the rivers Marañon and Orinoco, he treats of a certain nation of Indians, called, Choques, of whom he speaks as follows:

> For besides devouring mankind,
> A horror in which they delight,
> In all the serpents they find,
> They indulge to their full appetite.
> Their children and kindred they eat;
> Their bodies are tombs for the dead;
> They eat the worms under their feet,
> And even the hairs off their head."[3]

With a better intonation and a graver style as became

---

(1) Acosta: *Historia Moral y Natural de Indias*, lib. v., cap. xix.
(2) Part First: *Elegia*, vi., canto i.
(3) Segunda Parte: *Elegia* ii., canto ii.

him who used it, Don Alonso de Ercilla, on describing a great sterility which the lands of Arauco suffered in the year 1554, treats of the same criminal customs in the following manner:

> I made a great inquiry,
> Exact within the place;
> For human flesh was ate, you see;
> (Oh! cruel, frightful case);
> And brothers brothers ate;
> The thing may look false on its face—
> But a mother there was, who devouring her son,
> To her entrails returned, from whence he had sprung.[1]

It seems to me, nevertheless, that Ercilla is mistaken in supposing that this enormous crime was then practised for the first time, for it appears impossible that a mother would eat her own child as he says in the last verse, if the custom had not been well established before. I could quote many similar passages of the history of the Indies from various authors who have been in those parts and who related what they had seen, adding, that the jurisprudence of the Indians as to the property of individuals caused them to commit without any compunction, the most cruel act as though it was the most natural thing in the world. And this is confirmed in other verses of Juan de Castellanos, who does not allow me to be as sparing in my quotations as I would wish to be, owing to his witty and very natural eloquence in the present case, saying:—

> A certain chief of this tribe, was
> In strong terms well reproved,
> Because with his voracious jaws,
> He, his good subjects chewed.—
> Quoth he: "*I eat them up because
> They're mine; those of another brood
> I care not for:*" Yet, I believe such was
> His emendation, he ne'er again did have
> The chance of dining off his nation. [2]

The author would seem, in the coupling of these verses, to convey the idea that the Spaniards killed the Indian; which, if it so happened, will not have failed to form an important link in the chain of evidence in the indictment found against us by foreign nations for our barbarous inhumanity. And it must be observed, since we touch

---

(1) *La Araucana*, canto ix.
(2) Elegia á Benalcaza: canto viii.

upon this point, not at random as some of our readers might imagine, considering the task as a digression; that although in the first voyages of our celebrated discoverers of the New World, no foreigners, nor even the subjects of the crown of Aragon, were permitted to go there; afterwards by virtue of royal letters patent and under the protection of our rights and our honor, the privilege was extended to the people of all the countries of Europe, and of course, turned to advantage by the worst part of each nation. Oviedo seeing this, and jealous of our reputation which already began to be tarnished by those very persons, perhaps, who disgraced it by their acts, said on this account:—

"And because in the progress of these histories and of these new discoveries some mutinies and riots and ugly deeds have occurred, and may again take place, mixed up with treason and disloyalty and want of constancy on the part of some men who have come hither: believe not, reader, that Spaniards only have committed all these offences, for of all the languages spoken in Christendom there is none which is not represented here: here are found natives of Italy as well as of Germany, of Scotland and England, and also Frenchmen, Hungarians, Poles, Greeks, Portuguese, and people of all the nations in Asia, of Africa and of Europe: some of whom, not having come with the intention of converting the Indians nor of populating the country and remaining in it for any greater length of time than that required for the acquisition of gold and the accumulating of wealth in every possible manner, put aside shame, conscience and truth, apply themselves to every kind of fraud and homicide, and commit innumerable depravities."(2)

After what has been said here in relation to America, which is calculated to show, in comparatively recent times, the existence of cannibal nations, and also the practice of warfare and of human sacrifices as common institutions; aside of what may justify the conduct of the Spaniards in their proceedings towards these barbarous nations; it would not be difficult for me to show the resemblance which exists between the mode of life of the Indians, and

---

(2) *Historia Natural de las Indias:* lib. xxiv. capítulo iv.

that of the African Negroes, which is characterized by still greater barbarism and cruelty.

I have before me various accounts of travelers, whose bloody and immoral pages fill the reader with horror and disgust.

"Voracity" says one of these writers, "is the ruling passion of the Negroes in their savage state: they subsist upon theft; they will steal now a chicken, now a cat or a dog, but delight above all, in rats, of which they are passionately fond; their fires are never idle; and whenever they find any of these animals either in the woods or in the road, not only dead, but even in a state of complete putrefaction, they eat them without the least reluctance. There are Negroes of the race of *Bibis* who, in the Colonies have seized children of four years of age, for the purpose of feasting their barbarous stomachs, for, as they themselves confess, the most delicious morsel for a *Bibi* is the well-roasted flesh of a child served up hot. They are competent judges on this matter, for in the midst of the continual wars which desolate their country, they have innumerable occasions to feast upon this class of food, as they almost always eat their prisoners. With the object of being able to devour their captives with greater ease, the *Bibis* and the *Montchiavas* file their incisors till they form sharp points; in both of these races to keep the teeth entirely black is considered the greatest type of perfect beauty, and they attain this end by burning them with lime and staining them with the shells of wild nuts."[1]

On the coast of Guinea there is also a nation of savages called the *Yolofs*, whose native ferocity is not less atrocious than that of the nations already named. Owing to their custom of eating their prisoners, they naturally imagine that such also is to be their lot when they are sold to the traders; and if they do not accomplish a successful revolt on the passage, as has often happened with the Negroes from the Gulf of Berrin or the Kalabars, they generally commit suicide by hanging themselves as soon as they have entered on their servitude in the colonies.

The *Congos* and *Carabalis* have the reputation in

---

(1) This narrative, which was afterwards transferred almost entire to a small treatise published anonymously subsequently to the abolition of slavery in the French Colonies, belongs to the collection of voyages of La Harpe.

Cuba, among the Negroes of milder customs, of being anthropophagi, or as they more naturally say, man-eaters.

I questioned one of these miserable beings myself, in Havana, enquiring if it were true that they eat one another when at war, and on his answering me affirmatively with blood-shot eyes, as though he were on the point of luxuriating once more in so horrible a feast, I must confess I began to doubt the fact of our springing from the same origin.

Some philanthropists of little reflection and, uninformed of the customs of savage nations, have supposed that the traffic which is still carried on with the Negroes in their respective countries is what keeps them in a permanent state of war. I confess that at one time I also held this opinion, though I have never expressed it in writing; but while studying this question of slavery with the most fervent desire to arrive at the truth, I have read all the authors who have written with some truth on the customs of said nations, and have found that they all agreed in representing the Negroes in a permanent state of warfare, long before the traffic was commenced or thought of.

Neither can it be doubted that they were sacrificers of human victims, although, owing to their not having as clear a notion of the Divinity and of a future life as the Indians had, their sacrifices were less frequent, and were not celebrated with the same solemnities.

Now at this very time, in this enlightened age and under the immediate vigilance of English philanthropists, who with the greatest coolness have announced the news; scenes of the most revolting and horrifying character are about to take place in the Western Coast of Africa. Not to detract from the character of these scenes, as they have been described, I will quote a paragraph from the *West African Herald*, (an English paper, of course) which reads as follows:—

"His majesty Badahung, King of Dahomey, is preparing to celebrate a grand festivity in honor of Gezo, his predecessor. Desirous of eclipsing all previous monarchs in the splendor of the ceremonies with which this object is to be performed, the grandest preparations for the feast have been made by Badahung. He has ordered an immense ditch to be dug which is to contain human blood in sufficient quantities to float launches. On this occasion

2,000 persons will be slain. The expedition against Abcokuta has been deferred; but the king has put his army in the field to make excursions among the weaker tribes; and has already succeeded in making some captures. The young and strong prisoners will be sold, and the old ones beheaded on the day of the feast."

If the above repugnant and bloody notice were not of itself sufficient evidence in favor of my assertion, it would at least decide all the points to the investigation of which I am applying myself; as they are proven not only by the permanent strife in which those Negro nations live, whose ransom it has been attempted to abolish, but also by the inhuman butcheries to which their respective prisoners are doomed.

It is remarkable what little effect has been produced in those regions by the continued intercourse of the English, their protectors and friends, who know beforehand, and announce to the world, acts of such barbarity, and yet do nothing to prevent their perpetration; as if the philanthropy, of which they so much boast, in favor of those unhappy beings would not be more opportunely exercised by preventing the horrible butchery which is announced to take place, than by permitting that the young and strong people, whom the King of Dahomey wishes to sell, should be slain also for the want of purchasers.

Finally, to close the catalogue of proofs which justify the deportation of savage Negroes, who eat human flesh, to other countries, on account of their being incapable of receiving any manner of culture, whether forced or spontaneous, in their own country, I avail myself of a very curious work which an enlightened friend of mine, D. Joaquin J. Navarro, Lieutenant of the Royal Navy, has just published, who speaks as an eye witness of the greater part of what he states.

Said officer, in Her Catholic Majesty's steamer *Vasco Nuñez de Balboa*, took part in the new and most recent colonization of our Islands in the Gulf of Guinea, and being given to study and anxious to benefit his country by his labors, he wrote with admirable judgment, unquestionable truth and great facility, some "*Notes on the state of the West Coast of Africa*," which the Spanish Government caused to be published at the public expense.

Although these *Notes* treat only incidentally of the

customs and social state of the Negroes, it happens, nevertheless, that the intercourse with the English and French factories which extend from Cape Verd to the Cape of Good Hope, have not been productive of an atom of civilization to their respective nations, they still continue to live in the same manner as they have lived from the first era of the world; because those establishments scarcely trouble themselves about anything further than the profits accrueing to them from the ivory, palm-oil, dyewoods and gold which they export from those countries in very great quantities. Thus it is that the *Kroumanes*, who are the most civilized Negroes and who willingly enter the service of Europeans, offering themselves to the establishments and to the vessels, practice polygamy to an extravagant degree as will be seen by the following paragraph :—

"A *Krouman* considers himself independent when he ceases to hire himself out to work, and has twenty or thirty wives at his disposal. At his death, the wives become the property of his son, as a part of his estate; so that many have their own mothers for wives!"[1]

Their willingness to serve the Europeans and their comparative state of civilization is not, however, without danger to the latter; so at least we must infer from the paragraph with which the said author in the *Notes* to which I refer, closes his description of that country, saying :—

"The object of the commander of the steamer was to obtain on this coast of Krou a certain number of individuals of this race, to ship in each of the vessels which composed this naval force, some for ship duty, constant duty in the tops while at sea, and other duties of this class, and also to work on board the tender; but it was impossible to accomplish it, because we made the land on this rocky coast under the worst possible circumstances. It was very dark and rainy, so that certain land marks were not visible. We had very doubtful confidence in the negroes who offered to pilot the vessel; and, finally, the well-founded apprehension that some accident might happen, the consequences of which, always disagreeable, would be still much more so on an inhospitable coast,

---

(1) Navarrete: *Apuntes, &c.* : *Costa de Krou*, p. 22.

where far from receiving efficient aid from its inhabitants, we could only expect to be under the necessity of keeping the vessel under military precautions, in order to avoid being plundered."[1]

Speaking of this race of *Kroumans*, my friend, the learned author of the *Notes* which I am now reviewing, also says, "they are possessed by foolish superstitions; they believe in their *jusjus*, guardian or evil angels, as do all the races who remain in a state of barbarism, and among whom the light of Christianity has not been diffused; but they have none of those horrible and bloody customs which are so common among the natives of the bay of Biafa."[2]

From this declaration, made with such unquestionable sincerity by Mr. Navarro, and confirmed in other parts of his work, we not only see that the light of Christianity has not yet been diffused among the *Kroumans* of Western Africa, who have the most communication with the Europeans, and also that the English established in those parts have taken more care to look after their own material interests than to Christianise the natives, for the purpose of extinguising idolatry, polygamy, and all such abominations, but also we draw as an irrefutable consequence what it is attempted to show in this chapter, viz.: that the savage negroes of Western Africa wage war against each other from instinct, and sacrifice one another as will be stated presently.

"In the interior of Cape Coast," says the above-mentioned author, "is situated he kingdom of Ashantee, which is one of the most powerful and despotic monarchies in all Africa. Its inhabitants are wrapt in the gloom of the most abject idolatry; they worship sharks and serpents, and they add to this, human sacrifices, in all their most horrible details. This remarkable thirst for blood, on the part of the monarch and his people, springs not only from a barbarous desire of vengeance on such enemies as fall into their hands, in legitimate warfare, but also from the belief that their deities are conciliated by such sacrifices; that the troubled manes of their departed herbes are thus appeased, and that the victims will be their slaves in the

---

(1) Navarrete: *Apuntes, &c.: Costa de Krou*, p. 22.
(2) Ibid. Ibid.

life to come. Sometimes they exhume the skulls and other bones of notable men, to wash them with the blood of their victims. The graves are saturated with blood; and, although it is supposed that some of their customs are those which prevailed in Asia in the days of Moses, they are, without doubt, the most cruel savages to be found on the face of the earth in the nineteenth century."[1]

I am not aware of the amount of data which will be required to convince the most suspicious credulity that the natural state of African negroes in their own country is of the most degraded character; but I fully believe that what I have here written will stand the test of the severest criticism. The remarks I have made in the present chapter, and those I shall hereafter put forth, will show in an irresistible manner, that the warlike propensity of these negroes has not been increased by the slave trade, neither have their bad customs been modified by the presence in those countries of the English, who turn their attention to everything except to the work of civilizing them.

For which reasons, and because the limits of this work will not allow me to give latitude to further investigations, I will consider as sufficient those already given, in order to pass on to another matter.

---

(1) Navarrete: Description of the coast between Cape Palmas and Cape Lopez, pp. 27 and 28.

CHAPTER II.

Respective condition of the nations of Eastern Europe when discoveries in Africa and Asia were made towards the South and East.—Why the civilization of said countries was not attempted by means of conquest, and why the enslaving of their inhabitants, for the purpose of civilizing them, by cultivating the New World was prefered.—First privileges granted to introduce African slaves in America.—These privileges were obtained by the Flemings and the Genoese, and afterwards by the Portuguese, the Dutch, the French, and the English, until the famous contract of ASIENTO was made.—Losses suffered in this undertaking by some Spanish companies and private individuals, arising from their humanity.—Beginning of Spanish legislation in reference to black slaves.—Its eminently moral and protective character.—Obstacles which were opposed to the introduction of slaves in the New World, and for what object.

WHEN the Spaniards and Portuguese began to visit the western coast of Africa, the former stimulated by their private interest, and the latter by a speculative idea, to them of vast importance, they found, as I have already stated, in the countries which extend to the Cape of Good Hope, previous to the doubling of it by the renowned Vasco de Gama, a multitude of savage nations, intractable and wild, who in many instances punished with death the daring of the intruders.

This suggested the idea of enslaving those miserable beings, singly or collectively, as opportunity served, and of conveying them to Spain, a custom which prevailed until towards the end of the 15th century, when the discovery of the New World brought forth material deviations from the course until then pursued.

At that period and owing to the spirit of discovery which engrossed the mind of the celebrated Infante Don Enrique of Portugal, after the capture of Ceuta in 1415,[1] the Portuguese, by means of their inroads into Africa, and their establishments on the coasts of that continent, ascertained that the native tribes of Negroes were in a perpetual state of barbarous warfare against each other, and that captives could be rescued with great facility from certain death by being exchanged for commodities of little value.

For this reason, and if we bear in mind what were at that period the principles of jurisprudence in regard to prisoners who were not Christians, even when taken in the Peninsula or in the Mediterranean during the subsequent wars against the Turks, we cannot be surprised that Spaniards, as well as Portuguese, should not have felt over scrupulous in making slaves of negroes, especially as they did so with the eminently Christian object of rescuing them from inevitable death.

Arguing upon the principles of modern philosophy, there is no denying that such proceedings were deserving of the strongest reproof, since it would have been more rational to introduce civilization among the African tribes by means of religion and the support of a moderate military force, than by subjecting the negroes to slavery and conveying them to distant countries.

But as it cannot be denied that the spirit which prevailed in former ages widely differed from that by which the actions of men were influenced and regulated at other and more recent periods, the exploring nations were satisfied with doing all that circumstances permitted in favor of these barbarians, which indeed was all that could be expected, considering that they rescued them from inevitable death at the foot of their satanic altars and conveyed them to civilized countries where they acquired a knowledge of their Creator and enjoyed the blessings of social life.[2]

---

(1) Freire, *Vida del Infante Don Enrique.* Book iii.

(2) The lack of judgment with which past events are commented on according to the ruling spirit of the time being, meets with an admirable reproof in the answer of Cato, when he was taken to task at the age of 86 for some imaginary transgression in his youth: "It is difficult, said he, to give an account of my actions to men who live in an age which is not mine."

Nor could any more be done at that time, when Spain, not yet entirely liberated from the thraldom of the Crescent, had to concentrate her efforts to drive the Mahometan legions to the other side of the Straits; and when this sacred object had been attained, and the cross had been raised on the tower of *la Vela*, in Granada, from the depths of a boundless Ocean arose the World which Queen Isabella I. and Columbus had called into existence so that Spain might civilize it without looking towards other conquests.

On the other hand, no accusation can be brought against the Portuguese, seeing that their efforts neither tended to acquire territory, nor to civilize the people in those parts of Africa. The report of the lucrative trade in spices, perfumes, and precious stones, carried on with the East Indies by the Venitians, who traversed the Mediterranean, the Red Sea, and the desert to reach those lands, had been widely diffused, since the fortunate voyage of Marco Paolo, and thus the minds of the Portuguese navigators were bent exclusively on discovering a new and shorter passage to those regions by doubling the coast of Africa towards the East.[1]

It is true that the infante Don Enrique, whilst encouraging this project, did not scorn the acquisition of some territory on the coast of Africa, for the Order of Christ, of which he was Grand Master,[2] but it is not less positive, that first the Moors, opposite the Canary Islands, and afterwards the negroes of the tropical latitudes beyond Sierra Leone, opposed a most determined resistance to the Portuguese who visited them for the aforesaid object. Antonio Gonzalez and Nuño Tristan, (two valiant youths, who gave the name of *Angra de los Caballos* (Horses' Cove), to that part of the coast where being pursued by the natives they were saved by the fleetness of their horses) testify to the fact, by their account of the contest in which both were engaged in 1441 at Cape Blanco, and by the violent death of the latter which took place five years later near the river which to this day bears his name. Also Gonzalo de Suitra, killed in the same place by the negroes, Antonio de Nola, Dionisio Fernandez Cadamasto, and numerous others, who owed their safety in

---

(1) Lopez de Castañeda: *Historia del descubrimiento y conquista de la India por los Portugueses*, lib. i, cap. i.

(2) Freire: *Vida del Infante D. Enrique*, lib. iii.

similar conflicts, to their good fortune, their stout hearts and their strong right arm.[1]

England at that time was not a maritime power, and had no consuls even in the most important settlements where the business of contracting for slaves was carried on; France was more occupied in invading Navarre and Rosellon, and in defending herself in Italy against the victorious armies of our generals, than in exploring unknown regions, with the object of making the inhabitants participants of civilization and the advantages of commerce; it is not therefore surprising that no plan for combining the efforts of enlightened nations in order to put a stop to the atrocious warfare among the Africans was resolved upon, or that its execution should be contemplated otherwise than on the small scale conceived by D. Enrique.[2]

It being universally known that the negroes were kept in a miserable state of perpetual slavery by the Moors on their frontiers,[1] and by those of their own race, it became evident that the only practicable means of ameliorating their condition was to redeem them, especially such as had been taken captives in war, from that state of barbarism and wretchedness. In this manner they could be rescued from the cruelty to which they all would, sooner or later fall victims; and this measure could be adopted with a strict regard to justice, as the negroes were entirely devoid of that moral sentiment from which arises our attachment to our native land and our kindred; and notwithstanding this strange want of feeling which was a characteristic of that wretched people, according to the testimony of reliable authors, all that were taken to Spain were treated with great kindness and gentleness by their masters,[3] that is to say, in accordance with the natural disposition of the Spanish people, who are always humane and generous towards the weak and defenceless.

---

(1) Barros: *Da Asia Portuguesa*; Decada primera, libro i., cap. v. Martinez de la Puente: *Compendio de la Historia de las Indias*, lib ii., cap. i. Freire: *Vida del Infante D. Enrique*, libros iii., y iv., &c.

(2) In one of the voyages to Cape Blanco made by Anton Gonzalvez and Nuño Tristan in 1443, they fought with the Moors, as usual, and having taken 10 prisoners, the moorish chief of that district redeemed them by giving an equal number of their negro slaves in exchange. Barros: *Da Asia Portuguesa:* Decada primera, libro i.

(3) Ortiz de Zuñiga: *Anales de Sevilla:* Lib. XII.

The practice of introducing negro slaves into the two kingdoms of the Peninsula, which existed from the commencement of the XIIIth century, under the provision of a legislation no wise resembling that of the ancients, and by which the condition of these unhappy beings was protected and guaranteed, now received the sanction of the law in matters of slaves. The discovery of the western hemisphere ocurring immediately afterwards, and it having been to a certain degree ascertained that the habits of the indians of the New World unfitted them for the arduous labor of agriculture, and more especially so those of the Islands, private interest prompted experiments to be made to test the aptitude of the negroes for this labor; which experiments produced such admirable results, that the redemption of these unfortunate beings was officially organized and a great number was taken to the new spanish dominions.

The first royal privilege, granted in due form for the importation of negroes into the West Indies, was dated 1517[1]; and Navarrete commenting on this fact in its bearings on the interference of Father Las Casas, in favor of the Indians of the New World, says: "He came to Spain to plead their cause, and in May 1517, arrived at Aranda where the Court was at that time, and where the celebrated Cardinal Ximenez de Cisneros lay ill; for this reason he could not confer with him but went to Valladolid, there to await the arrival of the king, Charles I, who did not reach that city till after the death of the Cardinal. The young prince, then 17 years of age, in a country where he was a stranger, thoroughly ignorant of the Spanish language, and controled by the Flemings who accompanied him, issued at their suggestion many warrants of apportionment and grants of lands in the Indies and divers licences to carry slaves to those dominions, notwithstanding the existing prohibitions. Las Casas well knew that the way to accomplish his object was to win the good will and follow in the footsteps of these Flemings, in which he succeeded, especially with Mr. de Laxas, Lord Chamberlain and one of the king's greatest favorites; but when he saw that his plan would meet with some dificulties owing to the cupidity of the new guests, he chan-

---

(1) La Sagra: *Historia Política*: página 32: nota.

ed his plan and proposed, among other remedies, that the right of importing slaves should be given to the Spaniards residing in the Indies, so that the Indians might be somewhat relieved on the plantations and in the mines. This brought up the question as to how many slaves would be requisite for the four islands: Hispaniola (Santo Domingo), Fernandina (Cuba), San Juan (Porto Rico), and Jamaica, and information having been demanded from the officials of the department whose seat was at Seville, and whose duty it was to take cognizance of all contracts having reference to the trade, the answer was that four thousand would be required. The Flemings then took advantage of their influence to obtain this privilege which they sold to the Genoese for 24,000 ducats, with the condition attached that the king should grant no other privilege for eight years. We therefore infer from this narrative, the veracity of which cannot be questioned, first: that Las Casas in order to relieve the Indians, established and authorized the traffic in negroes for the Islands of the New World, as if they were not rational beings; and secondly: that those who solicited this negotiation and intervened in it, were not Spaniards, but covetous Flemings and trafficking Genoese."[1]

Navarrete in this passage, reflects strongly on Father Las Casas, and not without a show of reason, though, in my opinion with a total disregard for the justification of the case to be found in the old and new Testaments; for what else but slavery and the transporting of negroes to the territories of the New World could the wise prophet Jeremiah have wished to announce when he said: "Like as ye have forsaken me and served strange Gods in your lands, so shall ye serve strangers in a land that is not yours?"[2] For which reason, and if we bear in mind the humanity with which the Spaniards and Portuguese proceeded in rescuing the African negroes from slavery and impending death, though benefitting themselves by their labor, I consider Navarrete's remark, "*as if the latter were not rational beings*" particularly uncall for.

Father Las Casas is reasonable in everything but when

---

(1) Navarrete: *Coleccion de viages y descubrimientos, etc:* Tomo I. Introduccion.

(2) *Prophecies of Jeremia:* Chapter V; verse 19.

he speaks of the state of the respective souls of the Indians and of the negroes, because although by the above quotation, his advice about enslaving the negroes might be justified, we can find in the sacred Scriptures, abundant texts that cannot but refer in a certain manner to what happened with the Indians; for besides what St. Luke has anounced in his version of the Gospel when he said in denouncing the Hebrews to convert them to the Lord: "Every tree therefore which bringeth not forth good fruit is hewn down and cast into the fire;" [1] in Exodus, as if foreseeing what would happen to the Indians for their iniquities, will be found the following:

"For mine angel shall go before thee unto the Amorites, and the Hittites and the Perizzites and the Canaanites, and the Hivites, and the Jebusites; and I will cut them off. Thou shalt not bow down to their Gods, nor serve them, nor do after their works; but thou shalt utterly overthrow them and quite break down their images. I will send my fear before thee, and will destroy all the people to whom thou shalt come; and I will make all thine enemies turn their backs unto thee; I will not drive them out from before thee in one year, lest the land should become desolate, and the beasts of the field multiply against thee. By little and little I will drive them out from before thee, until thou be increased and inherit the land." [2]

Navarrete was perfectly correct in stating that the Spaniards were not the first traders between Africa and America, not only at that time but for many years after; for, as I have shown, the first privilege of 1517, for this traffic was granted to some Flemings, who sold it to a company of Genoese; and when the grant expired, owing to the great number of slaves then in the West Indies, it was not renewed for some time, until the penury of the Royal Exchequer, induced Philip II. to make another grant to a Genoese company, which his successors extended to Gomez Reimel, a Fleming, from 1595 to 1600; with Coutinho brothers to 1609; with Antonio Fernandez de Eloa and Manuel Rodriguez de Lamego, all Portuguese, up to the date of the revolution in Portugal in 1640:

---

(1) Chapter III; verse 9.
(2) *Exodus:* chapter XXIII; verses 23, 24, 27, 29 y 30.

with the Dutchman Coimans to 1692; with the Portuguese company of Guinea to 1701; with the French company of Guinea to 1712; and finally, in 1750, that famous treaty with England was concluded, which gave the latter a pretext for all its outrages and arbitrary proceedings against our foreign possessions. (1)

It is true that during some intervals that occurred between the expiration of each successive grant and its renewal, the contractors at Seville and other Spanish companies, sometimes undertook to provide negroes for our possessions in America, and sometimes the proprietors of plantations were allowed to introduce them free from duty, for once only.

But these exceptions, which were not many, only served to prove that the Spaniards were not the best calculated to carry on this commerce on an extensive scale, even through motives of humanity, since we see that in order faithfully to comply with the rules that existed for the good treatment and comfort of the negroes in their transportation, which required ample means to satisfy their redemption, to carry the best men from the coast of Guinea, and to bring over also some females, all the enterprizes of the Spaniards became bankrupt before the expiration of the contract, and the contractors at Seville, when they did this business on account of the government, suffered enormous losses. (2)

Nothing else could be expected, if the trade was carried on in good faith, as we did, in conformity with our natural disposition and love of justice; for the traffic once established, the laws were more zealous in protecting the moral interests of the contracted than those of the contractors. Thus it was that in 1510, previous to any grant of privileges, when but few negroes had as yet been taken to the West Indies, and those few the property of private individuals, Ferdinand V recommended the respective

---

(1) Navarrete : *Colleccion de viages y descubrimientos:* Tomo I, Introduccion. Antunez: *Memorias Históricas:* Tomo I, pag. 391, y tomo II, pag. 263. Zamora : *Legislacion Ultramarina :* Tomo III, artículo titulado " Esclavitud y Esclavos." etc.

(2) It was ordered that one ton should be allowed for every two negroes according to the dimensions of the vessel, and although foreign contractors infringed this rule allowing them less space, the Spaniards never deviated from it nor from that relative to their food.

owners to encourage marriages among their slaves in order to promote a better state of tranquility and order;⁽¹⁾ and afterwards, by a series of Royal decrees he not only prohibited that those who had licence to trade in Guinea should bring away married negroes without their wives and children, although the latter could be of no use in the Colonies, but he also established as a general rule that one-third of every cargo of negroes intended for the Spanish possessions in the New World, should consist of women.⁽²⁾ Another guarantee given by our laws to protect the morals of the Spanish Colonies was that concerning the preservation of the integrity of the Christian faith; for which purpose many decrees and Royal ordinances were issued, directing that the slaves taken to the West Indies be exclusively from the coast of Cape Verd, Angola, Guinea and the adjacent Islands, of the race called Bozales: this decree was enacted because some unscrupulous contractors and speculators, seeing that the Bozales had advanced in price, rather than to redeem those wretched creatures from an ignominious life and inevitable death, hoping to increase their gains, went to the Islands of Sardinia, Mayorca and Minorca there to buy at a much lower price the natives of Barbary taken on the coast opposite to Spain, who were mostly mulatoes and negroes, but unfortunately some of whom were whites.

For this reason, on the 25th of February 1530, a decree was issued prohibiting the taking of white slaves to the Colonies ; another prohibition was promulgated the 19th of December 1531, respecting the natives of Barbary; and on the 1st of May 1543, a law was passed to the same effect relative to all mulatoes coming from the same place —" Because (said the law) the negroes who live in that part of the Levant say that they belong to the Moorish or Mahometan caste, and as others would associate with them in a new land where the Catholic faith is now being implanted, it is against our interest to introduce such people." ⁽³⁾

---

(1) La Sagra: *Historia Política*. Apéndice: No. 89.

(2) The former is in a Royal Letter Patent dated Feb'y. 1st 1570, and the latter in another of Jan'y. 2d 1586.

(3) Antuniz: *Memorias Históricas:* tomo I—*Recapitulacion de las leyes de India, &c.*

With the object of keeping the negroes already in the Spanish dominions in an orderly state, after some years of experience as to the qualities of the race or nation from which they came, with the view of guaranteeing the lives and property to the Spaniards who benefitted themselves by their labor, and which were not always secure among such servants, the Kings of Spain prohibited the carrying slaves to the Colonies from the territories where they were most valuable, even if those places were within the limits where the redemption was lawful.

The first decree in reference to the prohibition was issued the 11th of May 1526, immediately after some commotion caused by the insurrection of the negroes against their masters, and with the remembrance fresh on their minds of similar occurences in Santo Domingo in 1522. In this decree the shipping of crafty negroes (*ladinos*) was prohibited, without determining any place of embarkation, and merely because being of bad habits (undoubtedly cannibals) they were not wanted in Spain, and in the Indies they would do more harm than good by contaminating the slaves already reclaimed and submissive gentle and obedient. Subsequently on the 28th of September 1532, a new law was issued prohibiting that negroes be taken from the Island of Guadalupe, because they were of a passionate, disobedient, turbulent and incorrigible race, and were the cause of all the insurrections and consequent loss of life which had occured among the Christians in Porto Rico and the other Islands.[2]

By what has been said of the traffic in reference to its origin and continuance while it was carried on by contract, the equitable, humane, civilizing, and philanthropic feelings that prevailed among our legislators respecting the redemption and service of the negroes are fully demonstrated.

Yet, as this is but a slight sketch of the regulations which afterwards became laws in our Colonies, I will put aside all other considerations and enter at once and fully on the exposition and explanation of the laws existing at that period.

---

[2] Antuniz: *Memorias Históricas:* tomo I.—*Racapitulacion de las leyes de Indias, &c.*

CHAPTER III.

The ideas of the ancient laws in matters of slaves excite public sentiment against modern slavery.—Radical difference which exists between the legislation of the heathens and that of our times respecting said institution.—Manner in which the Spaniards practically exhibited this difference, from the time that they introduced slavery into their colonies.—Religious principles which predominated in the formation of their laws.—Royal letters patent and circular instructions to the Indies dated 31st May, 1789, respecting the education, treatment and occupation of the slaves.—Comments made on the preceding document for the purpose of doing away errors of great magnitude.

THE natural abhorrence with which persons possessed of humane feelings, and professing the Christian faith, look upon the fact that slavery is established as a legal institution in our enlightened age, does not proceed so much from the nature of the institution thus condemned, as from the name by which it is known. For, having learned from the pages of history that slavery, in the darker ages, was a total deprivation of human rights, and that the owners could dispose, at their caprice, not only of the persons, but also of the lives of their slaves, the mind must evidently revolt at so barbarous a legislation, although the terrible power of life and death may no longer exist.

And while admitting that "Slavery" is not an appropriate name for the status of the negroes, for the sole reason that their labor is compulsory, yet it is the general impresion that, though the owners have no longer the power of taking the lives of their slaves according to their caprice, they may mutilate their limbs, brand them with ignominious marks, inflict cruel punishments on them, destine them to immoral purposes and compel them to labor day and night without relaxation.

These inductions, which appear logical, and which certainly would be so, had not a great reform taken place, by which they are set at naught, have powerfully contributed to the clamorous, though groundless charges, which have been made against us, not only by foreigners, but even by some of our own people. For which reason and in order to enable my readers to form an unbiased judgment of our proceedings in matters of slavery, I shall insert in the following pages the regulations which have been made concerning the treatment of slaves in our colonies, where they are enforced and scrupulously observed.

No longer, as in former times, is slavery imposed indiscriminately and as a natural right on the vanquished, to whatever class, condition or race they belonged, whether apostles or sectarians of a sublime doctrine, philosophers cultivating the liberal arts and sciences, or proletarians enured to the hardships of manual or agricultural labor ; neither is it intended to enslave that mysterious excrescence of the human species which populates a considerable portion of South Western Africa, and who, neither in their local intercourse, nor when conveyed to the centre of civilization, have given proofs of their capability to contribute in the least degree to the universal progress which develops itself in all other human beings with the aid of intellect.

These wretched beings, who are only capable of imitating what they see, and who never perform any kind of labor except what is taught to them ;—whose mental capacity is confined exclusively to the retentive faculty, although, at times, the remarkable aptitude with which some individual, more favored than the rest, perfects himself in what he has been taught, may appear to proceed from faculties of a higher order ;—those unfortunate beings, who have been ranked, by Christianity, among the descendants of Noah, and have been endowed, by the law, with all the rights common to mankind, are not considered as *things*, as were the slaves of Rome, Greece, Gaul and the Northern nations (who had been chieftains and warriors, and owed the irreparable loss of their rank, power and freedom to chances of war), but live among us under the protection of the laws, with all the attributes of persons, and are treated as such, in their civil status, according to the codes of laws wherein it is so ordered.

They are not deprived of the sweet ties of kindred, nor are their children torn from them in infancy as was done to slaves in ancient times by the mere command of their masters. They are not exposed to bodily punishment at the caprice of their masters, but solely for proven faults, and, even then, the punishment is always moderate and of such a kind as to prove beneficial. They are not compelled to combat with wild beasts or their fellow-slaves in the amphitheatre, nor are they punished with severity for the veriest trifles. There is no danger that their blood will be made to flow to add to the gaieties of a festival, at the caprice of another Quintius Flaminius, nor will they be hurried to execution in masses of four hundred, to avenge the assassination of one man, although their innocence of the crime was clearly proved. [1] No! Christianity has invaded slavery to abolish that of the people of civilized nations, and to infuse the principle of its holy charity into that of those beings who are rescued from a state of barbarism by universal commerce, to be employed for the general good, and, evidently, for their own benefit. For the Holy Spirit, through the mouth of the Apostles, has spoken to both servants and masters ; and, if he has said to the former : " Servants be obedient to them that are your masters according to the flesh, with fear and trembling, in singleness of heart, as unto Christ ; not with eye-service as men pleasers, but as the servants of Christ, doing the will of God from the heart ; with good will doing service, as to the Lord, and not to men ; knowing that whatsoever good thing any man doeth, the same shall he receive of the Lord, whether he be bond or free ; " he has also said to the latter : "And ye masters do the same thing unto them, forbearing threatening, knowing that your Master is also in heaven ; neither is there respect of persons with him. [2]

Having contemplated the different aspects of slavery after the triumph of our Holy Religion, it is evident that all its fundamental principles have been changed, and we could almost say, technically, that slavery no longer exists, as will be demonstrated by the regulations already mentioned ; and I wish, here, to call attention to the fact

---

(1) Tacitus : *Annal*, lib. IX, 43.
(2) St. Paul's epist. to the Ephesians, vi, 5, 6, 7, 8 and 9.

that, from the commencement of the trade in negroes, no precautions have been omitted which could possibly be conducive to their welfare; and this humane policy was pursued, not only with the slaves in our own possessions, where the improvement of their condition was encouraged in every imaginable manner, and freedom was accessible to those who chose to earn it by their industry and honesty, but also with those in the neighboring colonies which were established in the course of time.

In order that my readers may see the truth of this statement, they must know that, in 1680, 1693, 1733, 1740 and 1759, a general ordinance was promulgated to the effect that: "all negroes, of both sexes, who should fly from the English and Dutch colonies, and take refuge in the provinces of New Spain, with the intention of embracing the Catholic faith, should at once be declared free, and should not be sold again nor returned to their former masters" [1]; which ordinance, though infringing the rights of said colonies to a certain extent, was, nevertheless, commendable considering the excellent intentions and Christian spirit from which it proceeded. This law was so scrupulously observed that, when the governor of the Island of Trinidad (then one of our possessions) ordered the restitution of a mulatto woman who, with six children, had taken refuge there, having escaped from her English owners, in the Island of Granada; and a free mulatto, daughter of said slave and resident of Trinidad, presented a petition interceding for the whole family, and offering to pay their ransom, a decree was issued forbiding the restitution of the fugitives in the most positive and conclusive terms; this decision being greatly influenced by the fact that *the English inflicted severe and inhuman punishments on their slaves in such cases*, as was shown in the petition of the mulatto, by which she obtained the freedom of her mother and brethren without paying any compensation to the owners. [2]

---

(1) Zamora: *Legislacion Ultramarina*, vol. III, article "Slavery, slaves."

(2) Ditto, *ditto*, ditto: However it is necessary to remark here that in the course of time, as the ideas of right became more correct, and the communication among neighboring colonies more frequent, agreements were entered into, for the return of fugitive slaves to their owners, stipulating always that they should be punished with moderation, and a garantee was required sufficient to ensure the fulfilment of this humane clause.

Our legislators took the most special pains with the regulations concerning religious matters, and these are expressed with such mildness and charity that they alone would suffice as an evidence of the spirit which predominated in the enactment of these laws. As an example, I will give the words of the fourth Constitution of the diocesan Synod of Cuba, which treats of the obligation of masters to see to the religious instruction and baptism of their slaves, that Synod being held in 1680, and approved by a Royal decree of August 9, 1682:

"God, our Lord, having given to the *Bozal* negroes, who have been brought to this Island, the blessing of living among Christians, there to enjoy, among other privileges, the rites of holy Baptism; and, as we understand that many owners of slaves have had them in their possession more than two or three years, and have not had them baptized, we direct that all those who possess slaves who have not received the waters of Holy Baptism, shall send them to be baptized, within two months, duly instructed in the Christian doctrine; and those who, in future, shall buy slaves from the vessels that arrive, shall teach them said doctrine, with all the care and vigilance which these poor negroes require, and send them, within the period of six months, to the parish church, to be baptized, under penalty of excommunication to the owners, and a fine of ten ducats, to be applied according to the Royal decree of H. M.; and under the same penalty, after they have bought them, shall give notice to the beneficiary priests of the parishes, so that they may be registered by them, and care be taken that, the six months being past, their owners shall have them baptized; and, if they should not be instructed in the Christian doctrine, we order the priests to personally instruct them, and the owners shall pay said priests a sufficient compensation for such instruction, as a penalty for such omission and neglect; and in order that this may take effect, we order the ecclesiastical judges to compel the owners to pay the stipend which these clergymen may claim, with penalties and censures, for which we give them full power.

"And because it is our province and that of said ministers to teach the Christian faith to the negroes and to ascertain that they are duly instructed therein; we order said clergymen (as it is commanded in one of the

Constitutions of this Synod) that on every Sunday in the afternoon, they shall ring the church-bell, calling every slave to go and learn the Christian Catechism and prayers, enquiring like vigilant pastors, who are the absent, and compelling their presence together withthat of their masters, it being the duty of both, as faithful Catholic Christians, to endeavor by all possible means, that the slaves be instructed in the Christian Religion, and baptized after being so instructed ; with the observance of which regulation we gravely charge the conscience of all concerned."[1]

Although for the object indicated, a few words of the foregoing Constitution would have been sufficient, I have prefered to copy it entire, for the purpose of showing how laws were made for those regions, sofar removed from the vigilance of the metropolis. Thus the laws, royal ordinances and regulations, which were written on matters concerning the West Indies, were so constructed as to insure their perfect fulfilment by arousing the interests and stimulating the competition of the different administrative jurisdictions in the discharge of their duties, besides appealing to their consciences.

An immense number of decrees all equally humane were issued by our monarchs and tribunals, as much in the aforesaid matters, as in all others appertaining to the moral and material existence of the negroes, so that, not only the good treatment of the slave was guaranteed by the law and at the same time by the interest of the proprietor, but also his civilization when compared to the miserable estate of his origin; and even his freedom, under much better conditions, could be held for certain.

Nevertheless, these ordinances and royal decrees which were issued for so laudable an object did not form a complete and uniform body of laws, being interspersed among others incompatible with their tendencies, in the Code of laws of the Indies, and in the collections of general instructions to the viceroys and governors. For which reason, and owing to the great importance of the matter, which will become evident when it is considered that the redemption of the negroes had been enormously developed by the privilege which was finally granted to all vessels,

---

(1) Zamora : *Legislation Ultramarina :* vol. III, art. "Esclavitud, esclavos."

national and foreign, to carry on the trade, so that in the French colonies slavery was already regulated by a special ordinance, entitled *Code Noir*,[1] the piety of king Charles IV, opportunely stimulated by his royal council of the Indies, ordered the compiling of all the statutes relating to the negroes, from which resulted the following :

ROYAL DECREE *and circular* LETTER *of* INSTRUCTION *to the Indies, of May* 31*st* 1789, *on the Education, Treatment and Occupation of Negroes.*

I, THE KING, &c., In the *Leyes de Partida* and other Codes of legislation regarding these realms, in the *Recopilacion de las Indias*, in the decrees both general and special, having reference to the administration of my dominions in America, from the time of their discovery, as also in the ordinances which, after having been examined by my council of the Indies, have been sanctioned with my Royal approbation, a system has been established tending to provide for the usefulness, education of the slaves, and defining their treatment and occupation in a manner conformable with principles and regulations dictated by religion, humanity and the good of the State, and compatible with the institution of slavery and the preservation of public tranquillity.

Nevertheless, considering that all my subjects in America who own slaves, cannot without great difficulty acquaint themselves sufficiently in all the dispositions of the laws comprised in said compendiums, and that, owing to this difficulty, notwithstanding the orders of my august predecessors respecting the education, welfare and occupation of slaves, many proprietors and overseers have introduced abuses in direct opposition to the object contemplated by the existing legislation and other general and special measures taken in the matter; considering also that the number of slaves in America is likely to be increased in consequence of the privilege to carry on the trade which I have granted to my subjects, by article 1 of my decree of 28 February last ; and whereas it is my duty to extend my royal protection to this class of the human family, in order to prevent the recurrence of such abuses, and while the laws for this highly important object

---

(1) Antunez: *Memorias Historicas;* vol. II.

are being digested and condensed in a *General Code*, especially adapted to the government of the Indies, I have resolved that, for the present, all owners and possessors of slaves in my dominions shall punctually conform with the following instructions:

"CHAPTER I: *Education.*—Every owner of slaves, of whatever class or condition he may be, shall instruct them in the principles of the Catholic faith and in the fundamental truths, so that they may be baptized within one year of their residence in my dominions. They shall take care that the christian doctrine be explained to them on all feast days of precept, on which days they shall not be allowed to labor either for themselves or for their masters, except in the harvest season, when it is customary to concede permission to that effect. On those days, and on all others when it is obligatory to attend Mass, the owners of plantations shall pay priests to come and celebrate divine service, to explain the christian doctrine and administer the Holy Sacraments, at the times appointed by the church, and at all other times when the slaves may require or demand them; moreover, on every week day after their work is over, they shall recite the Rosary, either in presence of their owner or overseer, with the greatest reverence and devotion."

"CHAPTER II: *Food and Clothing.*—It is obligatory on the part of owners properly to feed and clothe their slaves, both male and female, which obligation extends also to the children of said slaves, although neither males nor females are considered to afford any compensation for their maintenance whilst under the age of fourteen and twelve, respectively.

But, as it is impossible to establish any fixed regulation with regard to the quantity and quality of the food, and the kind of clothing that must be furnished to them, owing to the variety of climates, and other local peculiarities, it is hereby ordered that, with regard to these points, the judges of the respective districts, with the consent of the Corporation, and in the presence of the Attorney General, in his capacity of *Protector of the slaves*, shall indicate and determine the quantity, and quality of food, and kind of clothing which shall be furnished to the slaves by their owners, according to their age and sex, taking as a rule that both food and clothing shall be of the same kind and description as those that, in conformity with the customs of the country, are allowed to free laborers; which Regulation being approved by the District Court, shall be posted monthly in all the towns, on the doors of the Town-houses, and churches, and of the chapels belonging to the plantations, so that it may be seen by all, and none plead ignorance."

"CHAPTER III: *Occupation of the slaves.*—The first, and principal employment of the slaves, shall be agricultural and other field labor, and not the occupations of a sedentary life ; and in order that the owners and the State may derive the due advantage from their labors, and that the slaves may perform them properly, the judges of the cities and towns, in the manner prescribed in the foregoing chapter, shall regulate the amount of daily labor of the slaves, in proportion to their age, strength and power, in such a manner, that while their hours of labor last only from sunrise to sunset, two of these hours shall be exclusively employed by them in working for their own benefit. The owners and overseers shall not have power to compel slaves over 60 or under 17 years of age, to do full work, neither to employ females in labor not conformable to their sex, or where they have to mix with the males; nor shall they be made to work as field hands ; and whenever they shall be appointed to domestic service, the owners shall contribute a compensation of two ducats annually, as provided in the 8th chapter of the Royal Decree of February 28th last, which has been already cited."

"CHAPTER IV: *Amusements.*—On all feast days of obligation, on which the owners cannot oblige or permit their slaves to work, after the latter have heard Mass, and received religious instruction, the masters, and in their absence the overseers, shall encourage the slaves to engage in simple and innocent recreation, under their personal supervision, without permitting them to join the slaves of other plantations ; and the two sexes being kept apart, avoiding drunkenness, and causing the amusement to cease before the call to prayers, at sunset.

"CHAPTER V: *Dwellings and Sick Room.*—Separate

dwellings shall be provided for each sex, and cohabitation permitted to married couples only. Said dwellings must be comfortable, sufficiently ventilated, and calculated to shelter the occupants from the inclemencies of the weather. The rooms and cabins shall be furnished with raised beds, blankets and all the necessary bed-clothing, and separated from each other in such a manner as to afford accommodation for one or two persons only.—Another well-sheltered and comfortable room shall be appropriated to the sick, who shall be supplied by their owner with everything necessary; and in case there be no accommodations on the estate, or by reason of the proximity of a town, they prefer to send them to the hospital, the owner shall pay for their admission the daily sum designated in Chapter II; and in the event of the death of the slave, the owner shall pay the burial expenses."

"CHAPTER VI: *Of the aged and infirm.*—The slaves, who owing to their advanced age, or by reason of sickness are unable to work—and the same in reference to children and minors of either sex—shall be supported by the owners, the latter not being allowed to liberate them, unless they shall provide them with sufficient means, according to the judgment of the attorney, to enable them to maintain themselves without further assistance."

"CHAPTER VII: *Marriages of slaves.*—The owners of slaves should avoid all illicit intercourse between the two sexes, by encouraging marriage, without opposing their marriage with the slaves of other owners; in which case, if the estates should be distant from each other, so that the consorts should not be able to comply with the ends of matrimony, the wife shall follow her husband, being bought by the owner of the latter at a price fixed by two umpires named respectively by the interested parties; and in case of desagreement, by a third, who shall be judicially appointed. Should the owner of the husband decline to purchase the wife, the owner of the latter shall have the privilege of purchasing the husband."

"CHAPTER VIII: *Obligations of the slaves, and correctional penalties.*—It being the duty of the owners of slaves to feed, instruct and employ them in useful labors, proportionate to their strength and sex, without abandoning the minors, aged and infirm, it follows, as an obligation on the part of the slaves, to obey and respect their masters and overseers; to execute the tasks and labors assigned to them, according to their ability, and to venerate them as fathers of the family: therefore, he who shall fail in any of these duties, may, and ought to be correctionally punished for the faults he may commit, either at the hands of the owner of the estate or of the overseer, according to the nature of the offence or its gravity, by imprisonment, fetters, chains, or the stocks, (in which he must not be put in by the head,) or with lashes, not to exceed twenty-five, and with an instrument that will cause neither serious contusion nor effusion of blood; which corporeal punishment must not be inflicted on a slave by any other person than by his owner or overseer."

"CHAPTER IX: *Infliction of greater penalties.*—If a slave commits excesses, misdemeanors or crimes against his master, his master's wive or children, overseer or any other person, for the punishment and check of which the penalties specified in the preceding chapter should not be deemed sufficient, the delinquent being apprehended by the owner or overseer of the estate, or by those who may be present at the time of the committal of the outrage, the injured party, or the person representing him, shall give notice to the nearest magistrate, who, in conjunction with the owner (unless the latter should desinterest himself in the charge by abandoning his slave to the course of the law), but in all cases with the co-operation of the attorney general, in his character of protector of the slaves, shall proceed to a full investigation of the case, and sentence the delinquent to suffer the penalty which the law inflicts, according to the gravity of the offense, but in every respect in conformity with the provisions of the law, as would be applied under similar circumstances to free transgressors. And when the owner does not abandon the slave, and the latter is sentenced to pay damages to a third party, the owner shall be responsible for the same, which will not exclude the penalty which, according to the gravity of the crime, the slave shall suffer, after the approval of the district court, whether the penalty be death or mutilation."

"CHAPTER X : *Transgressions of the owners or overseers.*—The owner of slaves or overseer of an estate who does not comply with the regulations of this letter of instruction respecting the education of the slaves, their food, garments, moderation of labor and task, attendance to their innocent amusements, supplying of rooms and infirmaries, or who abandons minors, the aged or invalids unable to work, shall be fined $50 for the first offence; for the second, $100, and for the third, $200; which fine shall be paid by the owner, even in cases where the overseer alone is guilty, and may not have the means to pay; this fine will be distributed in three parts, to the plaintiff, the judge, and the fine-fund, as will be specified hereafter. And in case the above mentioned fines should not produce the desired effect, and there should be a repetition of the offense, the transgressor will be proceeded against, and greater penalties inflicted, for disobedience to my royal commands; independently of the more stringent measures which may be resorted to, upon proper evidence as to the gravity of the case being submitted to me. When the transgressions of owners or overseers be for excess of chastisement, causing grave contusions, effusion of blood or mutilation, besides suffering the same pecuniary penalties above mentioned, the owner or overseer shall be proceeded against criminally, according to law, at the instance of the attorney; and the penalty corresponding to the offense committed shall be inflicted upon the offender in the same maner as if the injured party were free, the slave, if able to work, shall be sold, and the amount applied to the fine fund; and when the slave prove unsaleable, he shall not be returned to the owner or overseer who inflicted the excessive chastisement, but the former will be obliged to pay a daily amount fixed by law, for his maintenance during the natural life of the slave, payable by thirds in advance."

"CHAPTER XI : *Of those who abuse slaves.*—As the owners and overseers are the only persons who, with the moderation above stated, can punish a slave correctionally, any other person who is not his owner or overseer shall not abuse, chastise, wound, or kill him, without incurring the penalties established by law against those who commit similar outrages or crimes on free persons; such cases will be tried and prosecuted at the request of the owner of the slave who may have been abused, chastised, or killed; and, should the owner not take steps to bring the aggressor to trial, the attorney general, in his character of protector of slaves, will have a right to open the prosecution in the former case, even if there should be no plaintiff."

"CHAPTER XII: *List of slaves.*—The owner of slaves shall, annually, present to the magistrate of the city or town in whose jurisdiction his plantation is situated, a list signed and sworn to, stating the age and sex of each one, so that it may be entered by the notary of the corporation, in a book which will be kept specially for this purpose, and preserved by the said corporation together with the list presented by the owner; and the latter, whenever any of his slaves die or absents himself from his estate, shall, within three days thereafter, notify the court of such death or absence, so that, with the knowledge of the attorney general, the fact may be noted down and all suspicion of a violent death be avoided. And should the owner fail to act upon this requisition, it will be necessary for him to prove either that the slave died from natural causes, or that his absence is not fictitious, in default of which proofs, suitable proceedings will be instituted against the owner, at the instance of the attorney general."

"CHAPTER XIII: *The manner of discovering the transgressions of owners and overseers.*—Owing to the distance between the plantations and towns, the difficulties which would inevitably result from allowing slaves to absent themselves without a pass from their owners or overseers, on the plea of entering their complaints, and the just provision of the law that slaves shall not be abetted, protected or concealed, it becomes necessary to institute some means, proportionate to the circumstances, by which to acquire a true knowledge of the treatment received by slaves on the plantations; one of these being that the priests who visit the plantations to celebrate Mass and explain the Christian doctrine, shall discover, either from their own observation or from the testimony of the slaves, what are the proceedings of the masters and overseers towards them, and how far the general instructions are obeyed, so that, information being privately and reservedly given to the attorney general of that section, city or town, he may take measures to ascertain whether the masters and overseers fail entirely or partially to their respective obligations. This notice or private information thus given by the priest in virtue of his ministry, or acquired from the complaint of the slaves, does not make the owners responsible for the facts alleged or deprive them of the right of justification, and can only authorize the attorney general to propose to the Court that a member of the corporation, or any other respectable person, be appointed to investigate the charge; and this person, after making the necessary investigation, shall hand his report to the Court, who shall substantiate and decide the case, reporting to the District Court, according to the laws and the letter of instructions, and admitting the right of appeal in those cases in which the right is recognised by law. Besides employing these means, it would be advisable to select, through the magistrates and with the concurrence of the corporation and the approbation of the attorney general, one or more persons of unblemished character, who should be appointed to visit and examine the plantations three times in the year, in order to discover how far the regulations laid down in the letter of instructions are obeyed, and to report the result of their investigations, so that the attorney general being duly notified, and proper evidence of the charges being furnished, the evils may be redressed; it should moreover be deemed a commendable action in any one to denounce any failing in the fulfilment of the requisitions expressed in all or any of the preceding chapters; and the informer should be assured that his name will always remain a secret, and that he will receive the part allotted to him out of the fine which has already been mentioned, without any responsibility attaching to him, except in the case where it is fully and notoriously proved that the charge was false and malicious. And, finally, it is in like manner declared that the magistrate and the attorney general, in his capacity of protector of the slaves, shall be held accountable, in the *Juicio de Residencia*, for any errors of omission or commission into which they may have fallen by neglecting to take the necessary measures to insure the desired effect of my Royal intentions as expressed in this letter of instructions."

CHAPTER XIV: *Depository of Fines.*—In the cities and villages where the aforesaid regulations are to be enforced and where justices and corporations are composed of Spaniards, there shall be kept in the Town House, a coffer with three keys, one of which shall be in the hands of the Alcalde, and the others in those of the senior magistrate and the Attorney General; this coffer shall be destined for the reception of the products of the penal fines proceeding from cases defined by this letter of instruction, and the amount invested according to the directions therein expressed, no authority being given to either party to abstract therefrom one single *maravidi* for a different purpose or object than the legal disbursements stipulated in said instructions; such disbursements must be accompanied with a certificate signed by the three key-holders expressing the object and use for which the money has been withdrawn, they being responsible for the funds disposed of for other purposes, in case that for some of these or other reasons the accounts of this department should not be approved by the Intendant of the provinces to whom they must be remitted annually, accompanied by vouchers showing the amount of these fines and their investment with the necessary documents to prove the charges and credits. To the end that all the rules prescribed in this letter of instruction may be duly and punctually obeyed, I annul whatsoever laws, decrees, royal orders, uses and customs, which are opposed to them, and I order my Supreme Council of the Indies, viceroys, &c."

The above ordinances, forming a protective and humane code, such as was never made by other nations for the most favored of the people, was, as has been said, and was also stated in its preamble, the abridgment and compendium of all the rules, laws and dispositions, which were found in all the codes existing at that time. From which it must be inferred, that the treatment and legislation observed in regard to the negroes from the time of their importation into the Spanish colonies, did not correspond with their condition of slaves; far from it, these ordinances appeared rather to be made for free colonies, subject to reasonable contract; the more so as the way to freedom was opened by means of industry and individual capacity, to all those negroes who desired it. So at least we infer from Art. III of the aforesaid ordinances, which treats of the *Occupation of the slaves*, where it says that their working hours, each day, shall be from sunrise to sunset, and no more, and that they shall daily have two hours to themselves which time they may employ in manual labor, or some other occupations, the product of which shall be for their own benefit. And this without taking into consideration the hours which, on each feast day, the industrious negroes, without a manifest, or, at least, a scandalous disregard of the precept of sanctifying the Sabbath and feast days, can turn to advantage by devoting themselves to the mechanical pursuits taught by the slaves long established in the colonies to those who have more recently arrived; some by working in the small farms which their masters bestow on the most deserving; others by raising domestic animals at a small cost which they can afterwards sell at remunerative prices in the neighboring estates and towns; by which means a sufficient profit can be made and capital accumulated to purchase themselves from slavery whenever they may desire.

I have seen a great many of these slaves who have become free through their own exertions, by such means as are here mentioned, and they are favored by the protection of the law on this matter, which accounts for the circumstance of the freedom of no less than one third of the colored population of the island of Cuba, among whom many are landed proprietors, and slave owners.[1]

The spirit of the foregoing ordinances which were, as I have already stated, a compendium of all the laws on slavery, promulgated from the time of the discovery of the New World until that date, went so far in its humane precautions that it even guaranted a sufficient provision for all those slaves who should be incapacitated for work. So that in Chapter VI masters are positively forbiden to give freedom to the aged or disabled, unless they at the same time appoint them a sufficient income to cover all their ordinary necessities for the rest of their lives.

And what shall we say of Chapter VII, in what re-

---

(1) At this prèsent time, there is in Havana, in Calle Teniente Rey n. 37, a boarding-house, whose proprietor is a negro woman, a dominican, who has many slaves in her service.

fers to keeping together those who are united by the holy ties of matrimony? The supposed power which some misinformed philanthropists have fancied to exist among propietors, to sell at their option either of the consorts, and keep the other, and which has so inflamed the imagination of romancers and poets,[2] is not more worthy of credit than other falsehoods of similar origin, whose tendencies among the ignorant can be easily imagined.

The fact is that not only are the proprietors unable to sell those negroes who are married, without selling both husband and wife, as well as their younger children, so that wherever they go, they go as a family; but, in the case of a marriage between negroes of different estates, the owner of the male is obliged to buy the female, except when, by an amicable arrangement between the respective proprietors, the owner of the wife buys the husband.

A great deal has been said about the power of inflicting arbitrary punishment on slaves, on the plantations. Arguing from the unquestionable right of the masters, and even of the overseers, to discover and punish the minor offenses of the negroes, our rivals and accusers have discoursed lengthily on this subject, with as little reason and judgment as on all other subjects of which we treat.

On the supposition that proprietors, authorized by the law as guardians and overseers of the idiotic, could maltreat them at their will, without any more restraint than their own interests in the capital invested in the acquisition of slaves, these persons exaggerate in their arguments the severity and even the forms of the punishments, representing them as frightful and even including among them the scaffold, all with the sinister purpose which explains itself; for, if we keep in view Chapter VIII of the beforementioned ordinances, which refers to punishments, and is so opposed, in spirit and letter, to an act of inhumanity, the injustice of these declaimers becomes obvious.

The negroes, in their transgression of lesser degree, such

---

[2] Among many of their productions which might be cited, is a comedy called *El Negro sensible*, which was well received, particularly in private Theatricals, and which gave me the first negative ideas on the subject which I am now treating.

as intentional absence from work, petty thefts, quarrels from which no grave consequences ensue, disobedience to their masters, etc., etc., could not be taken before a supreme judge or magistrate, or even punished by imprisonment, because they would thus find the best way of eluding work. And as impunity would prove an encouragement to more serious offenses, leaving aside the confusion which would be introduced by a mistaken lenity in punishment, it is palpable that the law ought to concede, as it does concede, to proprietors that advisable permission to punish summarily petty offenses and misdemeanors.

The whip, it is true, is applied to the number of twenty-five lashes, with great severity, for were the punishment less severe, it would not produce the desired effect on the negroes who may merit it. The stocks for feet and hands is also a common punishment on plantations in our colonies; but sometimes whipping is preferable, when the want of rationality of the culprit is considered. But it should not be believed that the whip and the stocks are always in action, for not only weeks and even months sometimes pass on every plantation without a sign of the slightest castigation; but also if the slave who is to be punished can find a white man to intercede and answer for him, that he will in future comply with his duty, which intercession is never disregarded by any white man, he is pardoned and escapes punishment for that time, until he shall commit another fault, and forever if he amends his conduct.

Vulgar prejudices, increased by the mystery of distances and by the images which such an odious name as that of slavery conjures up, have seen fearful scenes of a brutal domination, where in reality there are no other strictures than those necessary for the carrying out of labor under the auspices of evangelical charity.

There are also ordinances, and not very mild ones, against the wrongs committed by owners, as can be proved by what is said in Chapter XI. And it must not be supposed that these laws are merely nominal and are never really applied, owing to the impossibility of the negro's complaining ; for, putting aside the fact that the negroes do make themselves heard with all the persistence which their case may require, they have a protector in the person of the attorney general, whose obligation is to watch over them, which duty he performs in the manner explained in Chapter XIII.

In short, if the ordinances which I have cited and commented on were not the complement of a constant legislation, although scattered through many different codes and other collections of laws, so long as they are an evidence of the Christian spirit which ruled our monarchs and legislators in the matter of slavery, their exposition would prove the crucible in which a proceeding which is directly opposed to slavery would be purified from all the stigmas which have been attached to it, even though they might date from centuries back.

It is true that the said ordinances suffered some contradictions even at the commencement of their promulgation, owing to a petition preferred to His Majesty by some proprietors and farmers of the islands of Cuba and Santo Domingo, and of Caracas and the Continent, from which resulted much lucid information, from very able and reliable authorities, who, although desiring the suppression of certain articles, ratified all those which referred to the kindness of humane charity with which the negroes should be treated in all the Spanish colonies.

With this view, and as in the course of time these colonies had grown and improved according as they increased in importance, the institution of slavery could not exist without definite rules that should determine its practise by a clear jurisprudence. Those laws by which it was successively governed were formed on the basis of its former regulations, the last of which was that now in force in our possessions of the New World, and which forming an integral part of the government of the Island of Cuba, was issued and promulgated in Havana under date of 14th november 1842, in forty-eight articles, which will be inserted in the next chapter.

CHAPTER IV.

The change which took place in the political circumstances of the New World in the beginning of the XIX century, suggested, many years afterwards, some alteration in the legislation concerning the slaves. Suggestions to this effect made to the Spanish government by the interested parties. Scrupulous investigations ordered to be made before these suggestions were acted upon.—New ordinances for the regulation of the slaves, issued on the 14th of November, 1842. Extraordinary circumstances demand some strictness in the Island of Cuba. Conspiracy of the negroes against the whites in said Island, plotted and conducted by the English consul : an official record of the process is inserted to prove the truth of the assertion. Exceptional measures then dictated for the regulation of the slaves. They are not practically applied, the authorities being swayed by the impulse of humanity that governed the former laws, which after all, prevailed at that time, and are still in force.

The ordinances copied in the preceding chapter, which are based upon the most charitable and protecting spirit that exists in the human mind, not only as applied to the slaves coming from a savage country, but likewise to the Spanish colonists, were made at a time when the number of the colored population in our possessions, although large, was not so great in any one place as to create apprehensions of a general insurrection.

The slave population of Santo Domingo, which was the first among the colonies where slave labor was introduced, increased to such a degree, and the greatness of our colonies having suffered much from pirates and sudden attacks from seditious armed hords, the industrious owners of slaves on the island, apprehending some unforeseen calamity, sought for protection from the king, petitioning that certain clauses of this Code of ordinances should be revised and corrected, and others revoked.

His Majesty, however, did not accede to this request until he had inquired into the causes on which it was founded; and upon a scrupulous examination by the most experienced persons having been made on the subject, such portions of the regulations as were most objectionable and dangerous were modified.

There were, indeed, many objectionable ordinances which, on annalysis, appeared still more so, not in the light of charity, but in consideration of the character and tendencies of the people for whom they were made. For we must remember that Almighty God, in His inscrutable wisdom, has made a great difference, of mind and understanding, of wiews and tendencies, in creatures of different races: so that any legislation which might be excellent for a set of men united by common sentiment, degenerates into a useless and even prejudicial measure when those men for whom it is designed differ widely from each other.

Besides, when we consider the changes which successively took place in the social and political order of our colonies, the concentration of industrial and laboring forces on a given space of ground, when first Santo Domingo, and afterwards the colonies on the continent, became independent of the crown of Spain; and moreover, the efforts made by our enemies to wrest from us the little we were able to preserve in the Western World: all these circumstances justified a critical and equitable examination of these laws, and also the change operated in the jurisprudence of the negroes as stated in the preceding regulations, and which resulted in the laws for good government issued in Havana the 14th of November, as will be seen by the following articles:

1st. Every slave-owner shall instruct his slaves in the principles of the Holy, Roman, Catholic, Apostolic faith; that all those who have not been baptized may be so baptized; and in case of danger of death, such owner shall baptize them, as it is known that, in such urgent cases, any one is authorized to do so.

2d. The aforesaid instructions shall be imparted at night, after working hours, and immediately afterwards the slave shall recite the Rosary or some other devout prayers.

3d. On Sundays and feast days of obligation, after

having complied with their religious duties, the owners or overseers can employ the slaves for two hours, in cleaning the dwelling and out houses but in no case, for a greater length of time, or in labors of the plantation, except in harvest time or when delay is impossible; on such days, they shall work the same as on week days.

4th. They shall take care that, when those slaves who are baptized have arrived at the proper age, they receive the sacraments, whenever our Holy Mother the Church commands it, and also whenever they may require them.

5th. They shall take the greatest care to make them understand the obedience which they owe to the authorities, their obligation to reverence the clergy, to respect the whites, to behave well towards each other and to live in harmony with their companions.

6th. Owners shall give to their slaves in the country at least two or three meals a day, as they may think best; such meals shall be abundant and substantial, and in all respects suitable to men subjected to fatigue and hard labor, and must consist daily for each negro of six or eight plantains or their equivalent in sweet potatoes, yams, yucas, eight ounces of meat or codfish, four ounces of rice, flour or other nourishing food.[1]

7th. The owners shall supply them likewise with two suits of clothes a year, in the months of December and May; each suit to consist of a shirt, a pair of pants of nankeen or linen, and one handkerchief; and in December shall be added, one year a flannel shirt, and the next a blanket.

8th. The newly born and very small children, whose mothers are sent to labor in the field, shall be fed with very light food, such as broth, pap, milk and similar substances, until they are weaned entirely or have finished teething.

9th. While the mothers are out at work all the children shall remain in a cabin or room, which on every plantation should be reserved for them, which shall be under the special care of one female slave or more, as the owner

---

(1) The uninformed on this subject must not be alarmed at not seeing bread mentioned as an article of food, for in our colonies it is entirely an article of luxury, and there are many white persons of means who never tasted it.

or overseer shall deem necessary, according to the number of children.

10th. If the children should fall sick during their early infancy, they shall be nursed at the breasts of their own mothers, who for that purpose shall be exempt from field labor and occupied in domestic duties exclusively.

11th. Until they attain the age of three years, the children shall have shirts of striped gingham; from three to six, they may be of nankeen; the girls, from six to twelve, shall wear skirts or long chemises, and the boys, from six to fourteen, trowsers; and after these ages they shall dress like the adults.[1]

12th. In ordinary times slaves shall work nine or ten hours daily, the master arranging these hours as best he may. On the plantations, in harvest time, the working hours shall be sixteen, arranged in such a way that the slaves shall have two hours in the day to rest, and six in the night to sleep.

13th. On sundays and feast days of obligation, and in the hours of rest during week days, the slaves shall be allowed to employ themselves within the plantation, in mechanical labors, the product of which shall be for their own benefit, so as to acquire the means to purchase their freedom.

14th. The owners cannot oblige either male or female of over sixty years or under seventeen, to do full work, nor to employ slaves of either of these classes in labors not appropriate to their age, sex, strength or constitution.

15th. Those slaves who, from their advanced age or from sickness, are unable to work, shall be maintained by their owners, who shall not be permitted to give them their freedom in order to get rid of them, unless by providing them with sufficient means for their support without need of other assistance.

16th. In every plantation a room shall be reserved for the purpose of keeping the implements of labor, the key of which shall never be entrusted to a slave.

---

[1] Our own sense of decency, and not that of the negro, dictated these measures. They have not the slightest idea of modesty, and no matter what may be their origin, their condition, their age, or state, I have never seen any negro, male or female, who took the least trouble to go dressed in a way to denote the slightest shame of exposing any part of the body.

17th. On going out to work, each negro shall be furnished with the implements which he needs for the labor of the day; and on going back, they shall be taken from him and put away in the depository.

18th. No slave shall leave the plantation with any implement of labor, and much less with arms of any kind, unless accompanied by his master or overseer, or the family of either, in which case he may carry his cutlass, and nothing else.

19th. No slave shall be allowed to visit the slaves of another plantation without an express permission from the owners or overseers of both; and when obliged to go to another plantation or leave their own, they shall take a writen permit from the owner or overseer, with the description of the bearer, the date of the day, month and year, expressing the place to which he is going, and the time at which he must return.

20th. Any individual, of whatever class, color or condition he may be, is authorized to arrest any slave he may find out of the house or lands of his owner, unless he can show the written pass, which he should carry, or which, on being presented, shows that the bearer is not on the route which said pass describes, or whose leave of absence has expired; he shall conduct said slave to the nearest plantation, whose owner shall receive him and keep him securely, so as to return him to his owner if he belong to the same district, and if not, to the magistrate, so that the latter may give notice to the interested party, in order that the fugitive slave may be recovered by the person to whom he belongs.

21st. Owners and overseers shall not receive any remuneration for any fugitive slaves that they may take into custody or receive according to the foregoing article, that being an obligation to which they are mutually bound to each other; and which tends to their reciprocal advantage. All others who may apprehend fugitive slaves shall be remunerated by the owner with the amount of four dollars for each one, according to the fugitive slave law.

22nd. The owner likewise shall be obliged to pay all expenses for food and medical attendance, in case it should have been necessary, and all others, as expressed in the same fugitive slave law.

23rd. The owners shall permit their slaves to recreate

and amuse themselves decorously on holidays, after having complied with their religious obligations, but without leaving the plantation or joining with slaves of others; and always in open places and in the full view of their owners, overseers, or their assistants, until sunset or until the bell rings for evening prayer, and no longer.

24th. Owners and overseers are particularly requested to watch vigilantly that the negroes do not commit excess in drinking, and shall not permit many slaves of other plantations, or men of free condition, to participate in their amusements.

25th. The owner shall take particular care to construct for unmarried slaves spacious dwellings in a ventilated and dry locality; with separations for each sex, well closed and secured with lock and key, in which a light shall be kept burning all night; and where their means shall permit, there shall be separate rooms for each married couple.

26th. At the hours of retiring for rest (which in long nights shall be at eight o'clock and in the short ones at nine), the roll shall be called and each slave shall answer to his name, so that only the surveyors shall remain outside; one of whom shall be appointed to take care that the others keep silence and to inform the owner immediately of any disturbance on the part of his companions or of people from other plantations or of any other important ocurrence.

27th. There shall likewise be on each plantation, a room well closed and secured with a division for each sex, as also two more rooms for contagious diseases, where the slaves who may fall sick, shall be attended in severe cases by physicians, and in slight cases, where domestic remedies are sufficient, by nurses male or female; but always with good medicines, proper food and the greatest cleanliness.

28th. The sick, where it is possible, shall be placed in separate beds with bedding consisting of a straw mattrass, mat or skin, with a pillow, blanket and sheet, or or boards that shall be sufficiently convenient, but in all cases, raised from the floor.

29th. The owners shall endeavor to repress all illicit connection between the sexes, encouraging marriages and giving to the married means of living together under the same roof.

30th. To accomplish this end and that the consorts may fulfill the ends of matrimony, the wife shall follow the husband whose owner shall buy her at a price stipulated between the two owners, or else by umpires appointed by both sides, or by a third in case of desagreement, and if the owner of the husband should not wish to buy the wife, then her owner shall have the same priviledge as the former, and in case that neither of the owners should wish to make the purchase, then both husband and wife shall be sold together to a third party.

31st. When the owner of the husband shall buy the wife, he shall buy with her all her children under three years of age, as, according to law, their mothers are obliged to suckle and nurse them until they attain that age.

32d. The owners may be obliged by the magistrates to sell their slaves, when they have inflicted on them grave contusions, or commited against them any other excesses contrary to humanity and the rational means with which they ought to be treated. The sale shall be made in these cases, for the price named by umpires or by a magistrate in case one of these should refuse to act, or by a third person in case of desagreement, but in case there should be a buyer at the price that the owner exacts, then the sale shall be made in his favor.

33d. When the owners at their own option and for their own convenience desire to sell a slave, they will be at liberty to fix any price they please, according to their estimate of his value.

34th. When a slave wishes to purchase his freedom, the owner must not refuse to fix his price, on payment of at least fifty dollars by said slave on account of the same.

35th. The slaves whose value has thus been fixed shall not be sold for a higher price than that previously stipulated, and with this condition shall pass from owner to purchaser. Nevertheless, if the slave wishes to be sold against the will of his master, without just cause, or should by his bad conduct give cause to be sold, the master may add to said price the amount of the excise duty and the cost of the deed of sale.

36th. As the benefit of this privilege, is entirely personal, the children of mothers who enjoy it cannot be participants in it, and they can be sold like any other slave.

37th. Owners shall give freedom to their slaves as soon as they receive their price as legitimately fixed; which price in case the interested parties do not agree, shall be named by umpires; one appointed by the owner of the slave or in his absence by a magistrate, another by the attorney general in the name of the slave, and a third by the same magistrate in case of disagreement.

38th. The slave who shall discover and make known any conspiracy formed by any of his class or by any persons of free condition, to disturb the public peace, shall receive his freedom and besides, a reward of five hundred dollars. If the informers should be many and present themselves in such a way as to show that the last ones did not know that the disclosure had been already made, then all such informers shall receive their freedom, and the reward of five hundred dollars shall be devided among them all, equally. When the information given has reference to a conspiracy of slaves or of free men against the owner, his wife, children, or relations, the overseer or any assistant on the estate, owners are recommended to be liberal with such slaves who have fulfilled the duties of faithful servants, as it is much to their advantage to offer an encouragement to loyalty.

39th. The price of their liberation and the reward alluded to in the first paragraph of the preceding article, will be taken from the amount resulting from the fines imposed for the infraction of these regulations, or any others ordered by the government.

40th. Slaves also shall receive their freedom when it shall be granted them in a will or by another legally justified means, proceeding from an honorable and praiseworthy motive.

41st. Slaves are obliged to respect and obey their owners, overseers, and all other superiors, and, to fulfill the tasks set them, and he who shall fail in any of these obligations shall be punished by whatever person may be at the head of the plantation, according to the delinquency or excess he may have committed, with imprisonment, fetters, chain or the stocks, in which he shall be confined by the feet and never by the head, or with wipping, which must never exceed twenty-five lashes.

42nd. When a slave shall commit grave transgressions or some crime for which these punishments should not be deemed sufficient, he shall be bound and carried before a magistrate, so that in the presence of his owner, if he should not give him up entirely to justice, or before the attorney general if he should do so and will not continue the accusation, he may be proceded against, according to law; but in case the owner should not have given him up, and the slave should be condemned to the payment of damages and costs toward a third party, the owner shall be responsible for the same, which will not exempt the slave from punishment, corporeal or otherwise, according to the offence he has committed.

43rd. Only owners, overseers or stewards shall be authorised to punish the slaves correctionally and with the moderation and under the penalties aforesaid; and any other person who may do so, without the special order of the owner or against his will, or cause him, by so doing, any other injury or wrong, shall incur in the penalities established by the laws, the case being opened at the instance of the owner, or in his absence by the attorney general as protector of slaves, if the transgression should not be so great as to affect the public good, or in his official character, if it should belong to this latter class.

44th. The owner in charge or the assistants in the plantations who may desobey or infringe any of these rules, shall be fined for the first time from twenty to fifty dollars; for the second time, from forty to one hundred, and for the third, from eighty to two hundred, according to the importance of the rule infringed.

45th. The fines shall be paid by the owner of the plantation or any other person who has been guilty of the infraction, and in case that he should not be able to do so for want of means, he shall suffer one day's imprisonment for every dollar that he has been fined.

46th. If the offense of the owners of slaves on plantations, should consist in excessive corporal punishment, causing grave contusions, wounds, mutilation, or more serious injury, besides being fined as stated, the person who shall have committed said offense shall be prosecuted criminally, at the instance of the attorney general, or officially, so as to impose on him the penalty due to his misdemeanor; and the owner shall be obliged to sell the slave, if he be still saleable, or to give him his freedom if he should be disabled, paying him, during his natural life, a daily stipend, which shall be determined by a magistrate, for his food and clothing, payable monthly, in advance.

47th. The fines shall be applied in the following manner: one third of their amount shall be given to the magistrate or any justice who may impose them, and the other two shall be applied to the fund which shall be formed in the political administration of each district, for the cases named in article 38, for which end they shall be paid into the secretary's office of said district, against his receipt.

48th. The lieutenant governors, magistrates and justices shall see to the punctual observance of these regulations, and they shall be responsible for any omission or excess in their carrying out.

Havanah, etc." [1]

Besides the forty-eight preceding articles, the Captain General of Cuba, in accordance with and at the recommendation of the *Junta de Fomento*, issued on the 31st of May 1844, (that is to say two years after the promulgation of the preceding ordinances,) other regulations which contained more stringent measures; but this was not done without a just cause, for many and very dangerous elements had combined, at that time, to annihilate our authority in those possessions which are still recognized with such glorious titles in the western hemisphere.

On this point, respecting which several preventive articles in the ordinances of 1842 had already become notorious, such as those offering premiums of liberty and a pecuniary reward to negroes who should denounce any conspiracy tending to disturb public order, it is necessary to give some explanation, not only to support with sufficient proofs the charge which I have already preferred against foreign machinations, but also to justify certain appearances of cruelty and rigor in the regulations of 1844. I do not like to declaim, nor to give vent to angry feelings in a work of such an especial nature as that which I am writing, and which I wish to make acceptable to all; but it would not be proper to allow to pass unnoticed the charges that might be brought against the harshness of our laws, should the motives for such harshness remain unexplained.

These are to be seen in several legal papers, relating to a suit, unfortunately notorious, which was formed on the

---

(1) *Biblioteca de Legislacion de Ultramar;* article on "Slavery," vol. III, page 136, etc.

island of Cuba in 1841, 42 and 43, on account of a vast conspiracy set on foot by the English consul, against the existence not only of our flag, but of the entire white race in the Antilles. And so that, in an ocurrence of such importance, we may not be led away in the exposition of deeds and the logical deductions to be drawn therefrom, we will leave entire the whole history, such as it was writen by the supreme judge who conducted the cause, as will be seen in the following decision, which presents a clear view of the case:

Don Francisco Yllas, *Captain of cavalry, Judge and Recorder of the Military Commission, etc.*

"This committee entrusted with the investigation of the alleged complicity of certain foreigners in the conspiracy of the blacks, already discovered, they having been accused by the criminals themselves, at different stages of the important trial of said case now in progress, and which has been conducted in accordance with our code of procedure in such cases, to-day presents to the court the necessary data to properly appreciate the facts elicited respecting each of the accused, and to pass judgment thereon, with that impartial and even-handed justice so emminently its attribute.

" On giving my opinion on a subject so grave and at the same time of such immense importance to the interests of the Metropolis, I may be permitted to trace cursorily the history of the facts which have led to these proceedings, beginning with the appointment of Mr. David Trumbull to discharge the duties of H. B. M.'s consulate in Havana. This fanatical abolitionist had already made known his opinions and principles in a work published in the year 1840, entitled " Travels in the West Indies;" and it is a remarkable fact that, in the communication directed by lord Palmerston to Mr. Acton, on the 17 of March 1842, on complaints being made by our Government against the conduct of the ex-consul, the English minister should say that the book writen by that functionary, and his unequivocal opinion in favor of the liberty of the slaves, recommended him and fitted him for the office which he held in this Island : as if men blinded and inflexible in their principles, of turbulent spirit, and capable of committing any outrage, were the most fitting to preserve harmony between two friendly and allied nations.

"It is therefore not to be wondered at, that with these antecedents, the ex-consul should have arrived at the conclusion that, in this country, he could preach publicly the emancipation of slavery, and that, on the other hand, as the political state of the Peninsula, at that time so full of lamentable errors, favored him particularly, he should rush on his dreadful mission without fear, and promote the triumph of his doctrines by converting the most precious of the Antilles into a scene of cruelty and rapine, under the governement of an ignorant and ferocious race. And, truly, gentlemen, if we pause to consider the peculiar circumstances of our country, the classes which compose its population, the immense number of slaves, and the means which that man put in play to bring about the insurrection of this terrible mass, we cannot but acknowledge that by a miracle only we have been able to save ourselves from such imminent peril.

"The government of the Island, notwithstanding the difficulties of its position, caused by the events which had changed the political aspect of the Peninsula, watched very closely the steps of the agents of the ex-consul, and on the 1st of December 1842, it arrested José Michel, a free black, whose case was tried in the military commission, before an able and practical attorney general, who, by dint of zeal, activity and efficiency in the discharge of his duties, suceeded in discovering the origin of those evils which we now lament. In fact, in that celebrated suit, it was thoroughly proved by all the means that the law recognizes, that the project of the conspiracy existed, and that its author and principal promoter was Mr. David Trumbull.

"This is proved by many facts, some of which are publicly known. They have been witnessed by the whole Island, and their marked tendencies require no explanation. The first step taken by him after his appointment was to embark in the English steamer *Venezuela*, for the island of Demerara. He engaged to pay the expenses to said island and back of four free negroes named as follows: José del Carmen Lamozano, Felix Rodriguez, José del Carmen Reitia, and Trinidad Baldemoa, with the assistance of the Emigration Society, at that time established in that port, his object being that they should visit the British Islands, and on their return to this country they should give to their countrymen an exalted idea of them. The persons who informed in a legal manner and gave the particular circumstances attending these facts bear a character of veracity entirely reliable, viz: the Spanish vice-consul at Jamaica, where the travellers made a stay; the vice-consul of the United States, at the same place; the captain of the steamer that conveyed them thither, through his boatswain; Don José Cabalzas, merchant, who was commissioned to furnish them with passports, who however excused himself from doing so; and even the secretary of H. B. M.'s consul, Mr. Francis Ross y Coguen, who moreover certified in his deposition the very important circumstance that Trumbull attempted to have these individuals embarked on board of a man-of-war, without passports; and the only reason why he did not do so was because the commander would not receive them; which step, on the part of Trumbull, clearly shows how little he cared to fulfil the requirements of our laws, and how ready he was to infringe them when they offered any obstacle to the accomplishment of his wild and criminal design. These facts are attested to in the indictment and shown in the report of the attorney general.

"The governor being apprised of the departure of the four emissaries, gave the necessary order for their apprehension on their return to the Island; and thanks to the vigilance of the authorities of this city, the arrest of the negro Lamorano was effected. This Lamorano is a man of understanding and of extraordinary sagacity, and possessed of intelligence not very common among men of his class. What might not have been the effect produced in this country by the preaching of these negroes, holding forth to the slaves an exalted idea of the advantages enjoyed by the colored poeple in the islands they had just visited?

"Almost at the same time when that expedition of conspirators left Havana, other agents of the ex-consul scoured the Island and prepared, so to speak, the ground on which the travelers were afterwards to conduct their operations. The council should bear in mind the arrival of the mulatto Luis Gigant in this place, about the middle of the year 1841; the steps taken by him to engage in the plan of the uprising of the free colored people; the offers he made them in the name of those who sent him, the expectation that he raised in them, as to the ultimate success of the enterprise, and lastly the meetings they held, the opinions there discussed, the mandates given to the members to make proselytes in the interior, and to prepare the minds of the slaves for the approaching outbreak and for the extermination of their masters, over whose dead bodies they would raise the edifice of their liberty.

" But undoubtedly the efforts of his emissaries appeared very ineffectual to the ex-consul, for in November of the same year, 1841, we find him again in this city endeavouring to convince some negroes of the right they had to be free. Information having been received by the Government, that he had come without a passport from his Excellency the Captain General, warning was given him that he must return to Havana, and that he must not be permitted to stop at Cárdenas or on any of the plantations which lay on his way, as he intended to do. Don Eugenio Balben, proprietor of the hotel at which he put up, testifies that, during the time he remained there, none but free negroes and slaves entered his room: George Becher and Francisco Huerta, known as Adams, (men who, according to the testimonies of the attorney generals Don Ramon Gonzales and Don Mariano Fortun, figured as chiefs and active promotors of the conspiracy in this place,) attracted attention by their frequent visits. Guillermo and Susano, slaves of Don Juan Torres, also declare, in fos. 41 and 43, that they were sent for by him to impress it on their minds that they ought to be free, the same as the negroes of Providence; the object of his journey being, as he said, to make himself acquainted with the manner in which they were treated in this province and in the district of Cardenas, which he intended to visit; and that they must have confidence in the means he would furnish them to obtain their freedom. The former of these negroes added that he had told them that an armed force would arrive from Santo Domingo, previous to which some emissaries would come for the purpose of instructing them in what they must do. Let it not be said that these three negroes were not reliable, and may have deposed falsely, for, in addition to the citations of folios 67 and 573, translated by the government interpreter, Don Martin Fort, they agree with the testimony of the free negro Miguel

Michel, who was fully acquainted with all the circumstances. Trumbull himself has furnished some facts which tally equally with both these declarations, and which can leave no doubt in regard to their truthfulness besides being confirmed by the papers found in his possession when arrested in Guibara, having reference to these same negroes of Forbs, with whom he had held conferences in this place in the manner we have just seen.

"Thus it was that this man commenced his career by spreading the seeds of insurrection until he was most fortunately checked in his progress by the order which relieved him of his office, an order which, although it disconcerted his plans, as shown by the letters from his agents taken from Michel, did not in the least diminish the audacity and energy with which they were conceived and put in execution. From the Island of Providence, where he went to reside, we were astonished to see him cross over to the port of Gibara in a sloop entirely manned by negroes as if careless to conceal the object of his undertaking. Observe how well his partisans were initiated in all he proposed to do, it being stated in one of the letters found upon Michel, that he had returned to the Island with the determination to revenge himself or die in the attempt.

"It would seem that he really had come to this resolution, for after having been arrested by order of the Captain General, and whilst in charge of an officer to be conveyed from Holguin to Gibara, he failed in the respect due to the authority, and abusing the kindness and forbearance shown to him by his conductor, he forced himself into the plantation La Caridad where he held forth to the negroes' the right they had to be free, and wrote threatening letters to their owner hoping that fear for his personal safety would compell him to give them their freedom.

"When the representative of a powerful nation thus entices and stimulates ignorant men, ever ready to shake off the yoke of slavery, to deeds of open rebellion; when the promise of future welfare with the acquisition of honors, and affluence is held out to free negroes, and when the attainment of those blessings is represented as easy, what must be the inevitable result of such proceedings? The numerous cases submitted to its decision have made the answer painfully evident to this committee. The slaves of hundreds of plantations are coaleseing and preparing to rise in rebellion; the free negroes employed in the country are inciting and animating them in their resolutions, and those living in towns are resolving in their meetings the ruin of the country and the extermination of thousands of families, who, impressed with gratitude now bless the hand that saved them."

It has been a source of satisfaction to me to find in the foregoing document a cause of gratitude towards the English government, for having removed a consul, who so invidiously and unworthily fulfilled his duties in the Island of Cuba. Justice and an unalterable desire of conciliation oblige me to make this acknowledgment, whilst a sincere regard for our national honor, by which the legal proceedings in this deplorable affair were influenced, have induced me to insert the preceding document before adverting to the following decree, so that the reasons which dictated its promulgation may be better understood and appreciated.

" 1st. The owners of slaves destined to agricultural labors shall see that they are instructed in the principles and mysteries of our holy religion, by the overseer, the steward, or administrator of each plantation, that they comply with the precepts of the Church, and that they receive the sacraments when so ordained.

" 2nd. Said owners, using in all cases the full power granted them by law over their slaves, as the only means to keep them in subordination, shall order that through the said substitutes they shall receive their food, clothing and necessary attendance during sickness : and also, that said slaves shall be punished, when they commit any offence, by whipping or imprisonment to a degree that they may consider in accordance with the instructions received from the master; who in no case shall whip the slaves himself, and to whom it is recommended in all punishments to incline rather to clemency than to excessive rigor.

" 3rd. They shall direct said administrators, overseers, and stewards, first : that every evening after prayers, the doors be closed upon the slaves until day light the next morning, and that a guard be kept going the rounds of the plantation, headed by a white man. Second : that the administrator, overseer or steward, does not leave the plantation, on any day of the year, except on business concerning the owner, or by his express permission. Third: that any colored person either free or slave, or any white man of suspicious appearance who may be found on the plantation without presenting a letter or paper signed by the person by whom he is sent, shall be arrested and sent to the district judge, and the same shall be done to pedlars. Fourth: that the subordinates of the plantation shall vigilantly watch the conduct of the free negroes who are employed on them, and shall be held strictly responsible for their conduct.

"4th. They shall order the said administrators, overseers or stewards, that, in case of any murder or affray or any disturbance showing symptoms of insurrection on the plantation, they shall immediately notify the Captain of the district that he may proceed to make the corresponding summary of the case.

"5th. They shall be careful to employ none but whites as cartmen, muleteers, or messengers and generally in any capacity in which it is necessary to go beyond the limits of the plantation.

"6th. There shall be in each plantation a number of white employees equivalent to one-twentieth of the number of colored laborers.

For the carrying out of the above regulations, made by the board of protection, sanctioned and issued by the Captain General of the Island of Cuba, the following instructions issued the 31st of May 1844, were ordered to be observed:

"1st. All emancipated negroes on this Island whose term of civil and religious instruction shall have expired and are therefore free, shall be taken care of by the government who shall provide them the means of embarking and leaving this country in the manner and form that Her Majesty, who shall be informed on the matter, shall direct. [1]

"2nd. The number of negroes without trade, property, or the means of subsistence existing in the Island shall be ascertained, and all such shall be held by the courts as vagrants and hurtful to society.

---

(1) The word *emancipated* is applied to all such negroes as are seized at sea or at the time of landing by the forces or agents of the government. They are placed under the protection of the government, who, to effect their instruction in labor and in christian civilization, places them with persons of laborious habits; these persons, in consideration for the benefit they derive from the labor of said negroes pay a monthly sum into the treasury.

"3rd. After a given length of time, all free negroes coming from another country shall be expelled.

"4th. The prohibition of landing negroes either slaves or free, shall be punctually observed.

"5th. The local authorities shall keep a strict watch over all negro lessees.

"6th. The prohibition to colored people to hold meetings shall be rigorously observed, and any outrage they may commit against the whites shall be severely punished.

"7th. On no account shall negroes be employed in drug shops, and much less to be allowed to make up even the simplest prescription.

"8th. All taverns in the country, which, according to the investigation and report of the local authorities, are, owing to their locality or want of means, of no service to the public, shall be suppressed after I have been advised and given my sanction.

"9th. The sale of liquors is prohibited in the country, both by the wholesale and retail, and is only allowed in towns.

"10th. The owners of plantations adjacent to each other shall be recommended to employ clergymen of known virtue to instruct their negroes in our Holy Religion as well as in the duties of morality, obedience and submission imposed upon them by society and the laws of the land."

For the sake of clearness, and ever with the end of historically and legally demonstrating that the civil status of the negro in the Spanish possessions of the New World is not that of slavery, which name has been applied to it with so little foresight and such notorious injustice, it is necessary to note that the above regulations were transitory, and, indeed, that the most objectionable portions of them were never carried into effect.

The ordinary laws, such as they existed before the promulgation of said measures, were prompt in their action and sufficient always, to inflict on criminals with singular lenity the punishment which they deserved. Afterwards, the calm which followed that great agitation inspired confidence and restored things to their natural current, so that the expulsion of the emancipated negroes which had been decreed was never enforced; nor were there any complaints or suits instituted against free negroes for vagrancy

A few months having elapsed after the punishment of the ringleaders, which was slight, indeed, compared with the magnitude of their crime [1] every thing returned to its former state; mild, civilizing, and supremely humane, in conformity to the former rules and regulations herein transcribed. And the results corresponding eminently to the pious tendency shown in the spirit of our legislation relative to negroes, became patent in the progressive emancipation of slaves, owing to the advantages they enjoy on the estates of the country, in the domestic labor in the houses of their employers or overseers, or in industrial occupations in the cities. These beneficial results were further secured by the new acts emanating from the authorities for the purpose of rendering effective the protection which our legislators had in view on establishing a fundamental rule as regards this institution and in behalf of the weak.

To demonstrate the proposition set forth as a fundamental idea in these pages, viz: that the civil state of the negroes in the Spanish colonies is not that of slavery, which name has been erroneously applied to it, and is not conformable to facts, the legal proofs set forth in the preceding chapter as well as in this, would suffice. Nevertheless, as unfair reasoning sophistry might say that laws are one thing and their application another, when material interests are raised above their spirit; in order to dispel any doubts and for the purposé of showing the true

---

(1) In all countries, sedition and treason are punished with the greatest penalties, and our code, like that of all the nations who properly value the peace of society, punishes these crimes with death; notwithstanding all this only three of the ringleaders were executed on this occasion; and though it is to be lamented that among them a mind gifted with poetic talent perished, I refer to Plácido, a mulatto who apart from this intellectual privilege possessed no other virtue, for he was quarrelsome, intemperate, dissolute and vicious, whenever an occasion presented, it cannot be denied without injustice and opposition to truth and to our procedings that wonderful clemency and extraordinary prudence were displayed in the decision of the court. The crime was, indeed, of the greatest, since it purposed no less than the murdering of all the white people of Cuba first and afterwards of Porto Rico, so that the negroes might then take possession of both Islands. But considering the defective judgment of those who wished to realize such a bloody programme and the facility with which this plot could, without inflicting capital punishment on many of the criminals, the severity of the court was limited to the execution of those three individuals, and the transportation of some two or three dozens of the most guilty to the Peninsula there to be imprisoned. Our proceedings, of course were as usual food for slander, but my statements are essentially true.

state of things such as it will be presented to the views and understanding of all persons who choose to judge them for themselves, as I have done, I think it expedient to amplify this idea by an impartial statement of the manner in which the compulsory labor of the negroes is carried on in our possessions of the New World, and what are the results of the practice.

CHAPTER V.

The reason why the legislation and proceedings of the Spanish Colonies are taken in this work as the type of the legislation and proceedings concerning the slavery of negroes.—How the free people of color live in Cuba and Porto Rico, where slavery exists, and in Santo Domingo where it is abolished.—Domestic service by hire in said countries, both of slave and free servants.—Other classes of service public and private.—The slaves on the plantations.—Character of their services, and comparison with the services of the white people in free nations.—Means which negro slaves have of redeeming themselves from labor in the Spanish possessions.—Corporeal punishment: its legislation and application.—The punishment inflicted on the negro slaves and that applied to white soldiers and sailors in some of the European nations, especially in England, compared.—Legal means which delinquent slaves have to escape excessive chastisement.—Trustees for the protection of slaves: their authority and its application.—Right of the slaves to change their master for just cause and in accordance with law.—Rules which, in the Spanish possessions, govern in such cases.—Some historical considerations on the wrongs to which the beneficent institution of negro labor has been subjected.

In the preceding chapters I have intentionally refrained from noticing any law, ordinance or regulation concerning slavery or the treatment of the blacks, in any country where the institution existed or still exists, except such as had reference to the Spanish colonies. For, as we were the first who introduced slavery in the New World, though with such modifications as the progress of civilization required, and with the twofold and commendable purpose of redeeming the negro from his barbarous condition, and of relieving the Indians from the labor imposed on them, to which they were neither accustomed nor adapted, I think that it is with our own laws, and not with those of other nations, that we should respond to the universal reprobation with which the social evil is viewed, which has caused and is still causing such violent agitation among civilized nations.

I have equally abstained from alluding to the practical manner in which the abolition of slavery has been attempted in all the colonies, and carried out in some, as this would have led me into a disquisition on the justice and the opportuneness of the efforts which have been made, and moreover, as since the time we began to be considered a great nation (which we certainly were in the sixteenth century) we have been constantly accused of inhumanity.

It has been proven by an impartial analysis and comparison that we were not the least distinguished for humanity in the laws referring to slavery, and in their practical enforcement, any foreign laws which I might here insert would only tend to establish rivalries, encourage disputes and recriminations, and produce discussions contrary to the spirit of impartiality and moderation which presides over this work.

Such as we have always proved ourselves to be, and in our own light as founders of African slavery in America, I desire that we may be considered and judged; taking as a principle that we have organised in a permanent manner the labor of these agents of universal wealth, and that we have abolished the former odious system of slavery, as is fully shown by the existing regulations, which, if duly analized, will be found efficient to serve as a basis for another code of laws to be universally adopted and applied by all nations owning slaves; and if better or more complete regulations can be found among other nations, there is no reason why they should not be adopted, upon the interested parties coming to a general understanding, and agreeing as to the necessity of a general reform.

Premising this in order to justify our intentional omission, and to give a greater independence to the character of this work, let us boldly enter at once upon the matter which is to be considered in this chapter, viz: the manner in which the laws are interpreted in their practical application amongst the Spanish proprietors or lessees of the colonial possessions, in regard to the respective rights and duties of themselves and their laborers.

As in this work, we could not, without being guilty of a serious omission, neglect to mention the state of the free negroes, who, in the island of Cuba, amount to more than one-third of the colored population, in Porto Rico to one-half, and in Santo Domingo the whole, it will be well for me to give at once the result of the observations which I have made during the period of thirteen years, which I have devoted to a constant study of the subject, passing the time for this purpose in the cities and smaller towns, but more frequently in the country. And in case my testimony should not be sufficient to produce on the public mind the desired effect, I appeal to the testimony of all persons who have studied the question impartially, with the firm conviction that they will corroborate all my statements.

First of all, it will be necessary to observe that the customs of the free negroes in Cuba and Porto Rico, where slavery exists, and where social discipline is maintained by the restraints of a good government, differ greatly from, and are superior to those of Santo Domingo, where an undue political liberty has introduced among the negroes habits of indolence and vagrancy, which are almost incorrigible. The former being accustomed to work ever since their eyes first opened to the light of civilization, whether they be *Bozales* who have been fraudulently introduced into said islands to be employed in forced labor, and have subsequently been liberated, or Creoles born of free parents, or those who, having been slaves from their birth, and being freed according to the provisions of the law, generally exceed the proper bounds of their liberty, labor does not degenerate among them as it does among the negroes of Santo Domingo, and of all other places where slavery has been abolished.

Owing to the nature of the tropical climate, which is so bountiful as to afford spontaneously the necessary sustenance to man, and so mild that there is no necessity for any great precautions against intemperate of the weather, the negroes being left entirely to their own will, without check or curb, naturally return to their primitive state and abandon all manner of employment. In the island of Santo Domingo, after its re-annexation to Spain, I have seen them lounging the livelong day in their miserable cabins, in which they kept some pieces of raw beef, which they only half cooked for their meals when pressed by hunger, while at a short distance from the door they had a few plantains and yucas growing. Satisfied with these provisions, which can be procured by a quarter of an hour's labor each week, these miserable creatures look with indifference on the good wages offered to them as an inducement to employ their strength for the benefit of the country, and they invoke the respect due to their condition as freemen when endeavors have been made to persuade them to improve their condition by working. "With a piece of meat," they answer, "a handful of plantains and a young negress we can live comfortably enough." And, moreover, they do not clothe their bodies more than is absolutely necessary for the sake of common decency, while their children live and grow up in the state of nudity in which they were born, until instinct teaches them to cover themselves, and then, not through any feelings of shame, but solely in imitation of their parents. Such is the life of the free negroes in Santo Domingo, with very few exceptions, and such it will continue to be until this state of vagrancy shall be ended by a good law of immigration, and by the municipal ordinances which will naturally be made when our authority shall be firmly established, and other races shall people the island.

Let it not be said that the sad state of the negroes in this part of the West Indies is an exceptional case which has been caused by the peculiar circumstances to which this already extinct republic has always been subjected; for, although the adjacent republic of Hayti, on the same territory, has pretensions to a superior state of civilization, all those who have carefully considered the subject well know how ridiculous that fictitious civilization really is, and what constant persuasions and encouragements, from the consuls and other foreign agents, have been necesary to maintain their civil laws, in order to prevent their political existence from degenerating into a state similar to that of the negroes of St. Domingo. In order to confirm ourselves in this opinion, we have only to consider what has happened in the rest of the of the colonies of the West and Lucaya Isles, as well as in the European colonies of the Western Continent, where negro slavery has been violently abolished. I have also visited some of these, and at St. Thomas, for instance, where though not very fertile, there are nevertheless found some excellent lands for the cultivation of the sugar cane and other lucrative productions, not a negro laborer is to be had, except at very high wages, and then the proprietors by whom they are hired run the risk of being left with the work half done. They prefer to gain their living by the loading and unloading of vessels, as being a task less arduous and limited to stated hours, although it is for that very reason a less profitable occupation. There are some who will not even do this, except when they are in actual want of a few *reals*, prefering, while they last, to live upon cheap fruits, and vegetables.

The freedom of the negroes in Cuba and Porto Rico is very different, for such a state of things is expressly forbidden by the laws. In the country, where the sugar ad coffee plantations are the focus of slavery and the inexhaustible sources of wealth, but few free negroes are to be found, either because they cannot procure work by the day on the plantations, or because they do not choose to engage in agricultural employements under the supervision of overseers and superintendents.

I do not mean to say that no free colored families reside in the country, for they certainly do; and some of them own large plantations and negro slaves; this is especially the case in Porto Rico where this class of the population is very numerous in proportion to the extent of territory. But where there are such families labor is not abandoned through indolence, and much less as unnecessary, as all are subject to the police regulations and to the provisions of an excellent government by which vagrancy is prohibited, as I have already stated; for which reason their state of civilization, and consequently their customs are, similar to those of the white population, with whom they live in social intercourse and constant communication.

But with the exception of this obligation to work, the kind of employment being nevertheless left to their own option, and of the moderate restraint which is imposed on their habits, the free negroes are in every other respect as independent as the whites, and the law protects them in all the civil rights which are common to them and to us. In the cities they are at full liberty to be in the public streets, even at the most unseasonable hours without further restrictions than those which public order imposes on all good citizens; they have their *tertulias* and balls just the same as the whites, and no authourities have ever refused them, without just cause, permission to keep up the dancing, with due decorum, within doors from sunset to sunrise on their particular festivals, whenever such permision has been respectfully solicited.

Perhaps it will be thougt that free negroes of either sex, who, having no other means of support, engage their services to a family of whites, are placed upon the same footing and bound to perform the same duties as other servants in countries where slavery never existed. What less could be exacted from a domestic who, besides clothing, food etc, receives liberal wages, and perquisites amounting to as much more ?

Yet this is far from being the case with the hired negroes; he who has a situation as cook will refuse even to sweep a parlor or to do the slightest work which does not belong to what he considers his exclusive obligations in the kitchen, even though he may be offered his weight in gold, while the negress who acts, as laundress would not think of going into the kitchen to attend to the fire, in the absence of the cook, even if the house was in danger of being burned down.

Owing to this state of things, which is unfortunately prevalent in the colonies, that branch of the service is insufferable, as no family can be even indifferently served without employing at least three domestics, while the wages and board of each of these amount monthly to no less than twenty-four dollars, or say, for the three servants, seventy two dollars; which in almost any country would be sufficient to support the family itself.

In addition to this, let it be considered that, when these servants have fulfilled their obligations, according to their own judgment, though generally not as they ought to have done, they imagine that they are free to go whithersoever they please, and, according to their customs they certainly possess that right, and scarcely ever return to their master's until bed time; now I may venture to say that this class, who are so much pitied by those who know nothing of their life and customs, would not change places with the most favored among the laboring classes in Europe, or even with many persons of the middle classes who are making such an outcry in their favor.

This description of the domestic service of the free negroes applies equally to that of the slaves who are hired out and of those who serve their owners, except in the matter of going out at their will, for in this respect the latter are subject to certain restrictions, and so are the hired slaves, whenever their owners have so stipulated with the employers.

Negroes of this class, both male and female, who hire themselves out to such persons, who, having no slaves of their own, are compelled to submit to the inconvenience of this most expensive kind of service, stipulate with their owners that on payment of certain monthly or weekly instalments they shall be free to dispose of their time and labor, so that whatever they may earn over and above that amount shall be exclusively their own.

Such is the general practice which is carried out more fully, when the slaves on their own account and at their own risk go out as public hackmen, or as workmen or porters on the docks and in the custom houses; and it can positively be affirmed that those who have followed such employments for two or three years and have not then purchased their freedom, have not chosen to do so for particular reasons, or because actuated by more ambitious views; as by continuing in their occupations for a length of time they can acquire means not only to buy their freedom but also to procure lands, by the product of which they may live in comfort without having to work much; and in so doing they are generally sucessful, especially in the capitals of both islands, and in other parts of the coast where trade is active.

Those who follow trades and other profitable business, such as tailors, shoemakers, segar makers etc., of which there are great numbers, and those who apply themselves to music and learn to perform on some instrument, can also speedily acquire means to obtain this freedom, on paying the required amount by instalments as is ordered in the regulations.

In short, any slave in the large cities, or in domestic service in the small towns, can obtain his freedom in a few years through his own industry and good conduct.

I cannot say as much of those employed on the plantations, for their labor is more valuable and they have fewer advantages than the others. Their daily tasks never last less than ten hours and they sometimes exceed that when extra labor is required at particular seasons. I can easily believe that they find this labor any thing but agreable when it is at first imposed upoun them, being accustomed to a life of independence in their native land; and that it is owing to this that there have been occasional cases of suicide among the *bozal* negroes recently imported into the islands. This is one of the charges which can justly be made againts us by civilization, for it is true that these unfortunate beings when newly arrived, owing to their ignorance of our customs, cannot appeal to the authorities against any ill usage which they may receive at the hands of the overseers charged with superintending their labor. Yet I trust I may be allowed to say that, when that period of acclimatation has been passed through, there will be found nothing inhuman nor even extraordinary in the labor imposed on those negroes, as all our laboring classes are obliged to work at least ten hours daily.

On this point I disagree entirely with the abolitionist, for, having entered into an impartial and equitable investigation of the respective condition of free and slave field laborers, without taking their feeling into consideration, and looking only on the material side of the question, I have found that the latter are treated no worse than the former, and that to compensate for their privation of the privilege of working or not, at their option, they are placed beyond the terrible ravages of want which have produced such distress in the freest and most enlightened nations of the Old World.

I remember the time when, in Castile, farm laborers could only earn ten cents a day, which was all they had to support themselves and those who were dependent on them, most of them having families; to pay the house rent, to procure clothing and to lay by for the time when they should be out of employment. And, besides, in cases af sickness, which could not but be very frequent in such a wretched state of existence, medicines have to be procured out of that same sorry pittance, though medical attendance could be obtained at the expense of the municipality.

Those who have lived, as I have, in Simancas or in any other town of the province of Valladolid, in the years 1846 and 1848, will not find the slightest exageration in the picture which I have drawn. Those laborers went out to the field to work at daylight, that is, in summer from three to four in the morning, and did not give up work until sunset, which in those latitudes and at that season is at eigth o'clock if not later. During the course of the day and at meal-times, they rested two alternate hours; and thus there remained to them nine hours out of each twenty four, for rest, consequently they work quite as much as the negroes in harvest time, and no less than the same negroes, all the year round.

Though the negroes on the plantations cannot obtain their freedom with such ease as the others, they nevertheless have opportunities which they can turn to account, especially when they have proved themselves intelligent, honest and submissive, for then they are generally separated from the laborers, and employed in domestic service by the overseers, or even by the master, in which situation they can easily acquire means to buy their freedom by economizing and saving the gratuities and presents lavished upon them.

Some of my readers will suppose that very few can obtain their freedom in this manner, as the number of household servants must necessarily be limited. But this argument, which may naturally be set forth by persons unacquainted with the countries to which I refer, can be refuted at once by any one who has any khowledge of the matter, with the demonstration of the unlimited number of servants who are retained on the estates and in the dwellings of their owners, owing to the fact, which has been already mentioned, that no servant is ever employed in more than one particular occupation, nor even in that one in the service of two different persons. When the owner of large estates has a numerous family, and owns plenty of negroes, the number of servants of both sexes who are employed in the household would be considered fabulous, each individual in the family having one exclusively in his service; and, where there are infants to be nursed, the wet-nurses take with them their husbands and little ones, and though these remain in perfect idleness, they are not obliged to return to their labor in the fields so long as they behave themselves properly.

It is also customary, on the plantations, to teach some trade or bestow a small plot of ground to such negroes as may desire either; and by these means they all have the opportunity to earn, by their extra labor, sufficient to pay the price of their freedom, in instalments, which the proprietors have no right to decline, as has been seen in some articles of the regulations.

With regard to the punishments, it would be difficult to destroy the prejudices which exist on the matter in those places where this institution is known only theoretically. In order to condemn the punishment of slaves, poets and novelists have spared no extravagance nor monstrosity in their comedies and dramas, and in narratives of cruelty which are manifestly absurd, as also in novels abounding in impossibilities.

When a youth, I read some of these calumnious works, which were expressly designed to inflame the public mind against negro slavery, and I own that at one time I shared the common prejudices; believing that the principles of humanity and justice ought to prevail over all interested motives. At that time when I was as ignorant as the worst among them, I had often inwardly applauded the apostrophe, as destructive as it was eloquent, which resounded through the world: *Preserve the principles, and let the colonies perish.* Subsequently, when I had entered the military service, and even long before visiting America, my opinions in this matter were materially modified.

In any collective body of men formed for the purpose of common labor or any other end, whose members are not taken from the higher classes of society, but from the ignorant masses, it would be absurd to apply the ordinary codes of laws for the punishment of crimes and offenses that might be committed; for such application would speedily cause the dissolution of said organization, and the jails and prisons would be filled with criminals whose offenses might have been punished in some other manner which would interfere neither with their services nor with their labor.

It is for this reason that it was customary, until very recently, in the Spanish militia, to punish soldiers who had been guilty of misdemeanors, by making them run the gauntlet or by inflicting from twenty-five to fifty lashes, instead of sending them to prison. For this reason also punishment by the lash was continued in the Portuguese army until 1856, twenty-one years after it had been abolished in Spain; and it is perhaps on this account that the English still inflict it with such severity on their soldiers and sailors, I myself having witnessed the death of an individual of the auxiliary legion, in the city of Lugo, during the civil war in Spain, who suffered the penalty of EIGHT HUNDRED LASHES, to which he had been sentenced, the total number of lashes being inflicted on his body, although he expired long before the completion of his punishment.

And if freemen are subjected to this treatment in highly civilized nations, experience having demonstrated that, without such severity, discipline and subordination could not be maintained in their armies, why should it be a matter of wonder that the most humane codes in the world authorize the penalty of lashes, to be applied with moderation to negroes when they deserve punishment, knowing that any other mode of correction would be useless, because unintelligible to them in their all but irrational state?

It is necessary that all discussions with regard to these matters should be governed by moderation, and not by ignorance and intolerance, for these can produce nothing but arguments and discourses which, however plausible they may be, are entirely destitute of reason, and effect no manner of good. Twenty-five lashes, which is the maximum of the punishment permitted by the laws, and applied with an instrument which does not inflict very severe chastisement on the semi-barbarous culprits, are a very proper and appropriate punishment when it becomes necessary to regulate confused ideas, to eradicate ferocious habits, and to maintain good discipline among the masses of a dangerous part of the population.

The fact is that the said punishment is rarely inflicted with the severity prescribed by the law; at the same time I do not mean to say that the whip of the overseer does not occasionally fall, with warning eloquence, on the shoulders of the careless, the indolent and the unruly, who disturb the established order by their bad example. It is possible that abuses exist owing to this practice; but, so far as the punishments prescribed by the regulations are concerned, they being more severe and publicly known, it can be positively affirmed that they are never arbitrarily nor causelessly inflicted.

I once resided for six months on an estate, that of Buena Vista, in the valley of Trinidad, and during that time there were but very few cases in which the penalties prescribed by the regulations were enforced. One of these was that of a runaway slave, who, having escaped punishment through my intervention, again took to flight before the week had elapsed. Having been captured a second time, he again appealed to me to intercede for him; but, although I willingly acceded to his request, my intercession was this time disregarded. He received twenty-five lashes, face downward, and for three days had his feet placed in the stocks after working; and, being subjected for some time to extra surveillance, he subsequently became one of the best behaved and most industrious negroes on the estate.

Such is the true character of slavery and its punishments in the Spanish colonies, whatever may be said to the contrary by ignorant declaimers and interested abolitionists. It has already been seen that the law could not be more protective or humane, for it contains measures to prevent any abuses in the application of the regulations it prescribes.

The commendable office of the slave protecting syndics should be fulfilled with all the charitable zeal on which it was founded, and I have reason to believe that it is thus fulfilled, as the negroes always have free access to the superior authorities, to present their complaints in person.

In the palace at Havana on all the audience days, which are of frequent occurrence, the stairs are always crowded with colored people who personally appear before the Captain General to make known their difficulties. Generaly speaking, these are mere trifling matters as may be expected from the limited understanding of these individuals; some, however, are just complaints which are immediately attended to by the proper authorities, nor is there any lack of petitions or of all sorts of stratagems to obtain money, which are not familiar to the negroes in said condition; and this is the case not only at the palace of the Captain General, but also at the Lieutenancies of the Government, the inferior courts and the captaincies of the Districts; so that the rights of slaves are everywhere protected by the authorities.

They have also the right to change their master when they can show sufficient cause why the law should protect them on this point; and if a slave does not wish to leave the country or town wherein he lives, when his master intends to send him elsewhere, he can claim the right to remain in said place, being upheld therein by the special ordinances. And in order to show the spirit which governs the regulations of that class that have been lately promulgated in Havana, on which, for their greater efficiency, the respectable corporations had been consulted, I shall here insert the regulations issued by the present Governor and Captain General of the island of Cuba, when hardly two months had elapsed after he was entrusted with that eminent office.

"*Government House and office of the Captain General and delegated Superintendent of Finance of the ever loyal Island of Cuba.*

OFFICE OF THE SECRETARY OF GOVERNMENT.

" So as to carry out with due effect the power of enlargement reserved by the civil and Superior Governement in the regulations published by my worthy predecessor on the 18th of Septembre last, and bearing in mind what has been proposed by their Excellencies the corporation of this city, and the information given by their Excellencies, the Council of Administration, I have decreed the following:

Regulations for the Syndic offices in this city, on the appearance of slaves to prefer complaints against their owners.

" Article I.—Within twenty-four hours after a Slave has appeared to complain of his owner, the latter shall be notified; the day and hour being appointed when he shall appear before the Syndic, which conference must take place within three days after the application of the slave.

" Art. II.—The nature of the conference requires the personal appearance of the owner, who can only be excused on satisfactory grounds, in which case he must be represented by a duly authorized person.

" Art. III—If no agreement should be arrived at in the conference between the Syndic and the owner, or if the latter should not attend to the second summons, then the former shall institute a demand or act of peace before a competent Judge which shall be presented within eight days after the second summons.

" Art. IV.—The agreement made between the Syndic and

the owner of the slave, shall be written out in a book kept by the former and signed by both.

" Art. V.—When there should be a just cause for the sale of the slave, he shall not be allowed to return into the power of his master, but shall be placed in the house of some neighbor, considered reliable both by the owner and the Syndic; and if this cannot be done whilst the slave is seeking a new master he shall sleep at night in the judicial depot, and shall not be hired out during the next ensueing eight days.

" Art. VI.—When the complaints of the slave are not for cruelty, or where the Syndic may judge that he will not be badly treated on account of having entered his complaint, then he shall be returned to his owner, with whatever securities the Syndic may think prudent, while his complaint is being examined by judicial or extra-judicial acts.

" Art. VII.—The deposit in general for slaves, or their provisional detention is only intended for males. The women in all cases, and for whatever lenght of time, shall be placed in deposit inthe hospital of St. Francis, or in the Charitable Asylum, and shall be employed in the service of these establishments, where they shall be maintained without the owner having to pay more than two reals for each slave no matter how many days she may have to remain there. This contribution is destined for the superintendents of said establishments, for their trouble in keeping an account of those slaves who are received and discharged.

" Art. VIII.—The deposit or detention can be dispensed with when, a slave on making application for his freedom, pays over into the Royal Treasury, in the Bank of Spain, or in the Saving's Bank, a sum which, in the opinion of the Syndic, may be deemed sufficient for the purpose, and present the certificate of his deposit; in which case, being provided with a written permit by the Syndic, he can engage in some employment while the question of granting him his free papers is pending; his wages being placed in the Saving's Bank to be delivered to the proper parties.

" Art. IX.—With regard to the price of the freedom of a child yet unborn the usual custom shall be observed, and the owner of the mother can not prevent her suckling and bringing up her child for the length of time determined by the law and the Slave Regulations. Neither can children under seven years of age be separated from their mothers, by sale or ortherwise, unless it be for the good of the latter, and so ordered by the Syndic or by the Judge.

"Art. X.—If the slave should present himself wounded, hurt, or sick, in such a way as to require medical assistance, he shall be removed to the Hospital of Charity, and, according to the gravity of his case, the Syndic shall make it known to the judge to whose jurisdiction it may belong, so that he may proceed according to law; or else he shall make it known to the owner, at the same time that he summons him to the conference.

"Art. XI.—The owners of slaves whose price has been fixed, and who employ them in their personal service, owe them the difference between the sum that they actually earn with them, and that which they might earn if they worked on their own account; but this does not prevent the matter being amicably arranged between the master and the slave.

"Art. XII.—It not being just that an intelligent and well behaved slave who, knowing some trade, should experience greater difficulty in obtaining freedom through his savings, or other legitimate means, than one who is vicious and stupid, because the price of the former is greater than that of the latter, the appraiser, at the time of fixing the price for his liberation, shall only take into account the age, health and physical aspect of the slave, as also the amount of money expended by the owner in teaching him his trade, or what this instruction might reasonably amount to, if he has not already been indemnified by his work.

"Art. XIII.—When the slave has not given any motive or cause for his owner to sell him, and when such sale is only the result of the free will of the owner, the said slave has a right to request a delay of three days, that he may endeavor to find a new master, a paper to that effect being given to him by the owner; but, after the three days, his owner is privileged to sell him to whoever he may choose.

"Art. XIV.—The administrator of the judicial deposit, on hiring out slaves remitted to him by the Syndics, shall impose on all who may hire them, the condition of not taking them outside of the city and its suburbs, as also that they shall not prevent them from going to the office of the Syndic, with an officer, whenever their presence may be needed.

"Art. XV.—When a slave shall present himself to complain of his master, who belongs to another municipal district, the Syndic shall notify such master, inviting him to confer with him within the space of eight days, or asking him if he would prefer the slave to be sent to the Syndic of his own jurisdiction, accompanied by a sheriff, at his own cost; on receiving his answer, the Syndic will immediately send the slave, and if no answer be made, such slave shall be placed at the disposition of the superior civil government.

"Art. XVI.—Whenever any Syndic shall have notice of a grave abuse of an owner against his slave, he shall have recourse to the proper authority, so that he may apply an immediate remedy.

"Art. XVII.—The Syndics are obliged to take personal cognizance of the verbal demands which may be made, and only on account of sickness or urgent occupations can they be replaced by the prefects, who in those cases are obliged to fill their places.

"Art. XVIII.—The owners of slaves, in all the relations they may have with the Syndics, shall treat them with all the respect and consideration which are due to them as magistrates and as protectors of the slaves; a troublesome duty which they fulfill towards the public in general and the owners in particular.

"Art. XIX.—The delicate charge which our laws, customs and government confide to the Syndics is essentially one of justice and equity; and for this reason they should inculcate in the slaves maxims of obedience and fidelity to their masters, and in the latter those of humanity, affection and protection towards their slaves.

"Havana, January 28th, 1863. DOMINGO DULCE."

In order to strenghten the arguments and explanations which I have given respecting the nature of this institution, which is so justly condemned on account of the name by which it is called, I could quote many authorities who have preceded me in the investigation of this matter; but, not finding in any of them the spirit of moderation which is necessary to the proper discussion of a subjet of such importance, when the object is to enlighten all parties without offending any; and, moreover, as they cannot be more convincing than the observations which I have made already, I trust that the sound judgment of my readers and their reliance on my sincerity, will excuse me from producing the evidence which would be required under other circumstances.

The truth is that when an idea which is not firmly based on justice is set forth by its authors with the desire that it shall become generally prevalent and bear down all opposition, all the resources of the human mind are put in play to give it, in the opinion of the public, the importance and authority which it could never attain without artifice. For the better success of this design, the natural ignorance of the majority is taken advantage of, and the humane feelings of all are worked upon when the question can in any manner affect them; and by keeping these springs in motion perseveringly, it is easy to convert the greatest of iniquities into an universally just necessity.

We have seen a striking example of this in the general outcry which was raised against the Spaniards for the manner in which they treated the Indians, according to the false accounts with which Father Las Casas, through motives of self-interest, defamed our character. In order to despoil the crown of Spain of all that portion of the continent which we still possessed at the commencement of the present century, as a just recompense for its discovery and civilization at the cost of great sacrifices, there was not a single calumny, among all those made against us by that celebrated friar, which was not published and commented on in all languages, especially with the object of demonstrating that the barbarous tyranny of the Spaniards had wished to effect the total extermination of the Indians.

Nevertheless, at the same time that these calumnies were being levelled at us, the most learned sage among the eminent men of this and of the past century, a distinguished writer whose fame was universal, and who, being a German, and not connected with us in any manner, could not be accused of unjust partiality towards us, was demonstrating in the clearest manner, based on the most careful observations and the most solemn evidence, that in Mexico, the number of Indians was far greater in 1808 than at the time of its discovery, owing to the order established by the laws fort heir mode of living, preservation and prosperity, and to the paternal care lavished on them by the Spaniards who ruled them.[1] I am positively certain that, if the illustrious author had prosecuted the same line of studies in the other parts of Spanish America, he would have pronounced the same opinion with regard to them, with the exception of the islands wherein the aborigines were found in fewer numbers, and the agglomeration of the whites and negroes was much greater than in the other parts, owing to which the Indian race ere long disappeared, being amalgamated with the others. But the political tendencies, which had decreed the independence of Spanish America as a just punishment for our connivance in the independence of British America, would have utterly disregarded any such demonstrations, and would still have continued to indorse the calumnies of Father Las Casas, both in the council and in the pulpit.

Let no one be surprised, then, at the contradictions which may result between my impartial demonstrations on the slavery of the negroes as it exists at present in the Spanish possessions, which are taken from the existing regulations and from the actual practice, which cannot be contradicted, as it is open to the view of all the world, and the never ceasing aspersions to which our ears are so well accustomed, and which have caused such an increase in the number of abolitionists in countries where slavery is unknown, except by false representation.

God, in bestowing on us the gift of hearing, gave us two organs by which we might hear impartially both sides of every question, and thus be governed in our decisions by a true knowledge of the case, and, above all, by justice. Let the reader, then, listen patiently to the *pros* and *cons* of this question, and, moreover, let those who have as yet no suspicion of the purpose of this work, not be startled at the novelty of my opinions whenever they are found to clash with their prejudices.

---

(1) Humboldt, *Treatise on New Spain.*

CHAPTER VI.

The condition of the laboring negroes in America is not that of slavery, which nomenclature has been erroneously applied to it, and is utterly false.—Exertions of the abolitionists to destroy negro labor.—Investigation on the origin of this idea.—There is no truly moral principle practically involved in the prohibition of the redemption of negroes, which is called the slave trade.—The abolition of slavery such as it has hitherto been effected, is opposed to the civilization of the negroes, to the prosperity of the Colonies, and to the interests of the whole world.—Origin of the abolitionist idea, its propagation and diffusion in official spheres.—The London Philantropical Society.—Its agents and its organized propagation.—First concession made by Spain to England as to the abolition of slavery: additional articles to the treaty of 5th July 1814.—Spirit of the treaty of September 23, 1817, to abolish the slave trade.—Its effects are contrary to the moral end with which it was apparently made.—Treaty of 1835.

TOWARDS the close of the eighteenth century, as it has been shown, and according to the proofs adduced in the previous chapters, the redemption of the negroes from Africa was humane, civilizing, useful, and even eminently Christian; and their organized labor would have been equitable, protective and beneficent, if, from the commencement, it had been divested of the odious name which, with such want of propriety, was applied to it by the arrogance of some, the egotism of others, the vanity of the majority and the uniformity which custom had created.

The Encyclopedists of Europe, confounding facts with words, the positive with the suppositious, reason with sophistry, order with confusion, liberty with licence, and, in short, subverting all the social ideas on which the great edifice of Christian civilization rests, had even then succeeded in perverting the public mind, in changing the feelings, in distorting justice to suit their purposes, in perverting the existing law, and inflicting a deep injury on the rights of property, which, at a later day, would cause great losses to well deserving individuals and wealthy communities.

Their first expressions were heard in the British parliament, spoken in the house of commons by the celebrated Mr. Pitt, and were afterwards repeated in the French tribune by the eloquent Mirabeau, which produced the atrocities of Hayti, which cost the Republic so many sacrifices, to commerce so many losses, and to humanity so much precious blood.

When the mind pauses to reflect on that tremendous period of the revolution of ideas which is still progressing, curiosity is quickened by the desire to ascertain the true cause of the one so openly and absolutely proclaimed, as to the abolition of the redemption of the negroes, and the emancipation from all servitude in regard to those who were already redeemed.

Policy has two great motive powers, without which nothing could be resolved in its spheres, as by their means States are governed, harmonizing their respective interests. One of these powers is essentially moral, and is symbolized in justice; the other is material, and proceeds from political economy. With the former only appearances might seem in conflict with the question we are discussing; and the latter must not be accepted, either, as it is presented by private history. I will explain myself, and leave it to the judgment of the reader to draw his own inference.

The Spanish colonies were at that time of immense extent and wealth; their productions supplied the whole world; and, although smuggling defrauded the treasury of large sums, all the nations of the world contributed to the wealth of the government and of the landed proprietors of the colonies.

England, France, Portugal and the Dutch had colonies similar to ours and contiguous to them; but, although many of the productions of their soil were similar to those of the Spanish colonies, the quantity was so small, in comparison, that it would have been absurd to state it in this disertation.

At this time, the English government encouraged more than ever the idea of raising to the highest degree the productions of that part of the East Indies under their dominion; and, as this purpose coincided with that fervent extemporized zeal against the redemption of the negroes, to abolish slavery, many suspected that the question presented with such flattering show of justice and philanthropy, was but a question of local interest, founded on a principle of egotism, and this opinion was expressed by several authors in their works.

In order to argue in this way, it is necessary that we should analyze the case in its moral tendency; not as a question of feelings, without further data than those of the impulse of the moment, but looking to the principles and to the ends with all their advantages and disadvantages, which is the manner in which governments argue, and on this rests the justice of the appreciations.

We have already seen the manner in which the negroes on the coast of Africa lived previous to the time when the interest of the American colonies induced their redemption: vagrants without home or country, with but confused ideas of family ties; strangers to any sort of civilization, and in perpetual strife among the different tribes, sacrificing each other like idolaters, and devouring one another like wild beasts. The practice which, by arousing the cupidity of the conquerors, prevented them from sacrificing their captured foes, was an immense benefit to humanity, and a great pecuniary advantage to the colonies; and if this cannot be denied, after the expositions made in this book, and those which are still to be made, it is also positively established as a fact that the idea, which began to develop itself in the latter part of the eighteenth century, of suppressing the redemption of negroes in Africa, even though it was accompanied by the thought of subsequently abolishing slavery in America, was devoid of any principle of true morality, and was nothing more than the embodiment of the theories of visionaries.

The good and the evil, in this case, are represented by relative ideas, and cannot be taken for their application in an absolute sense. The abolition of slavery is a benefit that no one denies, that no one rejects, and to which the whole civilized world justly aspires. But suppression of redemption where it is carried on to mitigate the effects of a war of extermination, without contriving anything to substitute it, without any agreement among civilized nations for the prevention of human sacrifices in Africa, without establishing in that country some ideas of civilization and new customs, is not an idea worthy of the mind of great statesmen, nor of the support of truly generous nations.

And even the abolition of slavery considered in itself, without reference to the redemption in Africa, is injurious to property, unjust to the owners, and prejudicial to the negroes themselves; and we have full evidence that it has proved such in all those places where it has been carried out. The products of labor and the wealth of the proprietors being relative, as are also the number of the laborers and the means of their maintainance, if the established order which maintains the discipline of labor is substituted by individual will, which destroys it, the productive agents naturally decrease without a corresponding diminution in the number of consumers, and far from doing good to the class which it is intended to benefit, it inflicts on it a great injury; and to this fact the English colonies in America have given ample testimony.

I have seen multitudes of negroes begging where formerly public charity had never been called upon; and I have known proprietors of the English West Indies, formerly wealthy, soliciting situations as overseers on estates in the Spanish possessions.[1]

England being the first who injured herself in her general interests for the purpose of gratifying the feelings of a few, I think there can be no reason to attribute a sinister intention to the idea of Mr. Pitt which was afterwards realized in the sphere of the government. It first appeared at an opportune time whith the then predominant ideas, and if it was carried to an inconceivable extent, this was due to the philanthropy which it appeared to possess, owing to the distance from the lands where its disastrous efects were to be felt, and to the inexperience of those who received and adopted it, without either understanding or investigating the question, and guided only by their philanthropy.

Such is my opinion, though it may not agree with that of those who seek startling analogies among unforeseen coincidences; and I believe, moreover, that the efforts of En-

---

(1) One of these was from the island of Trinidad, with whom I was acquainted in 1852, in Trinidad de Cuba, acting in said capacity on the estate of my distinguished friend Mr. Juste German Cantero.

gland to raise the industrial and agricultural products in the East Indies to importance, is the consequence, not the premise, of the ruin of its West Indie Colonies.

Having touched on this question lightly and with the necessary prudence from the respect which, in my opinion, is due to the intention of others, I shall continue to state the progress made in the public mind which though eminently philanthropic was useless, nay, even destructive to the very individuals who were to have been benefited by it according to the belief of its supporters.

Mr. Pitt, as has been stated, set up the war cry against slavery in the House of Commons in 1788; it resounded subsequently in the French Tribune when the revolution was at its heigth, as it was to be expected, the idea being already evolved and sustained with the authority of its origin and the unsparing impulse which was given to it; and notwithstanding that the breezes which wafted to America that solemn apostrophe where the harbingers of the carnage and horrors which took place some years afterwards in a part of the French Colonies, in 1807 the British Lords approved the famous law which gave a death blow to the institution and to all the interests in any way connected with it.

The gigantic triumph of the abolitionist scarcely satisfied them, its operation being local and limited; for which reason and perseverance being the great agent to arrive at all ends, and organized order its most powerful auxiliary, those fanatical upholders of a wrongly interpreted idea, associated themselves in due form, to labor in every direction and in every way, until they successfully crowned their work as they had conceived and as they still continue to foster it.

In the midst of the war of independence in Spain, when the war of emancipation had also broken out in South America, a deputy raised his voice in the Cortes at Cadiz to second the labors of the philanthropic society of London. This was a generous outburst of feelings whose intention I do not condemn; but it was imprudent and foolish under the circumstances when our enemies took advantage of all available means, this being not one of the worst, owing to the object to which it referred and the countries which it affected.

About that time there was a lull in the storm which raged over our Western possessions and especialy over the

Indies, where the compulsory labor of the negroes had been recognized and declared to be of absolute necessity. But the restoration of the king to the throne of his ancestors which had been usurped by the Emperor Napoleon had been assisted by our English allies, and gratitude immediately wrought that, in the question of slavery, which would certainly not have been counselled by strict justice.

I will not say that the English forced the Spanish government to adopt the idea of putting an end to the redemption of Africans to insure the abolition of slavery in America which would naturally have followed had the prohibition been efectually carried out; but it can safely be presumed that in proposing that idea they took advantage of the existing circumstances, and exaggerated the merit of the services rendered by them, for we find the agreement to the prohibition inserted, in an additional article, in the treaty of peace, friendship and alliance made and signed at Madrid, on the 5th of July 1814, by the plenipotentiaries of Spain and England, and ratified, with the said additional article, by his Catholic Majesty, on the 28th of August of the same year: that is to say when the war of Independence had just terminated, and when King Ferdinand, inexperienced in matters of government, began to rule his vast, and at that time, complicated monarchy.

The additional article, which, in said treaty appears like an exotic plant and is unintelligible, aside from the spirit which dictated it with ulterior views, reads as follows:

" The sentiments of his Catholic Majesty being entirely the same as those of H. B. Majesty as to the injustice and inhumanity of the slave trade H. Catholic Majesty will take into consideration, with mature deliberation, the means of combining these sentiments with the necessities of his possessions in America. H. Catholic Majesty promises, moreover, to prohibit his subjects engaging in the slave trade, when it may be with the object of providing the Islands and possession not belonging to Spain; and also to prevent by regulation and other eficacious means, the protection of the Spanish flag from being afforded to foreigners engaged in said trade whether they be subjects of H. B. M. or of other States or Powers."

And, as a compensation for this act of compliance, whose interpretation, by the Spaniards well versed in the matter alluded to, could with difficulty be guessed at, another additional article followed the one above copied, which, to a certain extent, gives us the clue to remove the doubts and mysteries which envelop the former. If we take into account the seditious offices of the English and the material aid which they gave to the revolted provinces of Spanish America, leaving out of the question the analysis of what motives they may have had to pursue that policy, and looking only to the friendly remonstrances made by the Spanish government towards England, while demanding that the offenses committed by British subjects against our authority should in future be prevented, it will not appear strange that our friends and allies should have taken advantage of our respective situation, and exacted from us, as a reciprocal service, the above mentioned promise to put an end to the slave trade, in exchange for the promise given by them in the additional article, which is the following:

"H. B. Majesty being desirous that the evils and discord which unhappily reign in the dominions of H. C. Majesty in America, shall entirely cease, and that his subjects in those provinces shall return to the obedience of their legitimate sovereign, H. B. Majesty binds himself to adopt the most effective measures to prevent his subjects from furnishing either arms, ammunitions or other articles of war whatever to the rebels of Spanish America."

The strictness with which this engagement of Great Britain was fulfilled is written with Spanish blood in the history of the American independence. The whole world knows that the arms and the most skillful agents to make them useful against our dominions beyond the seas, were sent from England. Sometimes soldiers were openly enlisted, and the action of the English government to furnish the recruits with war materials and the means of transportation was also publicly known. And in the mean time Spain was not satisfied with having promised to modify and afterwards to abolish the slave trade; but, by new pressures and urgent necessities of her precarious situation, was at last under the necessity of making the first treaty to that effect with England.

This happened in 1817, when past trials on the one hand, and on the other recent defeats and shameful defections, had left the Spanish government without naval means with which to smother the insurrection in the New World. To overcome this difficulty, our shipyards being empty and the arsenals without armament, measures were devised to purchase a squadron of war vessels already equipped and ready for sea, in whatever direction it might be required; and Russia having been able to furnish us with five ships of 74 guns, and three 40 guns frigates, for the sum of thirteen millions six hundred thousand rubles, or three millions four hundred thousand dollars, England, no doubt, to relieve Spain from the burden which the new debt would impose upon her, hastened to offer us, in consideration of a concession, four hundrd thousand pounds sterling, or two millions of dollars, as an indemnification for our losses in the abolition of the slave trade, provided we acceded implicitly to her wishes on this point.

And as, in all the actions of life which can injure an individual or a community, the evil is in the first step taken, Spain could not avoid, in 1817, the natural consequences of the solemn promise made three years previous, which was the first step, and, worst than all, which has since been successively taken in the question now discussed.

We made a treaty with England for the abolition of the slave trade, or rather, of the redemption of negroes, on the 23d of September of the above mentioned year; but its terms were not binding nor absolute for all places, until three years afterwards, though, for some, it was to take effect immediately, that is to say, that the first article declared the abolition of the slave trade, in all the Spanish dominions, from the 30th of May, 1820, and, after said date, the absolute prohibition of the trade in any part of the coast of Africa; and, by the second article, this trade was allowed to be continued on the whole coast of Africa south of the equator, and by no means to the north of it, until the said 30th of May, 1820.

This, no doubt, was a concession made to the material interests which were about to be injured, and, as may be seen, was contrary to the moral principles which it was intended to preserve; because, if the object of the abolitionists was exclusively the extinction of slavery without its abolition, and if it only affected the redemption of the negroes, the continuation of the trade for three years more to the south of the Equator might so increase the number of slaves of both sexes in our colonies, that, by proper discipline and by means of restrictive regulations against emancipation, the abolition of slavery might have been made forever impossible, as would have been the case in the North American Confederation were it not for the possible results of the present war.

Due attention should be given to this observation, not only to be able to form a correct estimate of the ends of the English abolitionists, and of the means which they employed to accomplish their purpose, but also to understand the question, now under discussion, with a clear and defined idea of humanity and public law. For, if the ends of the abolitionists were really to abolish slavery by interfereing with the redemption, trusting for their final success to the future propagation of their idea, either through the compliance of the nations, such as France displayed with regard to her colonies, in imitation of England, or through the extinction of the colored races in such other places in which the emancipation should not be carried out, the fact is that they were most signally defeated, in both extremes, as the results of their labors were diametrically opposed to their cherished purposes.

Thus, for example, in the United States, where, owing to the greater knowledge and experience of the colonists, it was believed that it was more advantageous to perpetuate the institution, acclimating and reproducing it with the means existing at the time the treaties were made, without, however, renouncing the redemption, the facilities for emancipation, which might formerly have existed in the regulations for slaves, disappeared immediately, and the increase of the negro population, which formed an integral part of property, made it apparent ere long that it would be absolutely impossible to effect the abolition of slavery in those regions without a violent and destructive struggle.

Such were also the results in the Spanish colonies as soon as the government of the metropolis was convinced that it had already made to philanthropy all the concessions which its conscience and its duty demanded. And, in these colonies and in all the other countries which continued to hold slaves, in spite of the treaties made with England to prohibit the slave trade in Africa, the nulity of these treaties and the impotence of the abolitionists were made manifest by the illegal, but incorrigible continuance of the redemption, through the necessities of agriculture and the daring of the traders.

On this point, to which I have perhaps devoted too much space at this time, I will again occupy myself more minutely, continuing for the present the recital of the concession made to England by the colonial nations, and of the law established specially with Spain in the last treaty.

That of 1817, being as it was the first of these treaties, ought to appear entire in this work; but, in order to avoid so many repetitions, I prefer to insert only its fundamental principles, as I intend to give the one which was drawn up afterwards with the corrections and amendments which had been counselled by experience during the practice of the first.

It will easily be understood that England would not cease from her efforts until she had succeeded in obtaining from the other nations concessions similar to those which she had attained from us; and it will appear natural that she should have continued so persistently to obtrude her philanthropic ideas upon us in order to obtain still more advantageous results.

We were not alone in the attitude which we then took against any further concessions, as the same resistance was made by the other States, not even excepting France, as she did not abolish slavery in her colonies until the last revolution, in 1848. Nevertheless, when we were most seriously engaged in our seven years civil war, and were obliged to solicit the amplification of the treaty of the quadruple alliance, which provided for the presence of auxiliary forces on the Peninsula, to serve as a moral support to the throne of our Queen, England again recurred to us, as the treaty of 1817 was hardly observed at all after the death of our last king, and in a friendly manner urged us to furnish still another prop to her reigning idea.

Whereas many Spaniards have since blamed the government of that period for not having repelled this new demand, I hasten to show here that it deserved no such reproaches; for, if some weakness is observed in this concession, the evil should be traced to its original source, which is nothing less than the second additional article of the treaty of 1814, or, we could with better reason say, to the misfortunes which befel us during a period of nearly half a century. This ought to be well understood so that ignorant censures may no longer be levelled at the glorious memory of an illustrious and venerable patrician.

England's demand, which will appear just if we take into consideration the precedents and nature of the question, was at that time justly acceded to, in consequence of which the treaty now existing for the abolition of the slave trade was agreed upon, which treaty will herein be found entire, from beginning to end, with the accessory diplomas.

"His Majesty the King of the United Kingdom of Great Britain and Ireland, and Her Majesty the Queen Regent of Spain, during the minority of Her Daughter Donna Isabella the second, Queen of Spain, being desirous of rendering the means taken for abolishing the inhuman traffic in slaves more effective, have, in order to obtain this important object, resolved to conclude a new Convention, in the spirit of the Treaty contracted between both Powers on the 23rd of September 1817, naming respectively for this as their Plenipotentiaries, to wit: His Britannic Majesty, George Villiers, Esq., his Envoy Extraordinary and Minister Plenipotentiary at the Court of Madrid; and Her Majesty the Queen Regent of Spain, Don Francisco de Paula Martinez de la Rosa, Knight Grand Cross of the Royal and distinguished Spanish order of Charles the Third, of that of Christ of Portugal, and of that of Leopold of Belgium, who having duly communicated to each other their respective full powers, and found them in proper form, have agreed upon and concluded the following articles:

"Article I.—The slave trade is hereby again declared, on the part of Spain, to be henceforward totally and finally abolished in all parts of the world.

"Art. II.—Her Majesty the Queen Regent of Spain, during the minority of her daughter Donna Isabella the second, hereby engages that immediately after the exchange of the ratifications of the present Treaty, and from time to time afterwards, as it may become needful, Her Majesty will take the most effectual measures for preventing the subjects of Her Catholic Majesty from being concerned and her flag from being used, in carrying on, in any way, the trade in slaves; and especially that, within two months after the said exchange, she will promulgate throughout the dominions of Her Catholic Majesty a penal law inflicting a severe punishment on all those of Her Catholic Majesty's subjects who shall, under any pretext whatsoever, take any part whatever in the traffic in slaves.

"Art. III.—The captain, master, pilot and crew of a vessel condemned as good prize by virtue of the stipulations of this Treaty, shall be severely punished according to the laws of the country of which they are subjects: as also the owners of the said condemned vessel, unless they prove that they had no participation in the enterprise.

"Art. IV.—In order more completely to prevent all infringement of the spirit of the present Treaty, the two High contracting Parties mutually consent that those ships of their Royal Navies respectively, which shall be provided with special instructions for that purpose, as hereinafter mentioned, may visit such merchant vessels of the two Nations as may, upon reasonable grounds, be suspected of being engaged in the traffic in slaves; or of having been fitted out for that purpose, or of having, during the voyage on which they are met by the said cruizers, been engaged in the traffic in slaves, contrary to the provisions of this Treaty; and that such cruizers may detain and send, or carry away such vessels, in order that they may be brought to trial in the manner hereinafter agreed upon.

"In order to fix the reciprocal right of search in such a manner as shall be adapted to the attainment of the object of this Treaty, and at the same time avoid doubts, disputes and complaints, the said right of search shall be understood in the form and according to the rules following:

"Firstly. It shall never be exercised except by vessels of war, authorized expressly for that object, according to the stipulations of this Treaty.

"Secondly. In no case shall the right of search be exercised with respect to a vessel of the Royal Navy of either of the two Powers, but only as regards merchant vessels.

"Thirdly. Whenever a merchant vessel is searched by a ship of war, the commander of the said ship shall, in the act of so doing, exhibit to the commander of the merchant vessel the document by which he is duly authorized to that end, and shall deliver to him a certificate, signed by him, stating his rank in the naval service of his country, and the name of the vessel he commands, and which also declares that the only object of the search is to ascertain whether the vessel is employed in the slave traffic, or if it is fitted up for the said traffic. When the search is made by an officer of the cruizer who is not the commander, the said officer shall exhibit to the captain of the merchant vessel a copy of the before mentioned special orders, signed by the commander of the cruiser, and shall in like manner deliver a certificate signed by him, stating his rank in the Royal Navy, the name of the commander by whose orders he proceeds to make the search, that of the cruizer in which he sails, and the object of the search, as has been already laid down. If it appears from the search that the papers of the vessel are in regular order, and that it is employed in licit objects, the officer shall enter in the logbook of the vessel that the search has been made in pursuance of the aforesaid special orders, and the vessel shall be left at liberty to pursue its voyage. The rank of the officer who makes the search must not be less than that of lieutenant of the Royal Navy, unless the command, either by reason of death or other cause, is at the time held by an officer of inferior rank.

"Fourthly. The reciprocal right of search and detention shall not be exercised within the Mediterranean sea, or within the seas in Europe lying without the streights of Gibraltar, and which lye to the Northward of the thirty seventh parallel of North latitude, and also within and to the Eastward of the Meridian of longitude twenty degrees west of Greenwich.

"Art. V.—In order to regulate the mode of carrying the provisions of the preceding article into execution, it is agreed:

"Firstly. That all ships of the Royal Navies of the two Nations, which shall be hereafter employed to prevent the traffic in slaves, shall be furnished by their respective Governments with a copy in the English and Spanish languages, of the present Treaty; of the instructions for cruizers annexed thereto marked A, and of the regulations for the mixed Courts of justice annexed thereto marked B; which annexes respectively shall be considered as integral parts of the Treaty.

"Secondly. That each of the High contracting Parties shall, from time to time, communicate to the other the names of the several ships furnished with such instructions, the force of each and the names of their several commanders; the said commanders ought to hold the rank of captain in the Royal Navy, or at least of lieutenant; it being nevertheless understood that the instructions originally issued to an officer holding the rank of lieutenant of the Navy, or other superior rank, shall be sufficient, in case of death or temporary absence of the same, to authorize the officer on whom the command of the vessel has devolved, to make the search, although the said officer may not hold the aforesaid rank in the service.

"Thirdly. That if, at any time, the commander of a cruizer of either of the two Nations shall suspect that any merchant vessels under the escort or convoy of any ship or ships of war of the other Nation carries slaves on board, or has been engaged in the traffic in slaves, or is fitted out for the purpose thereof, the said commander of the cruizer shall communicate his suspicions to the commander of the convoy, who, accompanied by the commander of the cruizer, shall proceed to the search of the suspected vessel; and in case that the suspicions appear well founded, according to the tenor of this Treaty, then the said vessel shall be conducted or sent to one of the points where the mixed Courts of justice are stationed, in order that the just sentence may there be pronounced.

"Fourthly. It is further mutually agreed that the commanders of the ships of the two Royal Navies, respectively, who shall be employed on this service shall adhere strictly to the exact tenor of the aforesaid instructions.

"Art. VI.—As the two preceding articles are entirely reciprocal, the two High contracting Parties engage mutually to make good any losses which their respective subjects may incur by the arbitrary and illegal detention of their vessels; it being understood that this indemnity shall be borne by the Government whose cruizer shall have been guilty of such arbitrary and illegal detention, and that the visit and detention of vessels specified in the fourth article of this Treaty, shall only be effected by those British or Spanish ships which may form part of the two Royal Navies respectively, and by such of those ships only as are provided with the special instructions annexed to the present Treaty, in pursuance of the provisions thereof. The indemnification for the damages of which this article treats shall be made within the term of one year, reckoning from the day in which the mixed Court of justice pronounces its sentence.

"Art. VII.—In order to bring to adjudication, with as little delay and inconvenience as possible, the vessels which may be detained, according to the tenor of the fourth article of this Treaty, there shall be established, as soon as may be practicable, two mixed Courts of justice, formed of an equal number of individuals of the two Nations, and named for this purpose by their respective Sovereigns. These Courts shall reside, the one in a possession belonging to His Britannic Majesty, the other within the territories of Her Catholic Majesty; and at the period of the exchange of the ratifications of the present Treaty, the two Governments shall declare, each for its own dominions, in what places these Courts shall respectively reside.

"But each of the two High contracting Parties reserves to itself the right of changing, at his pleasure, the place of residence of the Court held within its own dominions; provided always that one of the two Courts shall always be held upon the coast of Africa, and the other in one of the colonial possessions of Her Catholic Majesty.

"These Courts, from which there shall be no appeal, shall judge the causes submitted to them according to the provisions of the present Treaty, and according to the regulations and instructions which are annexed to the present treaty, and which are considered an integral part thereof.

"Art. VIII.—It is hereby agreed, between the High contracting Parties, that the mixed Commissions which are at present established, and sitting under the Convention concluded between Great Britain and Spain on the 23rd September 1817, shall continue to sit, and shall during two months, to be reckoned from the exchange of the ratifications of this Treaty, and until the further appointment and definitive establishment of the mixed Courts of justice under the present Treaty, adjudge, without appeal, according to the principles and stipulations of the same, and of the several annexes thereof, the cases of such vessels as may be sent or brought before them; and any vacancies which may occur in such mixed Commissions shall be filled up in the same manner in which vacancies of the mixed Courts of justice to be established under the provisions of this Treaty are to be supplied.

Art. IX.—In case the commanding officer of any of the ships of the Royal Navies of Great Britain and Spain respectively, duly commissioned, according to the provisions of the fourth article of this Treaty, shall deviate in any respect from the stipulations of the said Treaty, or from the instructions annexed to it, the Government which shall conceive itself to be wronged thereby, shall be entitled to demand reparation; and in such case the Government to which such commanding officer may belong binds itself to cause enquiry to be made into the subject of the complaint, and to inflict upon the said officer a punishment proportioned to any wilful transgression which he may have committed.

"Art. X.—It is hereby further mutually agreed that every merchant vessel, British or Spanish, which shall be visited by virtue of the present Treaty, may lawfully be detained and sent or brought before the mixed Courts of justice, established in pursuance of the provisions thereof, if in her equipment there shall be found any of the things hereinafter mentioned, namely:

"1st. Hatches with open gratings, instead of the close hatches which are usual in merchant vessels.

"2d. Divisions or bulkheads in the hold or on deck in greater number than are necessary for vessels engaged in lawful trade.

"3rd. Spare planks fitted for laying down as a second or slave deck.

"4th. Shackles, bolts, or handcuffs.

"5th. A larger quantity of water in casks or in tanks than is requisite for the consumption of the crew of the vessel, as a merchant vessel.

"6th. An extraordinary number of water casks or of other vessels for holding liquid, unless the master shall produce a certificate from the custom house at the place from which he cleared outwards, stating that a sufficient security had been given by the owners of such vessel, that such extra quantity of casks or of other vessels should only be used to hold palm oil, or for other purposes of lawful commerce.

"7th. A greater quantity of mess tubs or kids than

are requisite for the use of the crew of the vessel as a merchant vessel.

"8th. A boiler of an unusual size and larger than requisite for the use of the crew of the vessel as a merchant vessel, or more than one boiler of the ordinary size.

"9th. An extraordinary quantity either of rice, of the flour of Brazil, of manioc or cassada, commonly called farinha of maize or of Indian corn, beyond what might probably be requisite for the use of the crew; such rice, flour, maize or Indian corn not being entered on the manifest as part of the cargo for trade.

"Any one or more of these several circumstances, if proved, shall be considered as *prima facie* evidence of the actual employment of the vessel in the slave trade; and the vessel shall there upon be condemned and declared lawful prize, unless satisfactory evidence, upon the part of the master or owners, shall establish that such vessel was at the time of her detention or capture, employed in some legal pursuit.

"Art. XI.—If any of the things specified in the preceding article shall be found in any merchant vessel, neither the master nor owner nor any person whatever, interested in her equipment or cargo, shall be entitled to compensation for losses or damages even though the mixed courts of justice should not pronounce any sentence of condemnation, in consequence of her detention; but the same tribunal shall be authorized to pay out of the prize fund, if they shall think it in equity required, some sum of money proportionate to the demurrage suffered and according to the circumstances of the case.

"Art. XII.—It is hereby agreed between the two high contracting parties that in all cases in which a vessel shall be detained under this treaty by their respective cruizers, as having been engaged in the slave trade, or as having been fitted out for the purposes thereof, and shall consequently be adjudged and condemned by the mixed courts of justice to be established as aforesaid, the said vessel shall, immediately after its condemnation, be broken up entirely, and shall be sold in separate parts after having been so broken up.

"Art. XIII.—The negroes, who are found on board of a vessel detained by a cruizer and condemned by the mixed courts of justice, in conformity with the stipulations of this treaty, shall be placed at the disposition of the government whose cruizer has made the capture; but on the understanding that not only they shall be immediately put at liberty and kept free—the government to whom they have been delivered guaranteeing the same—but likewise engaging to afford, from time to time and whenever demanded by the other High contracting Party, the fullest information as to the state and condition of such negroes with a view of ensuring the due execution of the treaty in this respect.

"For this purpose the regulations annexed to this treaty *sub littera* C, as to the treatment of negroes liberated by sentence of the mixed courts of justice, have been drawn up and are declared to form an integral part of this treaty.

"The two High contracting Parties reserve to themselves the right to alter or suspend, by common consent and mutual agreement, but not otherwise, the terms and tenor of such regulations.

"Art. XIV.—The acts or instruments annexed to this treaty and which, it is mutually agreed, shall form an integral part thereof, are as follows:

"A. Instructions for the ships of the royal navies of both nations, destined to prevent the traffic in slaves.

"B. Regulations for the mixed courts of justice, which are to hold their sittings on the coast of Africa, and in one of the colonial possessions of her Catholic Majesty.

"C. Regulations as to the treatment of liberated negroes.

"Art. XV.—The present treaty, consisting of fifteen articles, shall be ratified, and the ratifications thereof exchanged within the space of two months from this date, or sooner if possible.

"In witness whereof the respective plenipotentiaries have signed in duplicate, two originals, English and Spanish, of the present treaty, and have thereunto affixed the seal of their arms.

"Madrid, this twenty-eighth day of June, in the year one thousand eight hundred and thirty-five.—(L. S.) GEORGE VILLIERS."

"ANNEX A

"TO THE TREATY BETWEEN GREAT BRITAIN AND SPAIN, FOR THE ABOLITION OF THE SLAVE TRADE, OF THE 28TH JUNE, 1835.

"*Instructions for the ships of the British and Spanish royal navies employed to prevent the traffic in slaves.*

"Article I.—The commander of any ship belonging to the royal Brtish or Spanish navy which shall be furnished with these instructions, shall have a right to search and detain any British or Spanish merchant vessel, which shall be actually engaged or suspected to be engaged in the slave trade, or to be fitted out for the purposes thereof; or to have been engaged in the traffic in slaves during the voyage in which she may be met with by such ship of the British or Spanish navy; and such commander shall thereupon bring or send such merchant vessel, as soon as possible, for judgment before that one of the two mixed courts of justice established in virtue of the seventh article of the said treaty, which shall be the nearest to the place of detention, or which such commander shall, upon his own responsibility, think can be soonest reached from such place.

"Art. II.—Whenever a ship of either royal navies, duly authorized as aforesaid, shall meet a merchant vessel liable to be visited under the provisions of said treaty, the search shall be conducted in the mildest manner and with every attention which ought to be observed between allied and friendly nations, and the search shall, in all cases, be made by an officer holding a rank not lower than that of Lieutenant in the navies of Great Britain and Spain respectively; or by the officer who, at the time, shall be second in command of the ship by which such search is made.

"Art. III.—The commander of any ship of the royal navies, duly authorized as aforesaid, who may detain any merchant vessel in pursuance of the tenor of the present instructions, shall leave, on board the vessel so detained, the master, the mate or boatswain, and two or three, at least, of the crew thereof; the whole of the slaves, if any; and all the cargo; the captor shall, at the time of detention, draw up, in writing, an authentic declaration, which shall exhibit the state in which he found the detained vessel ; such declaration to be signed by himself and to be given in or sent, together with the captured vessel, to the mixed court of justice before which such vessel shall be carried or sent for adjudication. He shall deliver to the master of the detained vessel a signed certificate of the papers seized on board the same, as well as of the number of slaves found on board at the moment of detention.

"In the authenticated declaration which the captor is hereby required to make, as well as in the certificate of the papers seized, he shall insert his own name and surname ; the name of the capturing ship ; the latitude and longitude of the place where the detention shall have taken place; and the number of slaves found on board of the vessel at the time of the detention.

"The officer in charge of the vessel detained shall, at the time of bringing the vessel's papers into the mixed court of justice, deliver into the court a paper signed by himself and verified on oath, stating the changes which have taken place in respect to the vessel, her crew, the slaves, if any, and her cargo, between the period of her detention and the time of delivering in such paper.

"Art. IV.—The slaves shall not be disembarked until after the vessel shall have arrived at the place of adjudication, in order that, in the event of the vessel not being adjudged legal prize, the loss of the proprietors may be more easily repaired ; and even after the arrival of the slaves at such place, they are not to be landed without the permission of the mixed court of justice.

"But if urgent reasons arising from the length of the voyage, from the state of health of the slaves, or from any other causes, should require that either the whole or a portion of the negroes should be disembarked before the vessel can arrive at the place at which one of the said courts is established, the commander of the capturing ship may take upon himself the responsibility of so disembarking the negroes, provided that the necessity of the disembarkation and the causes thereof, be stated in a certificate in proper form, and provided that this certificate shall be drawn up and entered at the time on the logbook of the detained vessel.

"The undersigned plenipotentiaries have agreed, in conformity with the fourteenth article of the treaty, signed by them on this day, the twenty-eighth of June, of 1835, that the present instructions shall be annexed to the said treaty, and be considered an integral part thereof.

" This day, the twenty-eighth of June, in the year one thousand eight hundred and thirty-five.—(L. S.) GEORGE VILLIERS."

"ANNEX B

"TO THE TREATY BETWEEN GREAT BRITAIN AND SPAIN, FOR THE ABOLITION OF THE SLAVE TRADE OF THE 28TH OF JUNE, 1835.

" *Regulations for the mixed courts of justice which are to reside on the coast of Africa and in a colonial possession of her Catholic Majesty.*

"Art. I.—The mixed courts of justice to be established under the provisions of the treaty of which these regulations are declared to be an integral part, shall be composed in the following manner:

" The two high contracting Parties shall each of them name a judge and an Arbitrator, who shall be authorized to hear and decide, without appeal, all cases of capture or detention of vessels which, in pursuance of the stipulations of the aforesaid treaty, shall be brought before them.

" The judges and the arbitrators shall, before they enter upon the duties of their office, respectively make oath before the principal magistrate of the place in which such courts respectively shall reside; that they will judge fairly and faithfully; that they will have no preference either for the claimant or for the captors, and that they will act in all their decisions in pursuance of the stipulations of the aforesaid treaty.

" There shall be attached to each of such courts a secretary or registrar, who shall be appointed by the sovereign in whose territories such court shall reside.

" Such secretary or registrar shall register all the acts of such court, and shall, before he enters upon his office, make oath before the court to which he is appointed, that he will conduct himself with due respect for its authority, and will act with fidelity and impartiality in all matters relating to his said office.

" The salary of the secretary or registrar of the court to be established on the coast of Africa, shall be paid by his Britannic Majesty, and that of the secretary or registrar of the court to be established in the colonial possessions of Spain shall be paid by her Catholic Majesty.

" Each of the two governments shall defray half of the aggregate amount of the expenses of such courts.

" Art. II.—The expenses incurred by the officer charged with the reception, maintenance and care of the detained vessel, slaves and cargo, and with the execution of the sentence ; and all disbursements occasioned by bringing a vessel to adjudication shall, in case of condemnation, be defrayed from the funds arising out of the sale of the vessel, after the vessel shall have been broken up ; of the ship's stores and of such parts of the cargo as shall consist of merchandize. And in case the proceeds arising out of this sale shall not prove sufficient to defray such expenses, the deficiency shall be made good by the government of the country within whose territories the adjudication shall have taken place.

" If the detained vessel shall be released, the expenses occasioned by bringing her to adjudication shall be defrayed by the captors, except in the cases specified and otherwise provided for under article the eleventh of the treaty to which these regulations form an annex, and under article the seventh of these regulations.

"'Art. III.—The mixed courts of justice are to decide upon the legality of the detention of such vessels as the cruizers of either nation shall in pursuance of the said treaty detain.

" These courts shall judge definitively and without appeal, all questions which shall arise out of the capture and detention of such vessels.

" The proceedings of these courts shall take place as summarily as possible ; and for this purpose the courts are required to decide each case as far as may be practicable, within the space of twenty days, to be dated from the day on which the detained vessel shall have been brought into the port where the deciding court shall reside.

" The final sentence shall not, in any case, be delayed beyond the period of two months, whether on account of the absence of witnesses or for any other cause, except upon the application of any of the parties interested; but in that case, upon such party or parties giving satisfactory security that they will take upon themselves the expense and risks of the delay, the courts may, at their discretion, grant an additional delay, not exceeding four months.

"Either party shall be allowed to employ such counsel as he may think fit to assist him in the conduct of his cause.

"All the acts and essential parts of the proceedings of the said courts shall be written down in the language of the country in which the courts shall respectively reside.

"Art. IV.—The form of the process or mode of proceeding to judgment shall be as follows :

"The judges appointed by the two nations respectively shall, in the first place, proceed to examine the papers of the detained vessel, and shall take the depositions of the master or commander, and of two or three at least of the principal individuals on board of such vessel; and shall also take the declaration on oath of the captor, if it should appear to them necessary to do so in order to judge and to pronounce whether the said vessel has been justly detained or not, according to the stipulations of the aforesaid treaty; and in order that, according to this judgment, the vessel may be condemned or released. In the event of the two judges not agreeing as to the sentence which they ought to pronounce in any case brought before them, whether with respect to the legality of the detention, or the liability of the vessel to condemnation, or to the indemnification to be allowed, or as to any other question which may arise out of the said capture, or in case any difference of opinion should arise between them as to the mode of proceeding in the said Court, they shall draw by lot the name of one of the two arbitrators so appointed as aforesaid, which arbitrator, after having considered the proceedings which have taken place, shall consult with the two above mentioned judges on the case, and the final sentence or decision shall be pronounced conformably to the opinion of the majority of the three.

Art. V.—If the detained vessel shall be restored by the sentence of the court the vessel and the cargo, in the state in which they shall then be found, shall fortwith be given up to the master or to the person who represents him; and such master or other person may, before the same court, claim a valuation of the damages which he may have a right to demand. The captor himself, and in his default his government, shall remain responsible for the damages to which the master of such vessel or the owners, either of the vessel or of her cargo may be pronounced to be entitled.

"The two high contracting parties bind themselves to pay within the term of a year from the date of the sentence, the costs and damages which may be awarded by the above named court; it being mutually understood and agreed that such costs and damages shall be made good by the government of the country of which the captor shall be a subject.

"Art. VI.—If the detained vessel shall be condemned, she shall be declared lawful prize, together with her cargo, of whatever description it may be, with the exception of the slaves who shall have been brought on board for the purposes of commerce, and the said vessel, subject to the regulations in article twelfth of the treaty of this date, shall, as well as her cargo, be sold by public sale for the profit of the two governments, subject to the payment of the expenses hereinafter mentioned.

"The slaves shall receive from the court a certificate of emancipation, and shall be delivered over to the government to whom the cruizer which made the capture belongs, to be dealt with according to the regulations and conditions contained in the Annex to this treaty, *sub littera* C.

"Art. VII.—The mixed courts of justice shall also take cognizance of, and shall decide definitively and without appeal, all claims for compensation on account of losses occasioned to vessels and cargoes which shall have been detained under the provisions of this treaty, but which shall not have been condemned as legal prize by the said courts; and in all cases wherein restitution of such vessels and cargoes shall be decreed, save as mentioned in article eleventh of the treaty to which these regulations form an Annex, and in a subsequent part of these regulations the court shall award to the claimant or claimants, or to his or to their lawful attorney or attornies, for his or their use, a just and complete indemnification for all costs of suit, and for all losses and damages which the owner or owners may have actually sustained by such capture and detention; and it is agreed that the indemnification shall be as follows:

" First. In case of total losses,

" The claimant or claimants shall be indemnified:

"*A.* For the ship, her tackle, equipment and stores.

"*B.* For all freights due and payable.

"*C.* For the value of the cargo of merchandise, if any, deducting all charges and expenses payable upon the sale of such cargo, including the commission of sale.

"*D.* For all other regular charges in such case of total loss.

" Secondly. In all other cases (save as hereinafter mentioned) not of total loss, the claimant or claimants shall be indemnified:

"*A.* For all special damages and expenses occasioned to the ship by the detention, and for loss of freight, when due or payable.

"*B.* For demurrage when due, according to the schedule annexed to the present article.

"*C.* For any deterioration of the cargo.

"*D.* For all premium of insurance on additional risks.

" The claimant or claimants shall be entitled to interest at the rate of five per cent per annum on the sum awarded, until such sum is paid by the Government to which the capturing ship belongs. The whole amount of such indemnifications shall be calculated in the money of the country to which the detained vessel belongs, and shall be liquidated at the exchange current at the time of the award.

" The two High contracting Parties, however, have agreed that if it shall be proved to the satisfaction of the Judges of the two Nations, and without having recourse to the decision of an arbitrator, that the captor has been led into error by the fault of the master or commander of the detained vessel, the detained vessel, in that case, shall not have the right of receiving, for the time of her detention, the demurrage stipulated by the present article, nor any other compensation for losses, damages or expenses, consequent upon such detention.

"SCHEDULE OF DEMURRAGE, or daily allowance for a vessel of

100	tons	to 120	inclusive,	5 £s.
121	ditto	to 150	ditto	6
151	ditto	to 170	ditto	8
171	ditto	to 200	ditto	10
201	ditto	to 220	ditto	11
221	ditto	to 250	ditto	12
251	ditto	to 270	ditto	14
271	ditto	to 300	ditto	15

per diem.

and so on in proportion.

"Art. VIII.—Neither the Judges, nor the Arbitrators, nor the Secretaries of the mixed Courts of justice, shall demand or receive, from any of the parties concerned in the cases which shall be brought before such Courts, any emolument or gift under any pretext whatsoever, for the performance of the duties which such Judges, Arbitrators and Secretaries have to perform.

"Art. IX.—The two High contracting Parties have agreed that, in the event of death, sickness, absence on leave, or any other legal impediment, of one or more of the Judges or Arbitrators composing the above mentioned Courts respectively, the post of such Judge and of such Arbitrator shall be supplied *ad interim* in the following manner:

"1st. On the part of His Britannic Majesty, and in that Court which shall sit within the possessions of His said Majesty, if the vacancy be that of the British Judge, his place shall be filled by the British Arbitrator, and either in that case or in the case where the vacancy be originally that of the British Arbitrator, the place of such Arbitrator shall be filled successively by the Governor or Lieutenant Governor resident in such possession, by the principal Magistrate of the same, and by the Secretary of the Government; and the said Court, so constituted as above, shall sit and, in all cases brought before them for adjudication, shall proceed to adjudge the same, and to pass sentence accordingly.

" Secondly. On the part of Great Britain, and in that Court which shall sit within the possessions of Her Catholic Majesty, if the vacancy be that of the British Judge, his place shall be filled by the British Arbitrator; and either in that case or in the case where the vacancy be originally that of the British Arbitrator, his place shall be filled successively by the British Consul and British Vice Consul, if there be a British Consul or British Vice Consul appointed to, and resident in such possession; and in the case where the vacancy be both of the British Judge and of the British Arbitrator, then the vacancy of the British Judge shall be filled by the British Consul, and that of the British Arbitrator by the British Vice Consul, if there be a British Consul and British Vice Consul appointed to, and resident in such possession; and if there shall be no British Consul or British Vice Consul to fill the place of British Arbitrator, then the Spanish Arbitrator shall be called in, in those cases in which a British Arbitrator, were there any, would be called in; and in case the vacancy be, both of the British Judge and British Arbitrator, and there be neither British Consul nor British Vice Consul to fill *ad interim* the vacancies, then the Spanish Judge and Spanish Arbitrator shall sit, and, in all cases brought before them for adjudication, shall proceed to adjudge the same, and pass sentence accordingly.

"Thirdly. On the part of Spain, and in that Court which shall sit within the possessions of Her Catholic Majesty, if the vacancy be that of the Spanish Arbitrator, and either in that case or in the case where the vacancy be originally that of the Spanish Judge, his place shall be filled by the Spanish Arbitrator, the place of such Arbitrator shall be filled successively by the Governor or Lieutenant Governor resident in such possession, by the principal Magistrate of the same, and by the Secretary of the Government, and the said Court, so constituted as above, shall sit, and, in all cases brought before them for adjudication, shall proceed to adjudge the same, and pass sentence accordingly.

"Fourthly. On the part of Spain and in that Court which shall sit within the possessions of His Britannic Majesty, if the vacancy be that of the Spanish Judge, his place shall be filled by the Spanish Arbitrator, and either in that case or in the case where the vacancy be originally that of the Spanish Arbitrator, his place shall be filled successively by the Spanish Consul and Spanish Vice Consul, if there be a Spanish Consul or Spanish Vice Consul appointed to, and resident in such possession; and in the case where the vacancy be both of the Spanish Judge and of the Spanish Arbitrator, then the vacancy of the Judge shall be filled by the Spanish Consul, and that of the Spanish Arbitrator by the Spanish Vice Consul, if there be a Spanish Consul and Spanish Vice Consul appointed to, and resident in such possession; and in that case in which there be no Spanish Consul or Spanish Vice Consul to fill the place of Spanish Arbitrator, then the British Arbitrator shall be called in, in those cases in which a Spanish Arbitrator, were there any, would be called in; and in case the vacancy be both of the Spanish Judge and Spanish Arbitrator, and there be neither Spanish Consul nor Spanish Vice Consul to fill *ad interim* the vacancies, then the British Judge and the British Arbitrator shall sit, and, in all cases brought before them for adjudication, shall proceed to adjudge the same, and pass sentence accordingly.

"The Governor or Lieutenant Governor of the settlements wherein either of the mixed Courts of justice shall sit, in the event of a vacancy arising either of the Judge or the Arbitrator of the other High contracting Party, shall forthwith give notice of the same to the Governor or Lieutenant Governor of the nearest settlement of such other High contracting Party, in order that such vacancy may be supplied at the earliest possible period. And each of the High contracting Parties agrees to supply definitively, as soon as possible, the vacancies which may arise in the above mentioned Courts from death or from any other cause whatever.

"The undersigned Plenipotentiaries have agreed, in conformity with the fourteenth article of the Treaty signed by them on this day the twenty-eighth of June 1835, that the preceding Regulations, consisting of nine articles, shall be annexed to the said Treaty, and considered as an integral part thereof.

"This day the twenty-eighth of June in the year one thousand eight hundred and thirty-five.—(L. S.) GEORGE VILLIERS."

"ANNEX C.

"*Regulations for the good treatment of liberated negroes.*

"Art. I.—The object and spirit of these regulations is to secure to negroes liberated by virtue of the stipulations of the Treaty to which these regulations form an annex (marked C.) permanent good treatment and a full and complete emancipation, in conformity with the humane intentions of the High contracting Parties.

"Art. II.—Immediately after sentence of condemnation on a vessel charged with being concerned in illegal slave trade, shall have been passed by the mixed Court of justice established under the Treaty to which these regulations form an annex, all negroes who were on board of such vessel and who were brought on board for the purpose of traffic, shall be delivered over to the Government to whom belongs the cruiser which made the capture.

"Art. III.—If the cruiser which made the capture is English, the British Goverment engages that the negroes shall be treated in exact conformity with the laws in force in the British Colonies for the regulation of free apprenticed negroes.

"Art. IV.—If the cruiser which made the capture is Spanish, in this case the negroes shall be delivered to the Spanish authorities of the Havanah or of any other point of the Dominions of the Queen of Spain in which the mixed Court of justice is established, and the Spanish Government solemnly engages that they shall be there treated strictly according to the regulations lately promulgated, and now actually in force at the Havanah, with respect to the treatment of emancipated negroes, or according to such regulations as may in future be adopted, and which have and shall always have the humane object of improving and securing honestly and faithfully to the emancipated negroes the enjoyment of their acquired liberty, good treatment, a knowledge of the tenets of the Christian religion, their advancement in morality and civilization, and their sufficient instruction in the mechanical arts, in order that the said emancipated negroes may be put in a condition to earn their subsistence, whether as artisans, mechanics or servants.

" Art. V.—For the purpose which is explained in article six there shall be kept in the office of the Captain

General or Governor of the part of the dominions of the Queen of Spain where the mixed court of justice resides, a register of all the emancipated negroes, in which shall be entered with scrupulous exactness the names given to the negroes, the names of the vessels in which they were captured, the names of the persons to whose care they have been committed, and any other circumstance likely to contribute to the end in view.

"Art. VI.—The register to which the preceding article refers will serve to form a general return which the Governor or Captain General of the part of the dominions of the Queen of Spain, where the mixed court of justice resides, shall be bound to deliver every six months to the aforesaid mixed commission, in order to show the existence of the negroes emancipated under this treaty, the decease of such as have died, the improvement in their condition, and the progress made in their instruction, both religious and moral, as also in the arts of life.

"Art. VII.—As the principal object of the treaty, of which the present annex forms an integral part, is no other than that of improving the condition of these unhappy victims of avarice, the high contracting parties, animated with the same sentiments of humanity, agree, that if in future it should appear necessary to adopt new measures for obtaining the said benevolent end, in consequence of those laid down in this annex turning out inefficacious, the said high contracting parties will consult together and agree upon other means better adapted for the complete attainment of the object proposed.

"Art. VIII.—The undersigned plenipotentiaries have agreed, in conformity with the fourteenth article of the treaty signed by them on this day, the 28th of June, 1835, that this annex, consisting of eight articles, shall be united to the said treaty and be considered an integral part thereof.

"This day, the twenty-eighth of June, in the year one thousand eight hundred and thirty-five.—(L. S.) GEORGE VILLIERS."

Before entering into an analysis of the spirit and practical consequences of this international compact, I shall here take up the history of the official and extra official labors which the abolitionists continued to pursue in the colonial nations and in the colonies themselves.

CHAPTER VII.

The system of apprenticeship instituted by the English in their Colonies by way of experiment as a substitute for slavery.—Character of said system and its negative results.—Considerations on the political ends which suggested such a system.—Uniform efforts of all the English agents to annihilate the slavery of the negroes in the other Colonies.—This system propagated in France.—The Colonies are officially consulted as to the freedom of the slaves.—Three systems are proposed by the French government to its Colonies.—Analysis and judgment of said systems.—Replies of the French Colonies to the consultation of the government.—The Republic of 1848 decrees the freedom of the slaves.—Operations of the abolitionists in Spain.—A ship of war manned by negroes is permanently stationed in the harbor of Havana.—The press is set to work.—They succeed in obtaining that the Spanish government should consult the Colonies on some points of abolitionism.—Evident tendencies to make the Island of Cuba a State similar to that of Haiti.—Charges and defences of the facts stated.—Remarkable letter of Lord Howden to Mr. Corbin: some erroneous statements containing offensive allusions to Spain are rectified.—New steps taken by said minister at Madrid to obtain the unconditional freedom of all the people of color in the Island of Cuba.—Lord Palmerston's despatch to Lord Howden on the same subject.—System of diplomatic and parliamentary recriminations. To introduce disorder in the colonial possessions of Spain, the right of search on the estates is proposed.—Important considerations on all these matters.—The English recommend the substitution of the negroes by contracted Chinese.—Reply of the United States to said proposition.

I have said that the success of the abolitionists in committing all the colonial nations to an agreement for the abolition of the redemption of Africans, was a gigantic step towards the fulfilment of their aspirations, and such it will undoubtedly appear to all if they will but consider that this agreement, founded as it was on a principle of true humanity, was, from the misapplication of that principle, destined to produce ulterior consequences of the most transcendental nature, and that, too, at no very distant period.

Its most immediate result was the complete ruin of the English colonies of the New World, which could not be averted, or even delayed, by the most consummate forecast nor by the most scrupulous care in carrying out the new experiment which was intended to prepare the way for a reasonable freedom.

The law which abolished slavery contemplated its substitution by an apprenticeship which was to last some years, during which the negroes who were to be emancipated remained subject to their former masters as to labor and discipline, and also as to their earnings in their respective trades. And in order that the collective or individual action of those indispensable productive agents of property should not be weakened by the ideas which their new civil state might suggest to them, the aforesaid emancipation law, setting aside all the consideration for the sentiment which had given it birth, and mindful only of the true character of the negroes, yielding rather to the existing state of things than to the fanaticism of absolute theories, confirmed to the masters the right which they formerly had as owners, of inflicting corporeal punishment on the apprentices, in the same manner and with as much vigor as though they were slaves.

Any one might venture to affirm that with a measure of so much foresight, labor would not degenerate in the English colonies until after the expiration of the term of apprenticeship; nevertheless, such an assertion, though entirely logical and very natural according to all the rules of common sense, would be but a gross and evident historical falsehood. For, whether the fundamental spirit of the law had infused itself in the minds of the negroes with more impulsive force than is to be surmised, or whether by means of the law itself the most fanatical abolitionists conveyed the propagation of their doctrines to the colonies, the fact is that the labor of the apprentices became immediately unproductive to their masters, who, seeing themselves burdened with the maintenance and all the other expenses attending the keeping of these miserable beings, after having been more or less sureptitiously deprived of their property, hastened to get rid of them when scarcely four years had elapsed, willingly relinquishing all the favorable provisions of the law, solely with the very justifiable end of not completing their own ruin.

This brought about the absolute freedom of the negroes in the English colonies, which thenceforward became a bug-bear to the others, on account of the bad example they set to the negroes who were still slaves, and also from the jealousy which was engendered by the contrast between their own ruin and the ever increasing prosperity of the other colonies.

From these premises, then, I do not hesitate to deduce, nor should any one be astonished at the fact affirmed by so many writers and orators, viz., that England, having effected the ruin of her West Indian possessions, and devoted her attention to the East Indies, formed the purpose of carrying out the abolition idea by making every imaginable effort to extinguish the slavery of the negroes wheresoever it might exist, in order to destroy all competition with her East Indian productions. And if it be true that the policy of that nation originated in this exclusive tendency, as a number of events have shown it to be probable, it is evident that England does not deserve the bitter reproaches lavished upon her, aside from those errors and illegalities which her agents have committed through excess of zeal and from want of knowledge.

As long as the cosmopolitan idea is confined to the desire of some few individuals, and is not a universal sentiment identified with moral interests, blotting out intervening boundaries, giving unity to all languages, and destroying individual nationalities, it is absurd to condemn a uniform policy maintained by a nation who aims at her own agrandizement at the expense of others, so long as she does not succeed by unlawful means or by disregarding public rights.

For this reason I, who extenuate the motives of such things as the rest of us would do if we knew how, am more apt to condemn whatever is contrary to the sentiment that tries to exalt itself in the minds of all, and for this reason, also, on entering fully and candidly into the analysis of the absolute emancipation of the negroes and of the prevention of their redemption, I will condemn with freedom and energy, and within the bounds of truth, all that is contrary to the moral end which should be the positive and unfeigned rule of the abolitionists.

From that time it was a permanent rule for all English agents, both diplomatic and consular, in other nations and especially in the colonies, to make every possible effort within the law, of course, to obtain daily some additional concession towards the freedom of the slaves. And in honor of truth it may be said that no idea in the world was ever better served than that of emancipation has been by the agents of England.

What these agents did both in the colonies and their respective scenes of action to arrive at the desired end, would furnish sufficient matter to fill an endless number of volumes. On the slightest suspicion of the transgression of the treaties by individuals who had nothing to do with the authorities or with the laws, and which were frequently imaginary, they made the most serious charges against the countries. And in the political disturbances which, in the present century, have agitated France and Spain, in the midst of revolutions and of less radical commotion, there was not an insurrection which the agents of Great Britain did not avail themselves to inculcate the ideas of emancipation in the minds of the rulers, in the tendencies of the insurgents, or in the minds of the public speakers.

In France, previous to the revolution of 1848, three men at the height of power, three statesmen of more reputation than circumspection, in short, three ministers of the monarchy of Louis Philippe, Roussin, Thiers, and Guizot, had already been made to declare that the emancipation of the slaves in the French colonies was legally decided in the affirmative. And although, in Spain, all the successive governments had maintained their independence within the limits of existing treaties, nevertheless there were not wanting authorities of the first order who, carrying the susceptibility of their character to an extreme highly honorable to themselves, but very dangerous to the respect due to the authorities and to the established law, not only exercised the vigilance on the coasts as actively and strictly as did their predecessors, but, overstepping all proper bounds, made searches on the plantations, and granted new concessions to the slaves for the purpose of preventing the fraudulent importation of *Bozal* negroes, and, also, to substitute for forced labor a new system of apprenticeship.

And the fact is that the words of those high functionaries of France in the times of Louis Philippe did not constitute an isolated idea, nor simply a mere transitory concession to the sentiments of some orators. When the deputies Passy, Tracy and Tocqueville decided to petition the French parliament for the emancipation of slaves, and successively wrested these declarations from the ministers, the London Anti-Slavery Society had already instituted a branch of their own in Paris, founded entirely on French principles, having as president M. de Broglie, and commanding the suffrages of said capital and of the cities of Saint-Quentin, Rouen, Havre, Nantes, Bordeaux, Bayonne, Toulouse, Lyons and Marseilles. And by that time, not only was the propagation spreading rapidly in the minds of a people who, though generous, were ignorant of the question which they attempted to solve; but the same infection had penetrated even to the official regions, perverting good sense, extinguishing prudence, and putting to flight all ideas which might have favored other and worthier interests.

After these unpremeditated declarations were successively made by the ministers in the French Chambers, as has already been stated, a plan was officially organized to accomplish the design set forth in said declarations; and the administrative committee of colonial affairs, residing in Paris, resting their claims on this plan, not only proposed to the government, in a decisive manner, the abolition of slavery in the French colonies, submitting to its deliberation three different systems, in order that the emancipation of the slaves might be carried out in accordance with the plan they might think the most elligible; but they went so far as to petition government to the effect that the councils of the colonies should not be consulted on so momentous a question.

This petition deserves our attention as it will enable us to understand to what an extent the abolitionists had succeeded in diffusing their ideas and increasing their importance. Fortunately for the French colonies, the colonial minister in Paris refused at that time to accede to such an arrogant demand, and the colonial councils and governors, and even a special council in each locality, were separately consulted; though at the same time the improper course recommended by the ministers in thè Chambers was followed, inasmuch as the colonists were forbidden all discussion of the expediency or inexpediency of negro emancipation, that measure being already *a principle decided in the affirmative*, and were only allowed the privilege of expressing their opinion respecting each of the three different systems which had been planned by the central administrative committee.

This measure was of great importance, owing to the light which it shed in gubernatorial spheres; and, as its analysis will not be out of place here, but rather appears indispensably necessary for the better acquaintance with the details of the important question which originated it, I will here relate its history, even though it must be in an abridged form.

The petition of the central administrative committee on colonial affairs, addressed to the French government through the Minister of Marine, who was also colonial minister, was made on the 19th of June, 1840. Three different systems for liberating the slaves were proposed in said petition, which were as follows: one, of partial and progressive emancipation, which had previously been devised by M. de Tracy, consisting principally in declaring the children of slaves free, and subjecting them, when of fitting age, to the jurisdiction of the owners of their mothers; the owners being benefitted by their labor until a certain period, and paying to the adults daily wages, by the savings of which they might successively be enabled to emancipate themselves. The colonists whose property might suffer by this system should, according to the by no means equitable idea of its author, be indemnified by a moderate compensation from the public treasury.

The second system, which emanated from a committee of the Chamber of Deputies, was also intended to effect a simultaneous emancipation, but by still more violent and less equitable means than those proposed in the first. The State was to take charge of the slaves, thus depriving the colonists of their property, in the name of the public good. The slaves would then be hired out, by the State, to their respective masters, and the proceeds of their labor were to be divided into two portions, one to cover the expenses for the maintenance and other wants of the negroes, and the other to pay to the owners the indemnification due to them by the State.

By the third system all the slaves were to be immediately declared free, and the colonists were to be indemnified for their loss. But the former were to remain subject to the latter during some years, in the character of apprentices, and the product of their labor was to be the remuneration of the owners for the expenses of apprenticeship. This was an exact imitation of the method adopted by the English in their colonies, which, as I have already stated, could not be carried into effect in all its parts, on account of the disastrous results which it produced from the very first day of its institution.

The French government, with far greater compliance than would have been counselled by a serious reflection on the subject and a proper regard for its own interests, did not hesitate to assume the responsability attached to these measures, and adopted them without further delay. To that effect a circular was sent to the governors of Martinique, Guadeloupe, Bourbon and Guiane, dated July 18, 1840, communicating to them that the council of ministers had resolved to order that, in each colony, a special council, presided over by the governor, and composed of the *ordonnateur*, the local director, the attorney general and the colonial inspector, should be formed, which council was to report to the government on the various points found in each of these three systems, and, at the same time, was to state the preparatory measures which, according to the opinion of its members, might be useful and necessary for the carrying out the legal project, on whatever system should be preferred.

At the same time another royal decree, bearing the same date, was issued to the governors already mentioned, ordering them to convene the colonial councils, and place the aforesaid question before them for their deliberation.

Our readers must naturally suppose that, in a question of such importance, no arguments would be spared. Those called forth by the circulars were really so numerous and so diffuse that it would be impossible to insert them all in less than two large volumes, it being a singular fact that, without any previous consultation or understanding between the different colonies, their opinions agreed so exactly that they all appeared to have emanated from one and the same colony.

The reports made were, in general, founded on a proposition presented in this form:

"Can paid labor and the free competition of laborers replace the compulsory labor of negroes in the colonies?"

This proposition, presented by some of the colonies in the same terms as above written, and by others, although in a different form, essentially the same in spirit, was unanimously decided in the negative on the following grounds:—The nature of the climate; the spontaneous vegetation of tropical soil, whereby life can be supported without labor; the natural tendencies of man not to labor more than is absolutely necessary to support life, when he undergoes a change of country, customs, wants, and, we might even say, of civilization; and the indifference with which he generally looks upon any other than his native land.

To strengthen these arguments the reporters adverted in the first place, as was natural, to the warning held up by the English colonies, which were then known to be ruined; and then entering into details on each of the systems proposed, they proved the positive spoliation contained in the idea of emancipation; not only by freeing the negroes, but by causing the abandonment of the lands which those agents cultivated and which without them would be unproductive.

To oppose the first of these systems, the incompatibility of the freedom of the children, while the mother remained a slave, was brought forward as an idea contrary to the laws of nature, and, although this argument cannot be classed among those distinguished for their soundness and conformity to truth, as, in this system the freedom of the mother was guaranteed so soon as her child should attain the age of discretion, there is no doubt that, at the first glance, it must have appeared of great weight.

But the opposition of the reporters appeared to be most strenuous against emancipation by the second and the third systems in that part relating to the indemnification of the owners with the salary they were required to pay to their laborers, who were neither more nor less than their own slaves. Such an indemnification was not real, owing to its origin, nor was it acceptable, owing to its form; inasmuch as in both senses it could with justice be declared null.

In short, after reiterating that the reports from all the colonies coincided in spirit though they differed in their form of expression, some of the councils obeying the order to consider the emancipation project as already decided in principle, whilst others respectfully, but energetically, presented their views against the measure, the arguments of the reporters may be summed up in the following conclusion:

The problem of paid labor and of the free competition of laborers has no affirmative solution in the actual condition of the colonies if we consider their secular organization and their pressing and future interests.

All transitory systems are bad in their nature, and, when protracted they produce the most destructive results. The social transformation of the colonies could not be effected except by the natural and steady course of things.

The most thorough examination of the three systems of emancipation which have been submitted to the deliberations of the colonial councils, demonstrates that the time to abolish slavery has not yet arrived.

The partial or gradual abolition of slavery by a legislative decision gives the colonists a right to a previous indemnification, which, to be just and equitable, according to the royal ordinance, dated the 24th of April, 1833, which guarantees the maintenance of the colonial institutions, ought not only to cover the total value of the slaves who are emancipated, but, also, that of the lands which will be ruined for want of culture.

It will be well to state that these reports, so absolutely opposed to the official and extra-official exigencies of the metropolis, did not emanate entirely and exclusively from interested parties; for it would be most notoriously unjust to class, as such, the Governors of the colonies, and the other administrative officials who formed the councils which had been created *ad-hoc*, as they had no landed property and were not permanent residents in these colonies. From the statements it will appear that, what with the inexperience on the one hand which lent itself to an exaggerated sentiment or hidden purpose by clamoring for the abolition of slavery, without knowing anything about that of the negro further than the ill sound of the word; and, on the other, the consummate experience in the government and in the administration of the colonies, which opposed the tendencies of these absurd though well intended clamors, there could not but arise an antagonism, which in fact did exist between the rule of the home government and the vast interests of the colonies.

That the council of Ministers saw their error as soon as their minds were enlightened by the colonial reports, cannot be denied, seeing that these clamors had no ulterior results except the damage done in the colonies by the distrust which they engendered for the future. Unfortunately, eight years afterwards, the French republic appeared with all its wild reforms, and in the name of equality the slavery of the negroes in the colonies was instantaneously abolished, never more to be renewed. This event would be laudable by every sentiment of humanity, if to destroy a work contrary to the dignity of man and the doctrine of Christ, they had not trampled under foot interests and rights that were in no manner opposed in their nature to the equity of the reform. But this is not the place for further considerations on a point of so much importance in the task we have undertaken, and therefore we will return to the history of the efforts made by the English abolitionists in the colonial nations.

In Spain, no less than in France, they labored to engraft the same ideas, taking advantage with singular ability of the political emigration in 1823, which obliged the most illustrious leaders of the liberal party on the Peninsula to live in England for the space of ten years.

This circumstance had a remarkable influence in the treaty of 1835, and the effects would have been much greater, if, in the excellent judgment of the Spanish government, the sterner duties of the public service had not out-weighed the impulses of personal gratitude. For which reason the agents of the Anti-slavery Society, knowing, that after said treaty, few if any official concessions could be obtained in Spain, had recourse to artifices to demoralize slavery wherever it was most successful.

With this end in view the Society, possessing at that time great influence with the English government, experienced no difficulty in obtaining that a ship-of-the-line of the royal navy, manned by negroes, should be stationed at the port of Havana; which vessel was, in fact, stationed there, ostensibly for the purpose of receiving the Africans taken from the slavers which might be captured before reaching their destination, but evidently, to serve as a focus and encouragement of insurrection to the slaves of the island of Cuba.

The next step was the appointment as consul in Havana, of the dangerous Mr. Turnbull, of whom mention has already been made in the official report, relative to the insurrection plotted by the negroes in Cuba in the year 1840; said functionary being a member of the Anti-slavery Society, and so fanatical, that he made himself ere long the object of strong remonstrances owing to the cool perseverance with which he acted in his labors of abolition.

At the same time or shortly after, other individuals belonging to the abolitionist society, presented themselves in Madrid, exciting the philanthrophy of journalists, and working on the general ignorance on colonial affairs, which, owing to the great distance between the countries, are very little known; and these individuals discharged their commission so fully through one of the said journals, called *El Corresponsal*, that in articles full of unquestionable sincerity, although without the least reflection, they went so far as to demand the absolute and immediate emancipation of the slaves.

By way of precaution, and with the view of supporting those philanthropic declamations, the *London Standard* had previously inserted a fictitious exposition, which was attributed to various planters in the island of Cuba, recommending the repression of the negro traffic as contrary to their own interests, from which absurd invention, which, in the opinion of the *Corresponsal*, was undoubtedly authentic, the abolitionists gained great favor with the unwary and in the sympathy of the aforesaid journal.

After which, and inasmuch as in the hearts of some generous and grateful persons, the remembrance of their own emigration or that of beloved friends could not be effaced, the Spanish government admitted in good faith and sincerity the remonstrances which, from that time, began to be made, with some asperity, by the English government, relative to the continuation of the traffic, and even consented to the plan of consulting the Captain General of the island of Cuba, as to the expediency of declaring all the negroes imported into the Island since 1820, free, in accordance with the demand set forth by the English government in a diplomatic despatch. As can be seen, then, the steps taken in Spain by the abolitionists were not less active than those that had been taken in France; and were it not that the discovery of the conspiracy for the insurrection of the negroes in the island of Cuba gave better evidence, than all the arguments that could be published against emancipation, of the dangers to which the security of our colonies was exposed by a course of indiscreet and even criminal compliance with such importunities, who knows but that, at this day, the most valuable gem of the Antilles, the pearl of the West, the coveted island of Cuba, would have been made another stain on civilization, like the western part of Santo Domingo?

What can be established as an undeniable fact is that the abolitionists desired this result, and that, for its accomplishment, various efforts of a private, and some of an official character, were made; and in order that this charge may not appear a mere supposition, should it not be established by corroborative evidence, I will present such proofs as are in my possession, some of which will be found in the reliable statements already made in this book, and other documents which will subsequently be inserted.

In the island of Cuba, which, from its exceptional circumstances, for seventy years back, differs completely from the other colonies, the colored people exceed in number and vigor the white population, as can be proved by consulting her statistics.

In 1850, the number of negroes and mulattoes, slaves and free, of the island in question, amounted to more than five hundred thousand, the whole population, both black and white, being a little over nine hundred thousand. Both elements have increased in the same proportion since that time, so that at present, of the total of one million three hundred thousand inhabitants, which Cuba contains, seven hundred thousand and some hundreds are colored. Add to this difference, which results in favor of the negroes, the circumstances of the discrepancy between the number of females and males, and consequently the proportional scarcity in the number of children, and the result will augment in a natural and incontestable manner, and in a manifestly dangerous proportion, the material strength of the negroes over the white population.

If we look upon this precedent, which must have been well known to the English Philanthropic Society which was laboring for the abolition of slavery, and then take into consideration the unmistakeable efforts made officially by the said abolition society and by the English government, firstly, to persuade Spain to proclaim the freedom of all negroes imported into the island of Cuba since 1820, and, afterwards, to induce her to adopt the total abolition of slavery, (as will be hereafter demonstrated) we cannot for a moment doubt that the africanization of Cuba would be the natural and logical consequence of those efforts, should they be crowned at last with success, and would, still more inevitably, be the result of a successful insurrection.

It would not be right for me to say that the English government took any active part in, or even had the slightest knowledge of the proceedings of its consul, Mr. Turnbull, in exciting the negroes of the island of Cuba to an insurrection against the whites; but neither would it be just to doubt the initiative taken by said consul in the conspiracy, since it appears officially in the judicial proceedings.[1] And, as he was a member and agent of the

---

(1) In another part of this procedure, which I have before me, there is an account which says as follows: "*Fiscal conclusion in the trial of the negro Juan Perez Basnuevo.*—This legal procedure arose from the celebrated case which must at present occupy public attention in every country where the news of the momentous event that caused it have reached. According to the data acquired in the various investigations in which I am

London Anti-Slavery Society, and owed his position as consul to his ardent zeal and well known works published in that cause, it is evident that to the said society, rather than to his private designs, we must attribute the attempt made by the negroes to exterminate the white population in the most flourishing of our possessions.

Moreover, and in order that the subject may be better understood, it will be well to add that the British government refused to recall its consul when the Spanish government was obliged to request his removal on account of the

> engaged, and those appearing from the investigations which the council has just attended to, it is a certain and positive fact that a very considerable number of free colored people had been secretly scheming, since the middle of 1841, to incite our slaves to insurrection, to exterminate all the white population, and afterwards to take possession of the Island. But what must most astonish us, what will appear impossible to all persons who have a knowledge of this event, is that the consul of a friendly and allied nation, the man who had the confidence of a government that ranks first in European civilization, should prove so false to his trust, and should abuse our friendship to the extent of inciting the rebellion himself, by sending emissaries over the whole Island, to undermine and shake the foundations upon which its well-being and tranquillity are based, and by putting in play all the springs that might contribute to the realization of such a horrible project. The name of Turnbull figures in every part of this great case as the arrogant author of the sad scenes we lament. The extermination of four hundred and nineteen thousand inhabitants, and the ruin and loss of the island of Cuba to the civilized world, seem to agree very well with the principles professed by this man, and with those so basely boasted of by the philanthropic society to which he belongs; as if we had not sufficient common sense to perceive that the freedom they wish to bestow on our servants is an evil for them a hundredfold greater than slavery itself, owing to the ignorance and barbarism inherent to these unfortunate beings.
>
> "If the agents of that society, which may well be called the would be destroyer of the white population of the Indies, instead of inciting our slaves to insurrection, would devote their energies to the study of the laws in favor of the slaves, to which one hundred and fifty-three thousand persons of color are indebted for the freedom which they now enjoy in the Island, their number, compared with that of free colored persons in the republic of the United States of North America, being in a ratio of more than two to one, according to the relative number of the slaves; if they would consider that these laws allow the negroes to acquire means whereby they can redeem themselves from servitude, which is a privilege that never was enjoyed by the slaves in the Roman republic; if these agents, I repeat, would devote their attention to this concise and simple legislation, which is replete with doctrines that breathe only true humanity and philanthropy, and which contained a prudent and wise system of emancipation, even at the time of their initiation, about the middle of the eighteenth century; they would undoubtedly be filled with shame at the idea of having brought about the unpleasant occurrences which are now occupying our attention, and filling us all with grief and sorrow, and, perhaps, would abandon at once and forever all their deplorable attempts."

bold and impudent declarations publicly made by Mr. Turnbull against slavery, in the presence of the slaves; and as, simultaneously with this attitude of the British government, a vessel of the English royal Navy, manned by negroes, was stationed at Havana, while its sable crew went continually on shore, clad in showy uniforms, the more effectually to arouse the ambition of their brethren in that city, calumny seized upon this coincidence as a pretext for attributing to the said government a complicity in the acts of its consul, and although this charge may have been unjust, the British government certainly took no steps to clear itself from the imputation.

It was undoubtedly on this account that this idea spread and became universal, not only at that time and with reference to the island of Cuba, but for many years after, and extending itself to the ordinary labors of the English representatives in the capital of Spain. And let it not be imagined that this suspicion existed only in the minds of Spanish visionaries, accustomed to view political questions through the narrow and hazy prism of their petty interests. No: the idea that England was trying to Africanize the island of Cuba had become generally diffused, and in such a manner that even the names of parties compromised in the question were well known; and, in Paris, Lord Howden, Minister of Great Britain in Madrid, was, in a friendly manner, requested to give an explanation of his real or supposed machinations, which had been exposed in some of the United States' journals.

The answer of the noble lord was not long delayed, as it was of the highest importance to him to exonerate himself from such a charge before the American Union, which had then a pro-slavery administration; and, rightly calculating that his answer would be published, he planned it with singular ability, making therein sundry charges and misrepresentations against Spain, with the two-fold object of diverting public attention from his evident culpability, and of furnishing to calumny fresh pretexts to continue its attacks against the Spanish administration in the Indies, such being at that time a commonly prevailing practice.

I might here omit the insertion of said answer were it not for the misrepresentations it contains, and the fact that it was published without any contradiction. Here, then, it will be found exactly as it was published in the year of its date; and my readers will allow me to make some comments on its contents.

"Paris, November 14, 1853.—My dear Corbin: I have just received your letter of yesterday, and I can assure you it by no means perplexes me. Our long continued friendship authorizes you to put to me all those questions, and I can answer them without failing in discretion or in the perfect discharge of my duties as public functionary; and you have sufficient discernment to know that in this case I am quite as anxious to tell you the truth as you can be that I should do so.

"I have read the extraordinary statements which you have sent me concerning the desire of England to Africanize Cuba, and the arrangements which I have been making in Madrid to that effect. In the most solemn manner which these ridiculous, though wicked inventions will admit, I declare that all that has been reported on the subject is entirely false. I have not the slightest objection to tell you what have been my negotiations with the Spanish Government respecting Cuba, for the last three years, and you will see that there is not the slightest foundation for the rumors which, it appears, have been spread in the United States.

"First: I have continually remonstrated with respect to the number of slaves which are annually imported into Cuba, and I have always complained of the public manner in which this traffic is carried on, with entire impunity, from the Captain General down to the lowest official, always excepting the excellent general Concha.

"Second: I have made fruitless efforts to induce the Spanish Government to follow the example of the United States in this particular, i. e. to declare the abominable traffic in human beings a piracy.

"Third: I have employed my time in diligent endeavors to obtain the complete and definite freedom of the negroes illegally detained as slaves since the year 1817, under the name of *emancipated negroes,* in contravention of the treaties; and I have the satisfaction of being able to say that the Spanish Government has at length listened to the dictates of justice and humanity, and has granted me this favor.

"Fourth: I have labored to procure the extinction of that intolerant and immoral law which obliges all foreigners desirous of establishing themselves in Cuba, to change their religion, upon the strange principle, which was held in no other part of the world, that the fact of a man's proving a renegade to his faith is a sufficient guarantee that he will make a good subject.

"Besides these official negociations, I have, in a friendly manner, and on several occasions, counselled the reform of the internal system of the Island, that the administration of justice might be improved, and the natives qualified to hold public offices.

"By this statement you will see that what I have really done, or, rather, attempted to do, is very different from what has been attributed to me in the American papers. When the true state of the case shall be made public, and ignorance and malevolence be put to flight, I trust that your countrymen will give the support of their approval to the reforms for which I have labored, and which are so consistent with your own laws and institutions.

"In all that I have made known to you with such entire frankness, the United States can see nothing but the natural workings of England's avowed and immutable policy in a cause which is so dear to her; and Spain must yet be convinced that, unless she modifies her intolerance and fulfils her agreements, she cannot at the present day expect to be ranked among civilized nations.

"Believe me, dear Corbin, to be, with the greatest consideration, sincerely yours.—HOWDEN."

A short time since a Spanish journal published in London, *El Español de Ambos Mundos,* said: "The Spanish Goverment has not yet understood the wonderful power of the press, from which so much advantage is drawn by the Governments of England and of the United States." This was expressed by said journal in order to show the effect which can be produced on public opinion by accusations and aspersions when they remain uncontradicted by the parties interested, who, by their silence, naturally appear convicted of their criminality; and there is no doubt that *El Español de Ambos Mundos* pronounced an important truth which is already too well known and acted upon by the enemies of the Spanish nation.

In the first place, Lord Howden deliberately wronged and calumniated all the Captain-Generals of the island of Cuba, who preceded general Concha, when it was evident to all the world that not one of them had authorized, with his knowledge or consent, the introduction of *bozal* negroes, notwithstanding that they were introduced on a large scale before and during the administration of general Concha. It would be unfair to the whole body of these officials to make mention of the integrity of any one in particular, in the strict discharge of his duties, and even to designate by name those whose premature recall has been attributed, by the ignorant, to their excessive zeal against the slave trade; let us, then, be satisfied with clearing the honor of all, knowing that it cannot be assailed with any positive foundation or even with any show of justice.

The introduction of *bozal* negroes into the island of Cuba, which has a periphery of two thousand one hundred miles, is carried on precisely in the same manner that slavers bear away their cargoes from the coasts of Africa; and the charge of bribery can be laid upon the English cruisers guarding those coasts, because they do not succeed in preventing the traffic, with as much reason as upon the Spanish authorities of the Island, because they cannot prevent the introduction of those cargoes, that being a natural and irremediable result of the necessities of agriculturists, and of the immense profits which are realized by those engaged in the trade.

The Spanish government, ever zealous in the observance of the letter and spirit of the existing treaties, could not legally do more than it had done, was doing, and still does to prove that those treaties did not exist only in name. If the fitters out of slavers were Spanish subjects alone, there would be no difficulty in declaring them pirates, according to the suggestion of the English Minister, and having them hung at the yard-arm, should such a proceeding appear equitable. But, in the first place, the treaties had already established laws and penalties for the slave traders and a special tribunal for their trial; so that, the penalty of hanging recommended by Lord Howden, not being authorized by the treaties initiated by his government, could not be adopted unless a new treaty was drawn up. In the second place, the majority of the traders were of other nations, and Spain did not see fit to create international conflicts for every slaver that she might capture. That the noble Lord sought to bring about such international difficulties may well be imagined, that is, if he did in fact recommend such measures, for the furtherance of his own philanthropic scheme; but it would be folly to suppose that the impertinent interference would be favorably received by the Spanish government, guided as it is by prudence and circumspection in politics and administration.

The absolute freedom of the emancipated negroes has always been secured in the Spanish possessions, in conformity with the regulations; and it is false that, at the date to which Lord Howden alludes, negroes captured from slavers in 1817 were held to forced service, as no prizes whatever were made until many years after, and certainly none could have been made until 1820, according to the first treaty. Neither does it seem probable that the English Minister had any reason for inserting the third exposition of his efforts, further than from puerile vanity and the desire of appearing to advantage at the expense of the honor of Spain.

In the Spanish colonies there is positively no law to compel foreigners, established there, to change their religion. The public observance of any other than the Catholic religion is not permitted in Spain, and this law is established in the colonies. Great numbers of Protestants of all the known sects reside in these islands, and their testimony can be appealed to in order that Lord Howden's fourth observation may appear in its true character before the tribunal of History. Article 66 of the Regulations, by which the heathen Chinese laborers on the island are governed, says:—"The master shall endeavor to teach the dogmas and morality of the true religion to the laborers, but without employing other means than persuasion and conviction; and should any of them manifest a desire to be converted to the Catholic faith, it shall be made known to the priest of that parish that he may take the proper measures to that effect." The impartial reader can compare the tolerance of this article with the accusations which Lord Howden makes against Spain with such a total disregard of truth, and draw thence the logical conclusions which his judgment shall dictate.

While I am on this subject I will also observe that, in

political and religious matters each nation follows that course which may appear most in accordance with its traditions, its most cherished interests, and its peculiar characteristics; and that Lord Howden, in writing to Mr. Corbin, a native of the United States, about the intolerance of the Spanish laws, only succeeded, though perhaps without being aware of it, in wounding the national vanity of his friend by the evident allusion to the positive defect of the laws of the United States which prohibit foreigners from establishing themselves in the country unless they become naturalized citizens. These two cases, however, are different, since the defect which really exists in the laws of the United States only affects an important point in political rights, whereas that of Spain, if it were indeed what Lord Howden asserts, would strike a mortal blow at the religious faith of those who should submit to its requirements.

Nevertheless, even if that were the case, such proceedings on the part of the Spanish government would not deserve the anathema pronounced on them by Lord Howden, who has gone so far as to declare that Spain is unworthy of ranking amongst the civilized nations ; because in matters of religious faith such absolute declarations are unseemly, it not being yet clearly defined, or, to avoid blasphemy, I should say rather, it being demonstrable by ample and unimpeachable evidence that, on a point so essential to human existence, that nation which cleaves exclusively to one faith, banishing all that sinful pride which leads the limited minds of mortals to attempt to grasp the Infinite as fully as God alone can comprehend it, is far wiser than those in which every change in the human mind produces a new creed, while from the infinite variety of these ideas there result as many different religious beliefs as there may be persons who chose to exercise their private judgment upon the spiritual interests of the world and upon the Divine cause of the universe.

The friendly counsels to which the English Minister refers, at the conclusion of his letter, will certainly appear very singular when they are compared with the real facts.

It is universally known that the great code of laws of the Indies is a monument of equity and wisdom, which, with the exception of the political part concerning modern institutions, has been preserved integral in nearly all the

Spanish American republics, since their independence. It is also known that, according to the same code the high functionaries of the law are required to give an account of their administration when they retire from office, and that they are held accountable, before the tribunal established according to law, not only for their own actions, but for the faults committed openly and with impunity under their jurisdiction by their subordinates. And it is furthermore known that the Spanish government, ever prudently deliberating on the reforms and alterations counselled by the changes of the times, and adopting all such as would not injure public interests, not only maintained in all their power the most beneficial dispositions of said code of the Indies, but also added new ones thereto whenever they appeared useful and necessary.

From these incontrovertible facts which are universally known, and which have caused justice to be done to the administration of Spain in her colonies, if not by the people at large, at least by the most eminent statesmen, we may draw the following conclusion : that the counsels to which Lord Howden refers in his letter to his friend at Paris, were either specially gotten up for effect in the case which obliged him to allude to them, or they were so unreasonable and exposed so much ignorance on the subjects to which they referred that the Spanish government utterly disregarded them as being useless or pernicious.

And what shall we say of that absurd and disgraceful counsel, recommending that the natives of the island of Cuba be qualified to hold office and discharge public functions ?

Being in Havana in the year 1852, and having seen a similar charge preferred against the Spanish government in a certain United States journal, I determined to ascertain how much truth that charge contained. At that time the island was governed by the ill-fated General Valentine Cañedo, and to his authority I had recourse, requesting him, by letter, that direct information might be furnished to me, from all the Lieutenancies of the government, the bureau of the Sub-Inspectors of the army, that of the Commandant General of the navy, the Captaincy General and the central offices, concerning all the employees, in every branch of the administration, who had not been born on the Peninsula. The General willingly granted this request, so that within the course of two months I found myself in possession of the desired data, which were so numerous as to form an exceedingly bulky package. It is true that in these papers were found some names of persons who had been born in Costa Firme and other parts of the Spanish American continent, but it is also a fact that the number of native Cubans who exercised public functions amounted with certainty to over seven hundred. As the fact which I have stated is official, and can be attested by the Lieutenancies of the government, to their testimony do I submit the defence of my assertions, and in case that there should be some indolent persons who might prefer still to doubt my words rather than trouble themselves to confront the truth by such means, I will proceed further to recall to their minds that previously to the date above alluded to, Don José de la Concha, a native of Costa Firme, had been Governor and Captain General; the unfortunate. Don Narciso Lopez, also a Spanish-American, had been Commandant General of Trinidad de Cuba; the Count of Villanueva, born in Havana, had been Superintendent General of the Public Treasury; the then Brigadier Don Juan de Herrera, also a native Cuban, was Commandant General or Sub-Inspector of Artillery; and a brother of the last mentioned officer; Don Francisco de Paula Michelena, a native Cuban, now living in the Island, retired from the military service, was Lieutenant Governor of Bejucal or of San Cristobal, I do not well remember which, and had also exercised the same functions, about that time, in another jurisdiction of the same department; and I had the honor of being on terms of deferential friendship with Don Matias Letamendi, also a Cuban, who held the post of Lieutenant Governor of Sancto Spiritus, where he displayed great loyalty and ability in the discharge of his duties. General La Vallette, the second in command on the Island, though not a creole, had nearly all of his relatives in Cuba, where they were born. The Chief Judges were all Cubans, with very rare exceptions; and, for the truth of this, I appeal to the testimony of the official Guide-Book, which would infallibly expose any mis-statement on my part; and native Cubans abounded especially in the army and navy, in which they held all grades, from the highest to the lowest.

With the aid of these explanations, which are not misplaced here, though they may appear foreign to the principal subject of this work, it will be easy to comprehend what is the real value of the contents of Lord Howden's letter to his friend Corbiń in the judgment of reflecting people. And the intrinsic value of said letter can be more accurately estimated when it becomes known that the charges preferred by the press in the United States of America, against that representative of Great Britain in the court of Madrid, were not without foundation, insomuch as they related to those concealed tendencies towards the africanization of Cuba, *i. e.* the delivering of the Island into the power of its African population, within a period of time which, though indefinite, would, according to their desires, infallibly come to pass.

This will be better understood if the reader bears in mind the computation, which has already been made in these pages, between the two races which people said Island, demonstrating that it would be difficult, nay, even impossible, to bestow unconditional freedom on the negroes without causing the violent extermination of the whites, owing to the material preponderance of the former over the latter; and then take into consideration the demonstration of the efforts made by Lord Howden to obtain, from the government of Madrid, a decree of entire and absolute freedom in favor of the negroes of the island of Cuba.

These efforts were made in the latter part of the year 1851, on the occasion of the unsuccessful Anglo-American expedition against that Island; for, the government of Spain having sent its expressions of gratitude to that of Great Britain, for its friendly offer to prevent, with English ships of war, any further attempts of like nature, the English, persevering in their idea of abolishing slavery, imagined that the circumstances were opportune to obtain a definite and favorable decision of the question.

This design was coincided with by a decree issued at that time in New Granada, abolishing the exiguous remains of negro slavery which still existed there, though, in the year 1817, if I recollect aright, and during the war of its political independence, the famous Bolivar had decreed that all children born of slaves in those territories which he governed, should be forever free; and, as if there was anything in common between the circumstances of that country and those of the lovely Antille, or as if English diplomacy was not aware of the disparity which existed between a country almost ruined for agriculture by its never ending civil wars, and a land whose inexhaustible productiveness is aided by its uninterrupted peace, the famous Lord Howden, who, two years after, was so solicitous in putting a wrong construction on the facts presented, when he was questioned as to his participation in the project of Africanizing Cuba, presented a note to the Spanish Government, on the 26th of September, in which the example of New Granada is held up to it to be blindly followed.

The Government of Madrid answered him with the prudence and circumspection demanded by the occasion; and, as it called Lord Howden's attention to some contradictions which existed between his despatch and those previously sent by the English chancellorship, lord Palmerston, who was his superior in the State department, endeavored, though not without great difficulty, to extricate himself from the muddle into which his blind confidence had placed him, to which effect he sent the following official letter:

"To Lord Howden, English Ambassador to Madrid.
"Office of Foreign affairs, October 20, 1851.
"My Lord: I have received your despatch of the 1st inst., inclosing a note received by you from the marquis of Miraflores, in answer to yours of the 26th of September, which expressed, in the name of H. M., the wish of seeing the Spanish Government imitate the example of New Granada, which has proclaimed the total abolition of slavery.

"With regard to the passage wherein, the marquis of Miraflores declares that the Spanish Government cannot understand how that of H. M. can recommend a measure which would prove fatal to the natives of Cuba, at the same time that it recommends Spain to conciliate their goodwill, I beg your Lordship will make the Marquis observe that the slaves form a considerable and an undeniably important part of the population of Cuba; that any steps taken towards the emancipation of these slaves will be in perfect harmony with the recommendation which H. M.'s government has made to the effect that measures should be taken to satisfy the natives of Cuba, in order to insure its union with the metropolis. And it is also very evident that if freedom was given to the colored population of Cuba, this fact would create a powerful element of resistance against the projects of annexing the Island to the United States, in which country slavery exists.

"As for the influence which the emancipation of the negroes would exert on the interests of the whites who are landed proprietors, it can be affirmed, without fear of contradiction, that free labor is less costly than that of the slaves; and it is undeniable that hired laborers would not be such dangerous neighbors to the wealthy classes as are ill-treated and revengeful slaves. Besides, it is a truth inherent to the principles of human nature that the slaves are necessarily more or less ill used; while it is equally evident that the resentment which ill treatment always provokes will be inevitable, whatever may be the efforts to smother it.

"For these reasons it appears to me that the communication which your Lordship was charged with making, concerning the measure adopted by the government of New Granada, does not deserve to be considered contrary to the benevolent sentiments which her Majesty's government expressed with regard to the natives of Cuba.—PALMERSTON."

From the perusal of this dispatch, which, as will be seen, proves the justice of the charges made by the American press against the representative of England in Madrid, even though his efforts to create a chaos in the island of Cuba by the unconditional freedom of five hundred thousand negroes were but the official expression of superior instructions, it is easy to perceive that the most difficult questions of the Western hemisphere are treated with levity in Europe, unless we should rather attribute the contents of said dispatch to the desire of reconciling, in any possible manner, the contradiction of the English chancellorship in its antithetical recommendations, in order to present it in the least unfavorable light.

Be this as it may, and since the consummate skill of the Marquis of Miraflores, aided by the power of justice, had amicably but energetically repelled the most dangerous suggestions which England had ever made against Cuba, the inextinguishable fanaticism of the English abolitionists, which learns nothing from the teachings of practical history but gathers therefrom only what may serve to destroy whatever may stand in the way of its exclusive interests, retired abashed for the moment within the limits of the constituted international laws; not with the purpose of remaining silent and inactive for any length of time, but rather to give a fresh impulse and another character to their projects by turbulent means, in order to see if they would thus prove more efficacious in their definite results. With this end in view, the notes advocating the repression of the slave trade were multiplied and made of daily recurrence, and so were the interpellations in both Houses of Parliament, and the most violent and unjust diatribes of the English Ministers against Spain and against the island of Cuba.

There were occasions when the Spanish government found it necessary to protest energetically against certain offensive censures which were utterly devoid of truth; but although by taking this attitude the government succeeded in obtaining the apologies which are so easily furnished in such cases by diplomatic courtesy, it could not prevent the English abolitionists from persevering in their shameful efforts against Spain and the Spaniards.

These noisy clamors, which daily became more exaggerated, were the prelude to a new combination which was formed in order to force upon Spain, in a novel manner, the adoption of measures which would prove ruinous to the negro question. These were nothing less than the establishment of the right of search, to interfere with the slave trade in the plantations of the colonial possessions, in which places such proceedings are forbidden by the laws; which would not only be the means of discrediting and perverting slavery, and of destroying the interior order by which that institution is supported, but would also convert the proprietors into bitter enemies of the government which should in such a manner disregard their laws, annul their claims to the obedience of the laborers and the respect of the public, and attack in so dangerous a manner their lawful interests.

This, as will readily be perceived, was another attempt

to introduce into the colonies, under a different form, the disorder and confusion which would have been caused by the absolute freedom of the negroes when it was proposed by Lord Palmerston through Lord Howden ; but, as the English had already reason to suppose that this proposition would be repelled with all the power that the Spanish government might boast, instead of proceeding personally and directly in the matter, they tried to compromise therein some other governments.

This plot was being concerted at the time when the war with Morocco was bringing into notice the moral and material progress of Spain ; and as this progress had become apparent to all the world, from the facility with which fifty thousand men, completely armed and equipped, had been thrown into Africa, without any neglect or even any weakening of the defences in the Peninsula and abroad; as well as from the abundance of specie with which the government attended to all the ordinary and extraordinary expenses, and to the payment of a debt which, though deferred without difficulty until that time, was suddenly and urgently claimed by the creditor, which was the English government. The French government, or, perhaps, the Emperor himself, thought the time had come for Spain to resume her former rank among the great powers. This was proposed by the Imperial government, the nation most interested in the matter taking no part therein ; and then it was that it occurred to the English Chancellor to propose to France and the United States the establishment of the right of search on the plantations of Cuba, the increase of the number of cruisers in the waters surrounding said Island, and the adoption of a plan of emigration, in China, which had been drawn up by the consular agents of the nations interested in the question in concert with the authorities of that vast and remote empire.

Of course, all the publicity which such a proposition demanded was given to it, with what object may be divined, and on this head the Spanish paper, published in London, which we have already quoted, made the following remarks :

"It is now high time that the Spanish government should seriously take this question into consideration, and refuse to allow any further trifling with its fame and that of the Spanish nation. In order to accomplish this it is necessary that Spain should thoroughly understand what is now transpiring, and that she should possess a perfect knowledge of all the secret springs which move the puppets in this show. Here Lord John Russell issues official notes, becomes excited and thunders forth his denunciations, not because his personal repose of mind is disturbed by the commerce in slaves, but because he is obliged to obey the wishes, the caprices, and even the extravagancies of influential persons, in order to retain his political position.

"These persons are, in turn, influenced by the employees of the different societies, which, being exposed to extinction from want of occupation, are obliged to get up some commotions in the world if they desire the continuance of their subscriptions, without which there would be no salaries for the secretaries, the employees, the reporters, and the rest of that innumerable hungry tribe who live in this country at the expense of certain manias and follies of the public. This is the secret cause of the outcry made here concerning the slave trade."

And afterwards, while reflecting on the apparent reasons on which the government of the United States founded its then natural desire to escape from seconding those propositions before the Spanish government, which apparent reasons formed another chapter of charges and recriminations against the authorities of the island of Cuba, this paper continued to treat the matter in the following words:

"As for the United States—what can be more acceptable for them than the amiable complicity and voluntary blindness of England, who allows them the undisturbed enjoyment of the abundant profits accruing from the slave trade, while she throws all the responsibility and all the odium upon Spain?

"To put an end to this interesting game, it is only necessary that Spain should display a little frankness and energy. Let her government commission its agents in New York to discover the operations of all the slavers fitted out in that port; let it, through its representative at Washington, unceasingly demand the detention of such vessels; let it publish in the *Madrid Gazette* the official notes in which such demands may be made; and the world will not delay in casting the odium and responsibility of the traffic on those who are really to blame. If the Spanish government will not act thus, Lord John Russell and the President of the United States will continue to play the game of shuttlecock with its reputation, that being an amusement which suits their interests and costs them but little, though it does incalculable damage to Spain."

It appears to me that these reasonings of the *Español de Ambos Mundos* were not far from right in their manner of sifting the question, nor were they devoid of justice. At the time that they appeared in answer to the charges preferred against Spain by the governments of England and of the United States, the latter had succeeded in freeing their vessels from the right of search, to which they had been ignominiously subjected by the treaties then in force, still no one can pretend to affirm—no one with any show of truth—can even simply state that the United States ships were not engaged in the slave trade. Just about that time an American slaver was caught *in fraganti*, and her captain was hung, in consequence of the excitement and antagonism which had already commenced to appear, with all the symptoms of an approaching civil war between the two great sections of that Republic, which are now engaged in the work of mutual destruction, and not because such punishment was customary in such cases; for, on the contrary, it is well known to those who are experienced in matters pertaining to the traffic, that, before this war broke out, four-fifths of the vessels engaged in the slave trade were Anglo-American, and that these slavers were fitted out and prepared in the ports of the Union without any attempts at secresy, and with full confidence in the success of their expeditions.

It was doubtless for this reason that the Federal government definitely and absolutely rejected the plan of introducing coolies into the States where negro labor was an institution. This government also said: "In the United States, where slavery exists, these heathen Chinese would demoralize the temperate, pacific and contented negroes, among whom there are great numbers who are sincere Christians."

Such is the history of England's efforts to abolish slavery in the principal countries where it existed and where it still flourishes. In the narration of these facts I have confined myself simply to those relating to the French and Spanish Colonies, omitting all mention of Brazil and the United States, because of the former I have but few data in my possession, and because it would now be extremely impolitic, in speaking of the latter, to enter into details which would scandalize the world, and, doubly so, to publish them in a work which is based on conciliatory principles.

Having ended this explanatory narration of facts which are supported by authentic documents, it is now time that we should analyze the effects produced on humanity and civilization by the absolute freedom of the negroes in those countries where slavery has been abolished ; on the public regard for international law, by the treaties which tend to the destruction of the right of redemption ; and on the future of Africa in its moral and material interests, by the philanthropic labors of the Society in London.

CHAPTER VIII.

Remarks on the unskillful manner in which the treaties that prohibit the redemption of the negroes were drawn up.—The prohibition of the redemption is opposed to the abolition of slavery: this proposition demonstrated.—The treaties now in force in these matters are also opposed to the liberal tendencies and ideas of progress which may havĕ originated them.—Historic results produced by this prohibition in countries peopled by negroes.—The bloody and already famous scenes in Dahomey. —Disastrous effects of said treaties in the slave holding countries which have emancipated their laborers.—The English Colonies.—The French Colonies.—The Republic of Haiti.—Moral and material state of the Spanish possessions.—In the countries where the institution of slavery exists, the number of slaves has increased since the redemption was prohibited. —The blame which on this account has been laid upon the authorities of those countries might be attributed, for the same causes and with greater reason, to the English cruisers.—The blame, however, belongs exclusively to the treaties on this matter now in force.

MANY times, upon consulting the data and bringing to mind the events which are to substantiate my views in this chapter, my conviction has been confirmed that the ideas of the most eminent men, when treating of facts bearing upon their own reputation, possess but little depth, if indeed they are not characterized by total want of force. And this conviction, which the vanity of men who have obtained no political prominence will not admit, and which a churlish wisdom would call unjustifiable, since I am myself open to the charge, can be justified, not alone by reference to the tempestuous and never properly understood question of slavery, but also to almost all questions of international polity in which it has been necessary to harmonize conflicting interests and views.

Consult the diplomatic history of peace and war; the substrata of offensive and defensive alliances, and the treaties which have ended wars, bearing carefully in mind the various interests brought to light by the contest, and nought will be found but ephemeral settlements; adjustments without positive results; flaws, unnoticed at the time, but leaving the door open for inevitable discord sooner or later, and affording pretexts for renewing the clash of arms, or for interminable disputes among lawmakers.

"Great men," said a deep thinker, "are like great mountains, they grow smaller the nearer we approach to them," and I assert that in the management of human affairs our intelligence is so limited, and our strength so unequal to the task, it may well happen that great mountains may form an exception to the rule, but not so with great men.

And this rule, the truth of which the generality of public transactions will easily demonstrate, becomes infallible when applied to slavery, for the most illustrious statesmen of the civilized world have in vain sought for the best method of treating it, and their efforts seem to have been only instrumental in increasing the chaos. This is evident in the present *status* of the negro, whose condition they have tried to ameliorate, as well in Africa as in the Colonies; in the laws concerning the rights of nations, as they exist to-day between all governments; in the industrial standing of those countries where the system of enforced labor once prevailed, but has been abolished; and in the arena where this vexed question, which both science and empiricism have handled so much and so fruitlessly, is now seeking a solution in blood.

The extremely limited intelligence with which God has endowed the negro, that, being of the human species, he might not be confounded with the lower animals, will inevitably render futile all efforts of the kind hitherto made in his behalf. Neither distinguished statesmen nor philanthropical societies, nor elaborate treaties, are of any avail, and so far have only resulted in bringing about the present deplorable state of affairs, and if persisted in will end in the subversion of order and the substitution of confusion; the well-being of a life of industry will be replaced by the license of an enervating and demoralizing indolence, the fruitfulness of honorable toil by the ruin of great territories, the respect due to international rights by vainglorious boastings and the bitter taunts of unjustifiable recrimination, the peaceful interchange of the necessaries and luxuries of life, by the divided interests of separate sections of a great nation, the views entertained by the one being antagonistical to and incompatible with the material wants of the other, and finally instead of peace, that inestimable boon which the genius of the age demands, the world will witness with abhorrence the recurrence of exterminating and cruel wars, only equaled by those which characterized the barbarous ages.

God forbid that I should deny the good intent of the efforts which have been the cause of so much disorder. Slavery! that barbarous institution, offspring of the primitive ages, criminal compromise between human liberty and an imperative necessity for labor, foul emission of that false policy which has been the accompaniment of conquest and invasion since the time of God's chosen people. Slavery, whose name became repugnant to the hearing, even where in reality it existed but in name, as soon as the idea of emancipation had reached its apogee in the course of the world's changes.

But it was said, they traffic in human flesh in Africa, and in America a part of the human family exists in a state of perpetual slavery. And this obtains and is practised legally among people with whom we are forced to commune, and the right so to do is guaranteed by existing codes in free nations!

Naturally enough, this ultraism prompted, no doubt, by true charity and unquestionable faith, took root among the masses and became the subject of fiery discussions. But although this occurred among the multitude whose manifestations are always passionate, and whose arguments are seldom if ever well digested, and notwithstanding the seeming injustice of opposing a pagan institution, even though it existed only in name, yet a careful analysis of the subject should have been resorted to as the only means of regulating these extravagant notions, so as not to exceed the bounds of the revolutionary spirit which had commenced to cry out against negro labor.

That the majority should protest against and demand the abolition of slavery, since under that name the redemption of the African race from barbarism, their civilization, and even their absolute eventual *emancipation* by means of labor, had been established, was but natural and praiseworthy, emanating, as it did, from a liberal people, ignorant though they were of the true merits of the case. But, that statesmen allowing themselves to be led by the horde, should endorse their errors, through sinful ignorance; that those invested with high powers and entrusted with the administration of justice, should attempt to solve by the criterion of public sentiment, and that alone, one of the most intricate questions which humanity could possibly submit to the judgment of the most privileged understandings; finally, that governments, supposed to be the abodes of greatest prudence and wisdom should unanimously agree upon a policy without the precedent of experiment, lay claim to infallibility and persevere in their folly after so many years of an experience with results contrary to their decision, is most wonderful, and suffices to form a chapter of terrible accusations against the authors and abettors thereof, when we reflect upon the endless heartburnings which their course is producing in the world.

I am ignorant of the course of procedure usual in matters of universal import when presented to governments for adjudication, but were one to judge of it by what has taken place respecting this matter of negro slavery, he would most probably be led to suppose that the private opinions of Ministers had alone been consulted, now enveloped in the haze of erroneous theories, and again clearly indicating the object arrived at. But, although I confess to this ignorance, never having been officially connected with the subject, I think myself capable of pointing out the course most likely to succeed, if I am not blinded by self conceit.

And I say this because the question referred to being in itself intricate and difficult to handle, even when shorn of the material interests liable to suffer in its solution, and confined to the principle which gave it birth, the first point which naturally suggests itself is to inquire if the demands of public opinion, in the shape presented to us, would be conducive to the desired end.

The prohibition of the slave trade and the abolition of slavery are by no means one and the same. I am even of the opinion that the first renders the other impossible; and I also believe that the truly humanitarian intent of the philanthropical people who clamored against the institution of enforced negro labor, on account of the name it bore, had in view the abolition of said system rather than the prevention of the redemption.

The prohibition of the slave trade being agreed upon without reference to the abolition of slavery, resulted in perpetuating the latter in the territories where it had but a precarious existence before, because the involuntary servitude of the blacks having been recognized as of imperative necessity wherever experience had established it, legislators at once commenced to draw the reins tighter and to deprive the industrious slave of the right which he before possessed to better his condition or ransom himself, while the cupidity of their masters prompted them to seek means for their reproduction by marriage. All, however, with the evident and very natural object of preventing a scarcity of labor on their plantations.

In addition to this inferred wrong against natural rights, the prohibition of the slave trade and the disposition to perpetuate servitude through the raising of negroes born in that condition without aspirations to better themselves in the countries where these means were adopted, all kinds of intellectual instruction was prohibited. And as physiology and phrenology both induced the supposition that cultivation would have its effect upon the race and improve its intellectual capacity, in the course of one or more generations, legislators actuated more by self-interest than regard for the poor unfortunates, forbid them all intellectual food as though it were poison, in order that their offspring might not be superior to their ancestors when with their savage tribes in Africa or Asia.

By this course, which moreover did not prevent the importation of slaves into said countries when it was thought they were needed, and which we might almost say continued without interruption worthy of note from the time the treaties were made against the slave trade until the war commenced in the Southern part of the United States, the philanthropy of the abolitionists miscarried even while confining itself within the limits of the compact, for many slave owners finding traffic in slaves more profitable than working their plantations, without giving up however, the latter, devoted themselves to the raising and sale of negroes upon a grand scale ; carrying them frequently in vessels freighted on purpose, and with all the requirements of legal commerce from one State to another.

To sum up, if the prohibition of the traffic in negroes in Africa was done with the view of doing away with slavery and of putting an end to the loathsome dealing in human flesh, its most immediate results were directly the opposite of those intended, since slavery was strengthened where before individual labor was allowed, and the trade in negroes which up to this time had been confined to African prisoners, not only increased to the scandal of public rights between Africa and America, but it also increased and was made legal under the very treaties which were intended to put an end to it.

This really happened in the United States, that is, in the most liberal country in the world, if we are to take into consideration the provisions of its republican and democratic constitution, and therefore it is not strange that among a people who could not, owing to the evident spirit of their laws, conscientiously oppose the freeing of such industrious slaves as might be able to acquire it as the fruit of their labor and good conduct, should attempt to take advantage of the weak points in the treaties which prohibited the slave trade, and carry it on in violation of the authorities.

And this course, according to them, was the more praiseworthy, as by this means legislation concerning the negro was enabled to preserve its liberal and protective features intact, without presenting the loathsome spectacle of human breeding pens for public sale, and without the transgression of the law concerning the slave trade being considered as of much moment either, since they knew that their action, although illegal, prevented the slaughter of these unfortunates, and by civilizing them, made them useful to mankind and themselves.

But laying these considerations aside and confining ourselves to the object of the present chapter, which is to show that all the concerted plans and international compacts made to abolish slavery, have brought about, when put in practice, the reverse of what was intended, which was, the moral improvement of the African race by means of liberty, and the prosperity of the colonies under a system of free labor, let us proceed to prove our position by means of such data as seem to be the most appropriate among those at hand. Should we succeed, the ravings of fanatical sects will be discredited, and by proving clearly the want of foresight of celebrated statesmen, the arrogant pretensions of human judgment to infallibility will receive one more reproof.

We have already said that the prohibition of the slave trade, without the abolition of slavery, riveted the chains of the latter in some places, and nowhere was it carried out effectually as a law; and to corroborate both assertions, I appeal to the laws of the slave States of the Anglo-American republic on the one hand, and on the other to the extraordinary increase of the colored population in the Spanish possessions, from the year 1835 up to this date, in which time it has doubled. This is a notorious fact, and figures in all the statistical reports which have been published during said interval, by which it is also seen, that said increase is equally divided between the slave and free population, and that nearly all of the former are imported, particularly in the island of Cuba.

As I do not intend to repel the charge which the abolitionists make against Spain on this account, nor much more to attempt to vindicate the Spanish authorities from that of having connived thereat, there can be no reason for concealing the truth.

Existing laws in the slave States tend to corroborate my assertions concerning slavery and the traffic in blacks in the United States, but lest some of my readers should believe that these laws are more honored in the breach than in the observance, which is the case in other places, I may be permitted to make some extracts from a letter, dated Boston, August 21, 1860, and published in the London *Morning Post*. It says as follows:

"Present occurrences prove that those who clamor for the restoration of the traffic in African slaves, are not actuated by mere caprice, but that the state of public opinion in America upon this subject, is such, that were the laws against the trade to be abolished, the measure would be received with great favor by not a small number of our business men. Restore it to the position it occupied in the beginning of the present century, and in three months, or even sooner, there would be five hundred American vessels engaged in it. Thirty years ago, public opinion would have sufficed to prevent this, but said opinion has changed very much since 1850. This is due to the efforts of the abolitionists, for, they having directed formidable attacks against slavery, its defenders were forced to bring to bear arguments which proved to be incontrovertible, and convincing not only to themselves, but *unfortunately to others also*, showing that the institution was in itself a very good one, from which it naturally followed that to reopen the trade would be both useful and proper.

"Logically, this cannot be contested, for there is no argument in favor of slavery which is not equally favorable to the slave trade. Moreover, does not the coasting trade in slaves exist? If an inhabitant of Virginia can legally send five hundred negroes to Texas, and if the cargo finds protection under the American flag, backed up by the cannon of the republic, why may not Texans be allowed to fit out a ship, send her to Africa, and obtain there five hundred chattels for fifty thousand dollars, instead of paying Virginia, at least, six hundred thousand dollars for them?

"I know merchants who would willingly contract, the law allowing it, to land five hundred Africans in Texas, at the rate of one hundred dollars each, and who would carry on the business with the same regularity with which they transport, to-day, white emigrants from Germany or Ireland to New York or Boston. To-day a Virginia negro is considered cheap at twelve hundred dollars, and a very likely woman is sometimes sold as high as twenty-five hundred dollars."

And now that we cannot doubt the practical results of legislation, nor justifiably deny the part which it had in preventing the redemption of Africans, or more properly speaking, of African prisoners, let us proceed to the consideration of what took place in Africa, in consequence of the prohibition, brought about by existing treaties, through the persistent initiative of England, and the blind sufferance of other nations.

It is proper to call to mind at this juncture what has been said in former chapters, respecting the status of the negro in his mother country. That uncivilized, pagan and barbarous state which is in some places that of cannabalism, and in all, most ferocious and bloody, looking as they do upon war as their ordinary avocation, and slaughtering their prisoners by thousands, before colonial nations invented a system for their redemption, and again doing so since the slave trade has been stopped.

We must also recollect the changes eminently favorable to humanity which took place in the conduct of these savages, as soon as their cupidity caused them to treat their captives with less ferocity, and also the transition which these poor unfortunates experienced from an abject and miserable life to one of Christian civilization, through the instrumentality of a system of moderate labor, as laid down in the regulations for their government.

In view of all this, it cannot be wondered at that we should take into account the evil caused by the prohibition of said system of redemption in those countries where it formally existed, nor that we should demonstrate beyond a peradventure and by the most horrible examples which history can produce, the fact that such evil was caused thereby.

I have before me a short treatise, published in France, at the time the emancipation of the slaves was then the order of the day. The authorship was shared by two travellers, perfectly well informed concerning the state of the negro, both in Africa and in the colonies, and whose opinions were entirely unbiassed, as is evident from the independent stand which they take. In fact upon reading it studiously and thoughtfully, one might at times readily imagine it to be the production of the London Antislavery Society, and at others that of some slaveholder of Bourbon or Martinique.

In this brochure, entitled, "Physiology of the Negro," there is mentioned an occurrence more criminal in those who quietly witnessed it, than in the ferocious actors themselves, and since any narative would not do justice to the account given by said travellers, I submit it to my readers in their own words :

"One of the terrible consequences of the prohibition of the slave trade, was the dreadful massacre of five hundred prisoners of war, which took place in Madagascar, a short time before the death of Radama.

"The King of the Ovas sent from his capital Zannanarivoce, at present Emyrna, a great army to subdue the negroes of Betanima, savage hords who had refused to recognize his authority. The two forces met and fought with fury; the number of dead and wounded on both sides being very great; but at last the Betanimans were defeated and left 500 captives in the hands of the conquerors, who were taken to the coast contiguous to Tamatava, to be sold, as the natives of the interior had no knowledge of the law which prohibited the slave trade.

" The orders of King Radama were decisive, viz., that at all hazards the prisoners should be sold; and great was the joy of the chiefs of the army, when from the highest peak of the *Ancaves* they beheld three vessels riding at anchor in the roads, which according to information communicated by the peaceable inhabitants, had come for the purpose of buying slaves.

"The prisoners were not long in reaching the coast; but great was the disappointment of their conductors when they found that one of the vessels was an English sloop-of-war, whose duty it was to enforce the law both on the coast of Madagascar and Bourbon.

" Notwithstanding this, the chiefs proposed, to the captains, the sale of their captives at the moderate price of twenty dollars a head—an offer which was of course declined. The price was then gradually lowered to fifteen, ten, and lastly to five dollars, but without any result; as the price had nothing to do with the law, which would in fact have been violated by any bargain whatever the amount might be. At last the Ova warriors offered to deliver their prisoners to the Europeans for the paltry sum of one dollar a head, which was again refused.

" The delirium of rage then succeeded to the anxiety for gain; they fell upon their defenceless captives, and the five hundred Betanimans were inhumanly butchered on the beach of Tamatava, without any interference being attempted by the captains to prevent this act of unparalleled ferocity.

" The captains should have bought the slaves, embarked them, and carried them to some distant part of the island far from their enemies. Humanity, which is so often invoked, demanded this transgression of the law. 'Those negroes would have been bought, it is true; but by giving them their freedom of which they would have been but temporarily deprived in order to save their lives, the violation of the law ceased. What! was it in accordance with the principles of humanity to coolly witness such terrible butchery, when three English vessels were provided with the means of preventing it?

"We leave it to the philanthropic abolitionists to solve this problem."

I fancy I see a smile of incredulity on the lips of those who, having no knowledge of facts in relation to the negroes, will look upon this dreadful narrative as an absurd and impertinent invention. And I even suspect that it will be disbelieved by other persons, who, though better informed are suspicious of the exaggerations of both tendencies, the anti-slavery and the pro-slavery, if in addition to it there were not more certain and undeniable evidence of horrors no less terrible, taken from an English journal.

In a previous chapter I have alluded to the barbarous instincts of the King of Dahomey; that stupid sovereign of a land of ferocious customs, who, to celebrate some festivity, actually floated his canoes through a lake of human blood. My readers have also seen that on ordering an attack to be made against the inhabitants of the neighboring country for that sinister purpose, this blood-thirsty villain had resolved, if possible, to sell the young and vigorous captives, or to sacrifice them with the rest if no opportunity of selling them presented itself.

From the detailed accounts, published by the English, who had commercial relations with that barbarian, these facts became known to the civilized nations in time to prevent, if they would, that butchery; and it would be but natural that, upon hearing such news, the Government of Great Britain, the then zealous initiator of benevolent intentions in behalf of the negroes, should hasten to prevent by every means in its power the butchery which was contemplated; and which was what all expected would be done, especially as the cruisers of the English royal navy frequent that neighborhood more particularly. The reader, then, may imagine our surprise when some months afterwards the democratic journal of Madrid, *La Discusion*, in its number of 30th of May, 1861, said as follows:

"We copy from an English newspaper the following news showing the horrible state in which the negroes in Africa live.

"The wholesale murder has taken place in Dahomey, notwithstanding all our philanthropic entreaties. Two thousand men and as many women and children have fallen victims to the cruelty of those rulers, as is the custom in that country, on the death of a King of Dahomey."

"This barbarous custom is founded on the popular belief that a sovereign ought to be served beyond the grave by an adequate number of his subjects; and as in paradise he continues to be king, he would consider himself humiliated if he had but a small retinue of attendants. The veneration in which he is held while living, cannot be compared with even that professed for the most despotic and theocratic monarchs of Asia.

"The principal personages cannot approach him without bowing their heads to the ground, and licking the dust as a proof of their humility. He is believed to be free from the ordinary passions and necessities of human kind, and in Dahomey it is considered criminal to say that the king eats, drinks, sleeps, or performs any other function proper to ordinary mortals. The human victims go willingly to death, as they believe they gain paradise in this way, although they do not expect better treatment there than they received in this world. Mahometanism is the basis of this superstition, and the Dahomians usually carry amulets with short sentences from the Koran inscribed upon them.

"What is most singular is, that the ferocious people are generally polite and even courteous, when the demon of war does not possess them. When this is the case their ferocity knows no bounds, and the women vie with the men in their cruelty. The King of Dahomey has a regiment of amazons who surpass in blood-thirstiness all the rest of his soldiers.

"The tutelar divinity of Dahomey is said to be a tiger! It is high time that European intervention should put an end to such atrocities. That country is worthy of a better fate. Few of the adjoining districts can surpass it in fertility. It is situated on the slave coast, with Ashantee on the west, and extends forty miles to the Gulf of Guinea. It produces pine apples, melons, oranges, sweet potatoes, and many other tropical fruits. Indigo is abundant, and tobacco grows well. A kind of indigenous cotton also grows here which is not of very inferior quality, notwithstanding the want of culture.

"It is more difficult, we know, to eradicate a barbarous custom when it is founded on an innate superstition, than when it is merely the result of tyranny in the rulers; but humanity requires us to destroy, if possible, the source of so many horrors; and the country, in a commercial point of view, well deserves our attention and our aid. [1]

---

(1) Owing to the exaggerations in which travellers are apt to indulge, I have often feared to be mistaken in my judgments and comments upon the affairs of Africa, and have therefore hesitated in accepting their accounts whenever they referred to such terrible acts. For this reason, which is worthy of the consideration of every just and upright mind, I have omitted to insert in this book some narratives of facts which are still more revolting and horrifying than those which appear in it. In order that such as appear in this work may not excite incredulity from the terrible nature of the facts which they expose, I think it well to insert in this place in the form of a note, the following letter of a Spanish missionary, recently published in *La Revista Católica* of Barcelona, and *La Verdad Católica* of Havana. The missionary, writer of this letter, is personally known in both the cities named; and from the encomiums made of his virtues by the Catalan paper, and the information I have personally obtained respecting him, in the island of Cuba recently (September 1, 1868), after having completed this work, I do not hesitate implicitly to believe the entire contents of his said letter, and to vouch for its veracity. Here, then, is the document alluded to, which on many accounts is very remarkable:

"Whydah, 14th February, 1863.—My dear Fathers and Friends:—My heart is witness that I have not missed a single opportunity to write to you since my departure from Europe, thus performing the most pleasant of duties. You must have noticed that none of my letters have as yet been dated from my mission house at Dahomey, having all been sent from various points of the coast of Africa, which during my lengthy travels I have been obliged to visit a great many times. During the four-and-a-half months of my transit from Vigo, in Galicia, to Whydah, in Africa, I have suffered greatly, especially as I had to pass most of the time on board of an ill-conditioned vessel, and upon the open ocean. In the midst of the many trials which are unavoidable in such a voyage as mine, some moments of peace and real happiness were not denied to me; but after all, these troubles came upon me when I was upon the ocean, or in some place where I was completely a stranger. Now, however, when, thanks to the Lord, I find myself in my own house and in the company of my missionary brethren; now that I am in the midst of the negroes of Dahomey, for whose sakes I have so often encountered danger of death; now it is that I write with exceeding gladness, my heart being filled with the sweetest emotions that I have experienced in a long time.

"It is now about three weeks since I disembarked with my companions, in Whydah, after having been driven hither and thither on the coast without being able to arrive at our destination. It would be needless as well as wasting time to describe the satisfaction which we all felt on arriving at the mission and meeting again our African companions; suffice it to say that an embrace was our only salutation, for being mute with joy, we were unable to utter a single word. Supposing that what will most interest you after hearing of my health will be the usages and customs of the country, I take pleasure in giving you an account of what passes in this uncivilized city. In the first place, our king reigns over a

I have not the courage to comment upon that dreadful narrative, for fear of offending those who furnished it, after knowingly allowing the scenes announced in it to take place. Humanity demanded some preventive measures to avoid the slaughter of so many human beings; and it cannot be conceived in conformity to what order of

---

million of subjects, and exercises over them the most absolute and despotic power. He sells them in great numbers, either to slave traders, or to the wealthy negroes of the country, who also treats them like slaves. He has a considerable number of troops, amongst which are more than six thousand women, armed with daggers, swords and clubs, which is his most formidable batallion, and consequently employed as the King's body guard. The King engages in war twice a year, and only yesterday, all the men in the kingdom were summoned to fight, without more ado, against another king, whom they will despoil of his troops and wealth, and who, no doubt, will be sold with the rest of the prisoners. When the King returns from the war with five or six thousand prisoners, he retains the majority to sell them, and the rest he will have beheaded or cut to pieces, and offered as a sacrifice to his idols. When the King receives a visit from some person of rank, he orders all the people to assemble in some public square and arrange themselves in the form of an amphitheatre, and there, in the presence of his visitor, he has three or four hundred prisoners beheaded; this ceremony is repeated twice a year in the feasts called *festival of the customs*. The King's palace is covered with skulls and human heads; the hall in which he gives audience is paved with human bones, and even his throne is raised upon the heads of the four kings who were his principal enemies, conquered by him in his capricious wars. When any one wishes to speak to the King, he receives him seated upon his magical and diabolical throne, having the executioner at his side with the axe (*destral*) on his shoulder, and the block (*tallado*) at his feet, and at the slightest signal from the King the head of the petitioner is made to fall. It is impossible for me to enumerate all the cruelties of the King; nevertheless, I must not forget to mention one with respect to the women. The King has six hundred wives whom he has chosen from his own kingdom, or whom he has reserved for himself from the prisoners of war taken from other kings. Upon the death of the King all these women will take their own lives by poison or the dagger, believing that they will resuscitate and live with the King in the other world. This horrible ceremony was performed a short while since upon the death of the father of the present King. The name of the late King was Guezo; the present one is Greré, and believes he is a son of the gods. When the King returns from the war he will bring more than two thousand women prisoners of war; he will confine them in a house which he has had constructed for the purpose, and all the men who are in want of a wife can go and buy one of them for the sum of forty *pesetas*, which is the fixed price of each one. But what is most singular is, that the King gives them the woman he chooses, while the poor fellows who buy them are not allowed to speak to or even to see them until they have payed down the price. However, they are at liberty to kill them if they do not suit them, and to buy others under the same conditions. It often happens that a boy buys an old woman, or an old man finds that he has purchased a child, and sometimes a man's purchase turns out to be his own mother, daughter or sister. My countrywomen can here learn to be grateful for the blessing of being born in a civilized country, and of

ideas this demand was delayed at that time, when two years afterwards, and according to the information given us, a short time since, by all the periodicals of the world, the government of England, assuming the garbe of civilized humanity, took possession, according to law, of those territories where such abominations were perpetrated.

knowing the sweet name of the Virgin Mary, which is entirely unknown to these barbarians.

"In this very city where I reside, and about three hundred feet from the chamber in which I write, is the house of the gods of these stupid and miserable savages. Do you wish to know what kind of a building this is, and what are their gods.? I will tell you, though with sorrow and the fear of horrifying you. The house is similar to a sentry box, with two doors, about nine feet high and three feet square, built of clay and thatched with the leaves of the cocoa nut tree; the gods who inhabit this temple are serpents!

"I went into this house yesterday and found twelve enormous serpents within, thicker than my arm, and proportionately long, and of the color of the salamander. They are very tame, and go about the city at pleasure. The sight of them caused me such a loathing that I was not able to eat my dinner. These are the principal gods of our unfortunate negroes. . . .

"In walking through the city I often stumble over some of these monsters, which are harmless so long as they are unmolested. If one of them should stray, after dark, about the city, and not be able to find its way home, it is the duty of every one to return it to its habitation, which they do by reverently carrying it in a basket or even in the hands, at a slow and majestic pace, to the palace from which it had inadvertently strayed. This palace hut is called the *House of the Serpents.* I must add that whenever any of the negroes of Whydah meet with any of these serpents about the streets, they bow down or even prostrate themselves at full length and cover their heads with dust, while the disgusting reptile crawls past in triumph.

"This is not the only spectacle which we are obliged to witness every time that we have to walk through the city, from curiosity or necessity, for whenever we go out we can hardly take a step without coming in contact with some of the stupid gods of Dahomey, which, in order to avoid giving them the appellation of *gods,* I will henceforth call *fetiches,* that being the name given to them by the hapless people of Dahomey, while the priests of the country are called fetishers. Well, as I said, whenever we walk out, we cannot take a step without encountering a number of *fetiches* of a thousand different kinds and forms. You will be astonished when I tell you that, besides the serpents, which are the great *fetiches,* there are any quantity of other lesser ones, such as the crocodile, the red owl, the bat, the ant, which are all fetiches, as are also some particular kinds of trees unknown in Europe, and small mounds of clay, of a pyramidal form, on the top of which the negroes place small gourds full of palm oil, decorating the other parts with the feathers of several kinds of birds of prey, which abound in Whydah. I confess, I rarely go out for a walk, for it is really disgusting to go about these streets, where your nostrils are continually assailed by the stench arising from innumerable puddles, where all the refuse of the city is thrown, emitting a fetid miasma, which, together with the equatorial sun of Whydah, would be enough to kill any one who should often venture into it. Everything in

Now, in the interval between the two opposite circumstances, viz.: the toleration with which the slaughter was allowed, (in accordance without doubt of the principle of non-intervention applied to the savages), and the violence afterwards exercised when there was no longer any fear of a similar occurrence, another Spanish period-

---

these streets excites loathing and abhorrence. More than twenty-four thousand negroes go about the city entirely naked, or with a small piece of cloth about half the size of a pocket handkerchief as their only covering. An infinite number of children of both sexes spring up like ants in every direction, and go about entirely naked, until the age of twelve and fourteen. This is a spectacle which strikes any one with amazement at first, but you soon get used to it, and seek for some new absurdities, which are never wanting in this country; in fact, I proceed on my way through the streets, and here I see a simple little tree, well taken care of and enclosed in a little house made of the trunks of trees. I ask what is the meaning of this, and am told that it is a god. I go on and see thousands of enormous and hideous bats, which are flying around a tree, and which confound and deafen me with their diabolical screams. I ask what that is, and receive for answer that they are gods. On my right hand there is a small mound of earth, sprinkled with palm oil, decorated with feathers and a number of little plates full of the blood of chickens and many other absurd and disgusting ingredients; on my left hand I see a hen nailed to the door of a hut by the wings or by the legs, the blood flowing from nostrils, bill, eyes and ears, which has been suffering this torture for three days. I am on the point of asking what this signifies, but abstain from doing so, knowing well what the answer will be—a sacrifice offered to the gods, to obtain something or other, such as the death of such a one, or the blindness of another one, &c. I wish to proceed, but cannot; I am no longer able to resist the effect of these stupid, disgusting and heartrending spectacles. I hardly dare to say more, or to relate to you any more of the cruelties and filthiness of the country. I fear I have already wearied you; nevertheless, I have still much more to tell, and that of a more horrible nature than anything I have yet related.

"To divert your thoughts, I will relate an anecdote. You have already heard me say that visits are not made here, as in Europe, in person or by means of visiting cards; persons of high rank pay their visits or carry on a conversation with their canes or staffs. Whenever the governor has anything to say to us, he sends his servant who carries his cane with the greatest respect; on his arriving at our house, one of us goes out immediately to meet him; the servant, after making a profound reverence, presents the staff, which we respectfully take in our hands—then, while we both bow our heads down, the servant delivers the message with which he has been charged by his master, we return him the staff, and after making another reverence to the very ground, the servant retires. The staff represents the owner, and each person has his. I have one in the shape of a salamander. Well, one day the servant of *Zerogan*, the governor, appeared, and after the customary ceremonies, he presented the staff to us and warned us on the part of Zerogan not to go out of the house during the following thirty nights, if we did not wish to expose ourselves to the insults of the people. In fact, the governor had good reason to warn us, as that very night such an awful uproar commenced throughout the city that we, although in the house, could not but tremble at the

ical, *La Correspondencia*, copied from an English paper the following information:
"The members of the London African Society had an interview, some time since, with Lord Palmerston, to present a petition asking for a subsidy for the king of Dahomey, who has abolished the hunting of slaves. The

---

sound of their infernal ceremonies. The cause of this excitement was tha a child had just been born who had the misfortune to come into the world with teeth, and in consequence was to be offered as a sacrifice to the god of the *toothed ones*. The whole city was assembled *en masse* before the house of the victim, with a thousand musical instruments of the most barbarous and ridiculous kinds which can be imagined. They commenced the ceremony by singing the most diabolical songs, after which they became intoxicated with the brandy which they make themselves, and then the *feticher* or priest took the child, and heading this immense crowd, directed his steps towards a lake which is about half a league from the city; all followed, and, leaping, yelling, and twisting their bodies into the most dreadful contortions, as though they were possessed, they arrived at the lake in about three hours and a half, and here all the horrors of their ceremonies were again renewed with such fiendish joy that it made our hair stand on end, though we were at a distance of half a league from them. At last, after having repeatedly stabbed the child, they threw it into the lake of crocodiles, to which the victim belonged, having been born with teeth. The infant was drowned after its sufferings were prolonged as long as possible, and then the crowd retired, yelling and dancing like a band of infernal imps, which they kept up every night for a whole month.

"I have visited the whole coast of Africa, and can assure you that I never witnessed such barbarous customs nor such fiendish usages in any other place. It is perfectly horrible! I might speak of many other cruelties witnessed by us, but I dare not, nor do I feel myself equal to the task. I am going to breakfast, as I hear the bell summoning me, and perhaps, afterwards I may have the courage to relate things which you have never read or heard of.

"I have breakfasted, and now I shall proceed. Besides all I have told you, we usually find a gourd full of palm oil and blood, whenever four roads cross each other; when three only cross, there is a mat with a dying hen upon it; when only two roads cross, the negroes place some other filthy thing upon it, as for example, a small mound of mud covered with feathers, which they take good care to sprinkle with blood every day, and all this is done by the counsel of their oracles to obtain some revenge, or the misfortune of a neighbor, and also to give thanks to their gods for the blessings they think they have received.

"This is not all, and it seems as nothing to me compared to the other barbarities which frequently happen in this country, governed by a tyrant who is surely inspired by Satan himself.

"One of our brethren belonging to this Mission, having gone on a visit to the capital some months since, spent some three months there, at the expiration of which he returned in very ill health, not so much on account of the inconveniences suffered in travelling by land, without roads or paths whatever, without a horse or any kind of carriage, being always carried on the shoulders of the negroes of the country, in a species of litter called *hamaque*, or *palanquin*, of which I intend to speak hereafter, if I do not forget to do so, as from the filthy and barbarous state of the country.

authors of this petition said that, to obtain this subsidy without drawing from the treasury, the reduction of the squadron on the coasts of Africa would suffice. They also propose to send a minister plenipotentiary to the king of Dahomey."

From which facts some captious persons have suspect-

"Our brother in question, being obliged to walk out every day, was compelled to witness the most horrible spectacles; oftentimes, on passing in the streets, he would find it closed up by heaps of hundreds of human heads; at other times he would go to the public square, and on a long rope, or on the tops and branches of trees, he would find dozens of men hung by the neck, by the arm, or by the feet, in the most horrible torture, bleeding from the mouth, nose, ears and eyes, some dead, others expiring, and others recently hung; while they had the consolation of seeing themselves surrounded by many thousands of men, (or rather ferocious beasts,) who were mocking and laughing at them. Another day he was invited by the king to witness the bravery of his amazons in a sham fight. He was conducted to an immense field, surrounded by three or four high and massive walls, formed of branches of trees covered with enormous and very sharp thorns; all the female warriors of the king, numbering six or seven thousand, ranged themselves in battle array, and at a simple sign from the king they charged on the wall and scaled this formidable barrier, before which, perhaps, our bravest European troops would recoil, if instead of having a dress of heavy cloth and leather, &c., they were in a state of nudity, as are our valorous female warriors of Dahomey. They leaped over the barrier, I repeat, and the blood streamed from all parts of their bodies. I now ask: Why does the barbarous king make them perform such an abominable feat? Because he wishes to please our companions of the Mission. Why do these inimitable female warriors labor so willingly and with such intrepidity? To please the king. Does this happen many times during the year? As many times as the king receives a visit from a white man, besides the three days in which all these sacrifices take place every year, to solemnize the feasts of the customs; it is no uncommon occurrence to see six, twelve, or twenty negroes drowned by order of the king, and the decapitation of a man who displeases the king is a thing seen every day.

"At the distance of three hundred paces from our house we have the magnificent Temple of the Bats. It consists of eight trees of an extraordinary height and luxuriant foliage, upon whose branches rest millions of these animals, which are as large as the young pigeons of our country, and who, with the tremendous battles which they have among themselves and the infernal cry which said battles produce, annoy and distract any one who is not accustomed to such a din.

"This is also the case with the Crow gods, which they have by the million. The money of this country is a species of small sea shell, one thousand of which make one hard dollar; the people require no other money; each shell is called a busa, and a shilling is called a galina. This very day I have to pay the governor of the city the duty for shipping my little negroes, which duty amounts to one hundred and forty thousand busas, which have to be counted one by one—who can have the patience to do this? I now have twelve women counting them, with two persons of the Mission watching them.

"I shall say something respecting certain customs of the negroes; but can only touch lightly on the subject, as I am very tired and in great haste:

ed that the fertility and spontaneous vegetation of the country of Dahomey had awakened in England, for some time back, the idea of acting as it has done; that is, to take forcible possession of it; and, in order to justify such a proceeding before other nations, nothing could be better than, coolly, to allow those awful butcheries to be

"*Revenge of the Negroes of Gabón.*—Peter offends Paul, robs him, for example, of a wife. Paul wishes to revenge himself on Peter, but if Peter is stronger than Paul, Paul goes out and robs or kills a child or a wife of Antonio, who is stronger than Peter, and then Antonio tears out the eyes of Peter or buries him alive, and Paul and Antonio thereafter remain at peace with each other. I do not know if a single reading will suffice to make this understood.

"*Funerals.*—When a negro dies he is buried with all he has in his house; one has recently died who was buried with fifty high-crowned hats . .

"*Weddings.*—Each negro has as many wives as he can support, and when he dies, his sons are married to the wives of their fathers.

"The man does nothing, the wife only works, and she alone has the privilege of carrying the parcels and the loads.

"*Births.*—When a male or female child is born with any defect, it is immediately killed by the parents.

"*Marriage Contracts.*—When a negro wishes to marry, he is obliged to supply the bride with hog's lard to dress her hair, and besides this, gives her a cat before they get married. What do you think of that?

"If I were not in such haste, I could relate a great deal more, but as I suppose you are already tired, (and with reason), I will conclude with an anecdote which, though it has its serious side, has also something amusing, so here you have it: One day I asked a negro if he believed in the Son of God. He answered me that he did, and added, that all the negroes believed it also. Why? I asked him; and the good man held forth in the following jargon: 'Two negroes, named *Baynayn* and *Ndulnaca*, went on a journey; which having been prolonged more than they had anticipated, their provisions failed them, hunger followed, causing the companions to fight, when one of them tore the eyes out of the other, upon this the Son of God, who was mending his drawers in Heaven, by chance looked downwards, and by so doing pricked his finger with the needle, he in a moment took out of his pocket a small pot of onguent, when seeing the negro who had just lost his eyes, and moved with compassion, he threw him down the whole pot of onguent, with which the negroes now-a-days cure all diseases without any diminution of the onguent.'

" Another : At a quarter of a league from our house, it happened that a woman was eating a fish in the presence of her slaves; it so happened that a bone stuck in the old woman's throat; she laid the blame on her slave, saying that he had bewitched the fish, in consequence thereof, she tied him up and confined him in a hovel leaving him to starve to death. What do you think of that ?

"Still another: While I was in Gabon, it happened that a missionary father having gone to bathe at a very short distance from the place where I also was bathing in the sea, a negro passed near him, and as he had only his head out of the water as he was swimming, the negro imagined that it was a monstrous fish which they call *bugari*, he therefore set up a cry that more people might come, and cried out incessantly in a very loud voice. *Yo-ó-go-lo, yo-go, yo-go*, which means—Come, a monster, come, come, On hearing this all the people of the neighboring tribe came; some with

committed, and, afterwards, give them publicity in all the languages in the world.

Be this as it may, the result which, with evident contradiction, has followed the suppression of the redemption of prisoners on the African coast, has been the return of the negroes to the state of barbarism and ferocity which characterized that race from centuries back. It must not be supposed that these are the only data on which I can base my assertions, for I have selected them from among many others equally important, that they may serve as specimens of the spirit which characterizes them all.

It has then, so far, been unquestionably demonstrated that the prohibition of the redemption of negroes has served only to perpetuate slavery, and to aggravate it in such places where the treaties have been neutralized by the reproduction of slaves for the market, and that it has also made the condition of African prisoners much worse wherever said treaties made by England with the slave holding nations have by chance produced their effects on the African coast. Having demonstrated these facts, let us proceed to consider what has happened in the colonies.

This new point of investigation has two phases, viz.: that of the colonies in which the prohibition of the redemption was the preamble to abolish slavery, and that of the other countries where slavery was confirmed with new ordinances, to avoid the disastrous results of the prohibition of the redemption.

---

clubs, others with irons, with guns, or with bows, &c., &c. ; but, in the meantime, while the negro who had given the *alarm* had gone to call the rest of the people, the missionary came out of the water and put on his cassock, and was walking quietly on the beach, the people came out with tremendous yells, and the missionary, seeing that they were all looking towards the place where he had been bathing, and that it was him who they sought, went towards them and told them smiling: 'It is I, it is I;' and the astonished negroes went away saying, '*Minisse, minisse,*' that is, the Minister, the minister.

" As I am very much occupied, and almost every day have an attack of fever, I cannot, without much trouble, write many letters, I therefore pray my Reverend Fathers to show this letter to my friends of Vich, Tarrasa, Viladran, S. Felio, Garriga, &c., &c. Do not write to me until further notice, for this very day, within six hours, I embark for Europe, but I do not know where I shall stop, whether at Fernando Po, Teneriffe, or Paris.

" BRRTOLOMEO M. SARRA, Missionary."

The first of these phases ougnt to be subdivided into two distinct cases, viz: that of those colonies in which slaveowners were deprived of their absolute authority and rendered dependent on the free labor of the negroes, and that of those other regions in which the slaves were suddenly transformed into masters, through a violent and sanguinary metamorphosis.

Leaving aside the second phase, to be analyzed afterwards, we will consider the two points of the first, separately.

I have often heard, and I regret that I have not at hand the proofs which could demonstrate it incontrovertibly, that Jamaica, before the abolition of slavery, had about twenty thousand inhabitants; and I know also, from repeated verbal information, that said population has degenerated to such an extent, since the freedom of the negroes, that at present it has hardly a sixth part of that number.

If any mistake be found in the numbers given, let it be considered unintentional; since the rapid and extraordinary decrease of the population of that Island is so true that no one would dare to deny it, being evident to all the world.

The same can be said of all the other English possessions in this part of the Ocean, which have degenerated more or less, according to the relative importance of each; and if the same general decrease cannot be shown in the French colonies, although the decrease has evidently been considerable in these also, it is because the time has not yet arrived for such disastrous results.

In either of these territories where the negroes have obtained their emancipation from forced labor, being left to their will to work or not, it may be that the life of these miserable creatures has been bettered in indolence, even if they are compelled to resort to public charity to be preserved from perishing from hunger; but it can also be asserted that their condition has become worse in every respect, for, from having been orderly and civilized, its present tendencies are towards the isolation of each individual and the abandonment of all social trammels and other requirements of civilization.

We could easily give any number of data to prove the disastrous results of the absolute freedom bestowed upon the negroes in the New World, and some have already been given in the chapter that treats of the respective condition of the free negroes and slaves in said colonies. But as, in the opinion of the abolitionists, the greatest advantage, not only to individuals, but to the country, results from the greater amount of freedom and independence, I believe that the best answer to this supposition will be a detailed and careful comparison on this matter in the republic of Hayti. For this purpose, that I may not be suspected of partiality, I shall make use of a work which was written on abolitionist principles, in an excellent article from *El Siglo*, an enlightened newspaper published in Havanna.

All the world is aware that the island known by the name of Hayti and also by that of Santo Domingo, and sometimes as La Española, is divided into two parts: the Western section, or Hayti proper, and what was until very recently the republic of Santo Domingo. It ranks next to Cuba in size, and is considered the most fertile of the West Indian Islands. The whole length of the island is four hundred and six miles, and its greatest breadth is one hundred and sixty-three. Twenty-seven thousand six hundred and ninety square miles have been measured, of which ten thousand and ninety-one belong to Hayti, and the rest to the Dominican section.

It is very difficult to ascertain with any degree of certainty the exact population of Hayti, as no definite statistics exist; but it is calculated to be about six hundred thousand. The climate, the natural productions and the fertility of the land cannot be surpassed in any other country in the world. Gold, silver, platina, copper, iron, quicksilver, tin, sulphur, saltpetre, jasper, marble, etc., are among its mineral productions. The gold mines have been abandoned for some time past, as well as all occupations requiring laborious industry. The climate is warm, but the sea breezes make it generally agreable, even during the heat of summer time. The vegetation is unsurpassably rich and exhuberant.

"It is extremely difficult," says a traveller, "to give any adequate idea of the magnificent beauty of the scenery of this island to those who are unacquainted with the richeness and variety of the tropical landscapes. The island rises up in the midst of a sea of crystal, clothed with a vegetation of unsurpassed luxuriance and splendor of every variety, from the stately and graceful palm-tree and the majestic mahogany, to the brillant flowers which seem to have stolen their colors from the sun, which gives them life. Birds of plumage as varied and beautiful as the colors of the rainbow, dart about the dark green foliage of the groves; and scarlet tinted flamingos adorn the shores. Fishes of many kinds and varied colors glide in the water, which is so transparent and pure that they can easily be distinguished at the depth of several fathoms.

"Turn your eyes wherever you will, on the sea or on land, and the most brillant colors will always be reflected. Nature, here, appears like a most beautiful queen adorned for a festival.

"In the island of Santo Domingo are found, combined with the tropical beauties, some of the loveliest landscapes in the world. The broad and fertile plains are covered with groves of orange and lime-trees and the coffee plant; spiral columns of smoke indicate the site of some invisible habitation; clusters of mango-trees, apparently growing in the waters, rise up gradually into sight, giving warning of some spot dangerous to navigation. There are no steep promontories as on our northern coasts: all the angles are delicatly finished off; all the outlines of the scenery are undulating and graceful."

To the beauty, so artistically delineated in the passages just copied, are added all the productions that could possibly be wished for. The mountains are covered with pine woods; enormous mahoganies, fustic, oak, acana, guiacum, quebrahacha, cinnamon, capa, laurel, spiraea, cavina, cedar, ebony, sabine, carey, and a thousand other precious woods. All the tropical fruits grow there spontaneously and in great abundance, including plantains, yams, corn, maize, pine-apples, melons, grapes, etc., as well as the agricultural products: coffee, cocao, sugar, indigo, cotton and tobacco.

It is a crime to permit the inexhaustible resources of a country so visibly blessed by its creator, to be left uncared for, without an effort to give them the developpement of which they are susceptible. In 1790, Hayti had reached a high state of prosperity, and was a colony the population of which amounted to five hundred thousand, of which thirty-eight thousand three hundred and sixty were white, four hundred and twenty-three thousand two hundred and seventy were colored slaves, and twenty-eight thousand three hundred and seventy were free negroes. In said year the French revolution broke out; and in 1793 the reforms were decreed, which, in the name of fraternity, have led to the results which the island of Hayti now presents to the world after a lapse of seventy years.

"If the present inhabitants of that island had any capacity to govern themselves," says, with sufficient fundation the periodical of Havanna to which I have already alluded, "had they any inherent or natural ability, or energy, they undoubtedly would have shown it during all that time. In a country whose natural resources and fertility cannot be doubted, this result would have been certain."

In cultivation, the island had risen to as high a rank and reached to as great mercantile prosperity as any country among those most favored by nature and art. It was delivered into the hands of its new masters as a terrestial paradise already cultivated; and all they had to do was to preserve it in the same state, and follow in the path of prosperity inaugurated under such good auspices. But some statistical data will prove more clearly than words how much the island has retrograded, and how fallacious were all the hopes that had been entertained respecting the industry of those inhabitants when left to their own resources.

In 1790 the value of the exports from Hayti amounted to twenty-seven million eight hundred and twenty-eight thousand Spanish dollars, the principal products being as follows:

Sugar, 163,405,220 lbs.; coffee, 68,151,180 lbs.; cotton, 6,286,126 lbs.; indigo, 930,016 lbs.

In 1826, nearly thirty years after the emancipation, these figures had dwindled down thus: sugar, 32,864 lbs.; coffee, 32,189,784 lbs.; cotton, 504,516 lbs., and indigo, none.

Sugar is no longer exported, coffee and lagwood being the articles of most importance. The sugar cane is gathered from the old plantations that have been abandoned by the Europeans, or from the mountains; and of the two articles that are still exported, one grows wild, and the other has only to be cut and carried to the marked, as its growth is spontaneous.

It is thus evident that all cultivation has disappeared, and that the only profitable articles are those which grow spontaneously and independent of any culture.

In 1849, the last certain date that the statistics furnish us with, and nearly sixty years after the emancipation, the exportation of the above mentioned articles was as follows:

Sugar, none; coffee, 30,608,343 lbs.; cotton, 504,516 lbs.; and indigo, none. [1]

It is impossible to say exactly what the insignificant exportations from Hayti amount to at present. The chancellor of the exchequer of that country, in a speech made by him some months ago, in the Senate, calculated them to amount to 2,573,000 Spanish dollars; and it is to be supposed, not without fundation, from what has sometimes happened, that this figure is double the real value of the articles exported.

A modern traveller says that he was not able to find any commercial statistics in Hayti; [2] and therefore the figures given by the minister are merely conjectural.

But, even admitting them to be correct, what a sad spectacle does it not present of the commercial ruin of that country! In 1790 the exportations amounted to about twenty-eight millions of dollars, and now the most exagerated official manifestations hardly make them exceed two millions and a half!

The same author whom we have quoted, a radical abolitionist, sent by the Baptist Missionary Society of London, to the colonies, with a philanthropic purpose that we can guess at, says further on: " This country has made no progress whatever since the emancipation. The inhabitants partially subsist on the production of the wild coffee plant, the remains of the agriculture in the time of the French. Properly speaking, there are no plantations here like those of the English in Jamaica, or of the Spaniards in Cuba. Hayti is the most beautiful and most fertile of the West India Islands. It has more mountains than Cuba and is more extensive than Jamaica. In no other place can the coffee plant be produced to such perfection as it is here, as it specially. requires a mountanous soil; *but the indolence of the negroes has been the ruin of these plantations, that were at one time so flourishing.* They only gather the coffee from the wild plant; the cultivation

---

(1) *Commercial Relations of the United States*, vol. I, p. 561.
(2) Underhill, *The West Indies; their moral and social condition.*

of the sugar cane has been entirely abandoned, and the island that once provided Europe with half of what it consumed of this article, is now obliged to provide its necessary wants in Jamaica and the United States."

Full of the abolitionist spirit which brought him to the New World, the aforementioned author sometimes attempts to lessen the fact of the decay of the republic of Hayti in favor of the negroes ; but as the real state of the country cannot but become evident, from his truthful statements, let us hear what he says in describing his impressions in his travels to Port-au-Prince:

"We passed," he says, "through a number of deserted plantations, on which the buildings were in ruins ; the machinery destroyed, the boilers broken and strewn about the road. If it were not for the law, which prohibits the exportation of any metals, these fragments of the former opulence of Hayti would have long since been sold to foreign speculators. During this long excursion we only saw one machine grinding cane, to extract the juice from which *tafia*, a species of rum, is made, with which the inhabitants of Hayti become intoxicated. This machine was impelled by a quantity of water that had been brought from a great distance through an aqueduct. With the exception of a few plantain trees, and some small plots of land, sown with corn around the huts, there was no sign of the surprising fertility of these magnificent plains.

"At the time when it was occupied by the French, before the revolution of 1793, thousands of hogsheads of sugar were made ; and *now not a single one is produced!* . . . All is ruin and desolation. The pastures are all destroyed, and the lands formerly so luxuriant with the sugar cane, are now barren and overrun with weeds.

"The hydraulic works constructed for irrigation, which cost immense sums, are nothing but heaps of ruins. The plough is an agricultural implement, the recollection of which has been lost among that people, although it is so perfectly adapted to its extensive fields and fruitful soil.

"A country that can produce so many articles for exportation, and consequently for the enrichment of its inhabitants, which, besides sugar and coffee, can produce cotton, tobacco, cocoa, spices, all kinds of tropical and some European fruits, lies uncultivated, lifeless and desolate. Only small quantities of logwood are exported ; of ebony, mahogany, and other precious woods, none; as the axe of the wood cutter is never employed, except it is for local uses. The present inhabitants despise labor, and the majority are content with the spontaneous productions of the woods."

The aforesaid Underhill, and Mr. Webley, also a missionary, have likewise written on the condition of the Haytiens. Leaving aside the Christian practices which the more civilized negroes of said country profess in their religious worship, they declare that the majority profess the religion of *Vandoux*, i. e., the worship of the serpent; which is an African superstition, and which no longer leaves a doubt of the retrocession of the negroes to their original state of barbarism.

This religious ceremony is described by both travellers in the same manner, differing but little in the wording as follows:

"On entering the selected spot, they take off their shoes, and tie a handkerchief, in which red is the predominant color, around their waists. The king is recognized by the scarlet band which encircles his forehead like a crown, and a scarf of the same color distinguishes the queen. The serpent is placed upon a platform, where certain savage adoration is paid to it, commencing with the following chorus:

"Eh! Eh! Bomba, hen! hen!—canga tafia te—
cangamourne de le—canga de ki li—canga li."

"The song ended, as well as the successive gesticulations, which are numerous and very strange, the serpent is placed in a box, upon which the queen climbs, and forces herself into a violent trembling fit, pronouncing oracles in answer to the prayers of the worshipers.

"Then the king lays his hand on the box which contains the idol, and is suddenly seized with the same trembling that the queen experienced, which is next communicated to the entire circle, so that they all shake as if possessed by fiends. A wild dance follows these exercises, after which *tafia* is drunk in abundance until the weaker ones fall apparently lifeless on the spot. The dissolute bacchanals continue to enact such scenes as decency forbids us to describe, and which would even cause the heathen gods, if such gods had ever existed, to shudder with horror."

What a horrible scene of barbarism does this present! Moreover, let it be borne in mind, though we have to repeat it once more, that the preceding lines were written by English abolitionists.

The following has also been written on the moral ideas of the Haytians, and published in the London *Missionary Herald:*

"Almost all of the negroes of that republic are Vandoux. They practice sorceries and mysticisms, and are extraordinary adepts in poisoning, the person whom they select as a victim very rarely escaping from their fiendish arts. From this the practice of oberism or sorcery appears to be as general in Hayti as it is in the interior of Africa."

What more is required to show that the negroes being emancipated from all civilizing laws through their independence, have returned to their original savage state? Commerce and its products have ceased in this island since it became independent, and its inhabitants have gone back to African heathenism.

Are additional proofs still required of the evils caused to humanity and to the civilization of those unhappy beings by the supreme means of freedom which was employed to better their condition?

What a striking contrast there is between the soil and inhabitants of Hayti and those of Cuba? And nevertheless, at the present time, in the latter, where everything bears the mark of social progress, including the characters of the negroes who live there, slavery exists (since that is the name applied to the institution of organized labor, in which there are but few traces of slavery, justly so called); while in Hayti, where the negroes have not only accomplished their civil emancipation but also enjoy political independence and self government, very soon there will not remain a single vestige of the civilization of the industrious people to whom these fertile lands once belonged.

And to give to these comparisons a better coloring in the minds of the politicians of good faith, and to the logical deductions which thinking men may draw from them, it is proper to say that the population of Hayti has not diminished owing to its independence, but has rather increased about one-fifth of what it was when it annihilated the whites who had been their masters; which fact makes the extraordinary decrease of their agricultural production the more censurable. And the island of Cuba, whose entire population scarcely amounted to two hundred thousand souls when Hayti made herself independent, that is to say, in the latter part of the eighteenth century, has since then multiplied in the proportion of seven to one, or in the same proportion as that of the English colonies has decreased since the emancipation of the slaves.

Adding to these figures the consideration of the actual state of the revenues of both colonies, it will be seen, that whilst those of England and France are retained only as stratgetic points, and their administrations and small garrisons respectively are maintained by allowances from the public treasury; while the exports of Jamaica which, thirty years ago, were estimated at ninety thousand tons, and five years ago, were reduced to only nineteen thousand; and whilst in the French colonies, after the fall of the Republic of 1848, the redemption of negroes was substituted by a voluntary contract, very similar to the slave trade, and which, though by a strange tolerance of the English government, was considered legal, was, nevertheless, the cause of bloody scenes, as in the case of the bark Regina Cœli, and of international difficulties, as in the case of the Charles et Georges; the Island of Porto Rico covers all her official obligations with ease, and the Island of Cuba, after maintaining on a war footing twenty-five thousand soldiers and thirty vessels of the Royal Navy as an ordinary garrison, after paying an organized administration which would almost govern a kingdom, and also paying the Spanish diplomatic and consular corps residing in the New World, remits annually, to the treasury of the Metropolis over two millions of dollars as the overplus of her colonies, or pays with this amount, which is sometimes duplicated, extraordinary expenses such as were incurred by the re-incorporation of St. Domingo, its sustenance and improvement, and by the expensive expedition to Mexico.

In order that these data may not be used as an argument against slavery, by supposing that this amount is obtained by the excessive labor exacted from the slaves and by the heavy contributions imposed upon property, I will add, that it is derived without much effort from the Custom-house duties, which are eminently liberal, with the exception of a few articles; and that, besides what has already been shown by the insertion of the code of laws in force for the good government of the slaves, and what has been said respecting the constant and the ever humane and protecting acts of the local authorities, there is not a single negro slave in the island of Cuba who, after having acquired the first notions of the work which he has to perform and of his civil status, is willing to return to his native country with his freedom.

Let the abolitionists hear this again, once for all, and draw their own deductions in good faith ; and let them not persist in their absurd idea of knowing the wants of the negroes better than they do themselves.

These details relative to the Spanish colonies serve admirably to analyze the second phase presented to the observation of men of good faith by this question, such as it has been established by the abolitionists.

I have already stated, and I now repeat, that in honor of truth I will not attempt to deny or even to express any doubt that the introduction of Bozal negroes is carried on in said colonies in spite of the treaties extant. Otherwise, as the practice of breeding slaves for the market has not been established in the colonies as it has been in the southern states of the Anglo-American republic, it would be impossible to account for the extraordinary increase o the colored population, and still more impossible that there should be in Cuba, at present, three times the number of slaves that it contained in 1835, when the carrying out of the treaties for the suppression of the slave trade had been agreed on definitely.

From these facts, which speak so eloquently of the inefficiency of said treaties, daily and hourly opportunities have been sought to attribute this non-fulfilment to the bad faith of the authorities charged with their execution.

The English, who are the most directly interested in the prohibition of the redemption, who have more numerous means of publicity, and whose political customs are better adapted to the purpose, have accused the said authorities in every known form, and, in some cases, in a manner not becoming international respect, without excluding the government in Madrid, which has sometimes been the object of rude attacks in parliament and in all the newspapers of England. And Spain and her public men, who attached but little importance to such freedom of speech, occasionally vouchsafing only such notice as was required to repel some offensive phrase, or some notoriously false and calumnious assertions, seeing that the English believe that clandestine redemption can be repressed with such facility, and that they accuse the Spanish authorities of fostering it, have finally commenced to suspect that this conviction and this suspicion emanate from the fact that the English themselves are addicted to the practices which they attribute to others.

To arrive at this conclusion, we have but to reflect that England has numerous vessels of her royal navy stationed on the entire coast of Africa, commanding an uninterrupted chain of strategic points which are in her possession, and that said vessels are commissioned solely and exclusively to prevent the redemption of Africans wherever it may be effected.

The logical and impartial inference which can be drawn from these facts just stated, is, either that the English cruisers accept bribes from the redeemers of negroes in the districts where the trade is carried on, as they have accused the Spanish authorities of doing, in which case they should not be allowed to escape unpunished, or else that the redeemers, being stimulated by the great profits accruing to them from their enterprise, evade the vigilence of the English in Africa with the same dexterity with which they elude that of the Spaniards in the New World.

The execution of the existing treaties being equally entrusted to the English and the Spaniards, to the former in Africa and to the latter in America, how can it be expected that those who can pass the lines of the former with impunity should not be equally successful in evading those of the latter?

It must be confessed that this argument is unanswerable, the more so as the points where the redemption is effected, though numerous and at long distances from each other, are perfectly well known and are constantly watched by the English cruisers. If their vigilance was exercised only out in the open sea, in the vast expanse of the ocean, it would then be an easy matter for the traders to avoid them by navigating by different parallels, and in that case there would be some justice in throwing all the responsibility on the Spanish authorities, their vigilance being confined to the coasts of their respective districts. But as this is far from being the case, and as both on the coast of Africa and in the Spanish West Indies, there are certain localities, well known to traders, where the slavers evade, in like manner, the operations of the authorities, and destroy the spirit of the treaties, it must be confessed that the responsibility lies upon the English, at least as fully as upon the Spaniards; and that those absurd charges and offensive recriminations, so unjustly made by the former against the latter, might on the same grounds be directed by the latter against the former.

The truth is, that the evil does not lie in the proceeding of the English cruisers, nor of the Spanish authorities, but in the spirit of the absurd treaties which are characterized in every respect by their short-sightedness, illegality and immorality. They were intended to improve the condition of the negroes in Africa, whereas, never until the date of the enforcement of the treaty, and from that time to this, had there been perpetrated there such bloody and revolting scenes, which have even compelled the English to commit an act of possession which looks like violent spoliation in a friendly land. It was intended also to destroy slavery in America by the prohibition of redemption, and slavery has on the contrary been perpetuated, and has increased in an extraordinary manner. It was attempted to foster colonial wealth by means of free labor, by giving absolute freedom to the negroes, and with it encouragement to work for wages, and these recovering their natural instincts through their civil freedom, have abandoned labor and have ruined the colonies where these desolating experiments were attempted. And finally, international law, reviled and scoffed at as it has been, with or without cause, in the sense which the declaimers against the clandestine traffic have adopted, has proved with still greater force what has resulted from former evidence that the treaties are absurd, being impracticable, if we are to believe the result of thirty years of continual experiments, and of innumerable and useless precautions, and that being absurd from the fact that they are impracticable, they cannot be considered legally binding.

CHAPTER IX.

Mutiny of the negroes on board the Ship *Regina Cœlis* and bloody destruction of the whites who composed the crew.—Repugnant demonstrations of joy exhibited in the British parliament on the occasion of that butchery.—Attempts made by the British government on the petition of its Colonies to renew the redemption of negroes under another name.—The same thing attempted by the French government.—Case of the Ship *Charles et Georges* captured by Portuguese cruisers.—International conflict it produced between France and Portugal.—The attitude taken by England in consequence of this conflict.—Imperial ordinance of Napoleon III ordering the suspension of the new form of the redemption of negroes, and announcing his treaty for obtaining Chinese in the English possessions in the East.—Detailed analysis of the regulations by which these laborers are governed in the Island of Cuba.—Their civil condition is the same as that of the negro slaves, and it is even worse in some respects.—Remarkable inconsistency which results between the idea of abolishing the redemption of negroes and stimulating the servitude of the Chinese.—Comments on these inconsistencies to show their true phases to public opinion.

I HAVE referred in a former chapter to two events, the relation of which should not be omitted, because one of them shows the lengths to which an idea may be carried in opposition to the theories which gave rise to it, and the other affords additional proof of the deplorable state to which public rights were reduced by the abolition of the slave trade, and shows also the pretended efforts of diplomacy ostensibly in favor of colonial interests, but in reality to establish the traffic under another system of laws.

The first of these incidents was both repugnant and blood-thirsty, and although it can by no means be attributed to the machinations of the fanatical abolitionists of the London society, since it took place entirely beyond the limits of their influence, still upon its immediate results being made manifest, they laid themselves open to the severest censure on account of their inhuman readiness to applaud it.

This occurrence was nothing less than a mutiny of negroes who had been contracted for the French colonies, in conformity to a new plan pursued by way of experiment by the emperor Napoleon III., which mutiny took place on board the French merchant ship "Regina Cœli." Owing either to the carelessness or the humanity of the captain of the vessel, or perhaps to a combination of both, the crew was surprised and attacked by the negroes on board, who were being conveyed to the colonies as free laborers, not by their own will, but by the rapacity of their captors, who had sold them for that purpose. The attack was as disastrous as it was sudden, so that one individual only succeeded in escaping the general massacre. The case was too horrible not to produce very great excitement, and naturally aroused in behalf of the victims that interest which in all similar catastrophies is felt by every humane heart. This occurrence was the more to be lamented, inasmuch as instead of emanating from a manifest transgression of the law, as would otherwise have been the case, it occurred on board of a vessel legally authorized by the nation to which it belonged, without any hindrance from other nations, to save from certain death those who, in return for the charity exercised towards them, thus barbarously treated their generous preservers.

There was, however, one exception to the universal feeling on the subject, which was the more strange and surprising, as it was publicly expressed in the British Parliament by one of the most illustrious orators of that distinguished assembly.

I shall not be the one to proclaim in this place the name of that great philanthropist, lest the just indignation which the fact will arouse in all well organized minds should convert that name into an object of public execration, but I will not refrain from saying that it was enrolled in the Anti-Slavery Society; and that though this society was founded by an impulse of exaggerated love of humanity, against all that can offend the spirit of Christianity, the sentiment expressed by the orator, lamenting that a single individual of the crew of the French ship should have escaped from being butchered by the negroes, could not be more opposed to that philanthropy so much cried up by the society, nor more disgraceful to the principles by which it is fictitiously governed.

The second case was still more heinous, and manifested itself under circumstances even more discreditable to international law, at least according to appearances.

As soon as the political passions were quieted among the French populace, after the revolution of 1848, the empire examined into the spirit of republican legislation, and finding that the abolition of slavery was already decreed and converted into an accomplished fact, and that in its natural consequences it was in a fair way to ruin the colonies, it not only made regulations against the vagrancy of the negroes with others intended to encourage labor, but, besides, with the tacit approbation of the English government, an experiment was made of the aforesaid system of free labor in Africa, by opening the doors of emigration, which had the character of being voluntary, in order to restore to the colonies their former prosperity.

This experiment was not wanting in precedent, it having been tried by the English themselves on a former occasion; and let it not be thought that I make this statement at random, I do it with the official evidence before me with which the Anti-Slavery Society remonstrated against the attempt.

This system originated in 1841, when, on the 15th of February, an expedition consisting of three vessels sailed from the Thames, under the orders of Mr. Barclay, bound to Sierra Leone. This gentleman was a member of the legislative assembly of Jamaica, and had gone to the English metropolis expressly to make known the absolute necessity of negro laborers in the colonies, and to point out the only way in which that necessity could be supplied, which was neither more nor less than the former redemption, under the appearance of voluntary emigration. A great inducement which undoubtedly moved the British government to accede to the request of the colony, was undoubtedly the vexation felt in England on account of the necessity of buying in Hayti the coffee needed for home consumption, which had hitherto been supplied exclusively from English possessions. For although it had been attempted to remove the annoyance by exacting that all vessels carrying coffee to British ports should touch at Cape Town, that measure did not destroy the fact of her having to provide herself with colonial products in foreign lands, while she herself had colonies equally fit for their culture.

Mr. Barclay's expedition undoubtedly produced the desired results in Jamaica, and I believe it gave rise to the custom of making similar expeditions to the rest of the English West India Islands, which, however, were undertaken with certain precautions so as not to scandalize the world. The truth is, that the re-engagement of laborers took a definite form, and that to insure the success of this contract, written instructions were given in the letter and spirit of which the actual practice of the system of redemption was made apparent. In said instructions, the contracts under this new system were notified that, as the negroes were unacquainted with the value of money, they should provide themselves with such articles as might be fancied by the natives, such as—powder, tobacco, rum, Manchester plaids, caps, laguli, and a few firearms.

"To engage laborers," said these instructions, "it is indispensable that the negroes should receive in advance the value of a months' labor in different articles, according to the amount which has been agreed upon to reward the labor of each man ; said reward to consist in general of a quarter of a keg of gunpowder, ten *manillas* of tobacco, and a bottle of rum, or else a piece of Manchester plaid, ten *manillas* of tobacco and a bottle of rum.

"From these amounts any one can calculate the exact proportions required to procure any number of laborers, say, for instance, to engage forty negroes it will be necessary to be supplied with twenty muskets, twenty-one kegs of powder, twenty gallons of rum, eighty pounds of tobacco, and four pieces of Manchester plaids."

If we take into consideration the amounts of these articles which are more than sufficient to remunerate the monthly labor of forty negro apprentices, we will see that their punctual payment would prove highly burdensome to the contractors, consequently we can well imagine that, as far as their salary is concerned, the condition of these negro laborers must have been similar to that of their predecessors under the new regulations issued and promulgated in the English colonies, which, after slavery was abolished, were not so liberal as they had formerly been. And we are further strengthened in this supposition by finding in the aforesaid instructions a recommendation to the effect that the chiefs of the tribes from which the laborers are procured, shall be propitiated by presents of some value, which, of course, are to consist of the articles above mentioned ; and as we have reason to suppose that only the power of the chiefs, and not the will of the negroes themselves, is consulted in the contract, it appears highly improbable that the contractors should fulfil their part of the agreement when they have secured their laborers, in their respective countries, where the customs, the wants, and the laws are so different from those of Africa.

It will appear natural to all that the London philanthropic society should have made a great outcry on hearing of Mr. Barclay's expedition and its results, but it would have been difficult to guess at the attitude which would be taken in that matter by Lord John Russell, at that time president of the council of ministers. This celebrated disclaimer who, in parliament, has so often directed unmerited reproof against the Spanish government, at the instigation of the Anti-Slavery Society; this man, famous as a philanthropist for his speeches, for which, whenever they allude to forced labor in the colonies, present him to the world as the chief defender of the negroes, not only granted Mr. Barclay's petition and authorized the redemption in Sierra Leone, limiting, however, the term of slavery of the negroes there redeemed to *fourteen years*, but he also insulted the Anti-Slavery Society by refusing to communicate with it personally, but referred them to his secretary, Mr. Vernon Smith, in a few brief lines which were openly contemptuous, and treated only on general topics.[1]

This precedent being established, and it being besides a well-known fact that the negroes seized from slavers, at sea, by the English cruisers, are not returned to their country, as would seem just and natural, but are taken to the English colonies for a certain number of years to work, under the name of apprentices, but, in reality, as slaves, it is not to be wondered at that the Government of Great Britain should agree so well with that of the Emperor Napoleon III. and tolerate the redemption of negroes, disguised under the name of emigration, in the manner in which it had been practiced by the French.

---

(1) My late esteemed friend, Don Mariano Torrente preceded me in investigating this matter, and I have formed the above statements on his works which treat of the Island of Cuba, and also on some explanations offered by Lord John Russell in the English Parliament.

This new system having been put into practice with great advantage to the French colonies, which owed to it their continued prosperity after slavery was abolished, although they did suffer some severe losses, the Portuguese men-of-war stationed on the coast of Africa, being determined to defend the treaties in force against the redemption, seized a French vessel, the *Charles et Georges*, which was engaged in shipping a cargo of the so-called free laborers. And on the said vessel being taken into the port of Lisbon as a legal prize, and its seizure and detention being approved by the Portuguese courts, the French Government, becoming at once acquainted with the facts of the case, and without any right further than that of its unquestionable power, claimed the absolute control of the trial of the cause, and imperatively demanded from Portugal that the captured vessel should be immediately released.

It was said at that time that this occurrence was a crafty and underhanded stroke instigated by the Anti-slavery Society, and sustained by the influence which Great Britain possessed with the court of Portugal; and though it is possible that this charge may have been unfounded, it will appear very natural in the eyes of the public, when it is taken into consideration that said Society had remonstrated very strongly with the English Government against the tacit concession which it made to the French authorities with regard to the practice of engaging negro laborers, and that the London ministerial papers were the most energetic defenders of the immunity of the Portuguese courts and of their executive decision against the captured vessel to which we have alluded.

Be it as it may, and much as the Ministers of King Pedro V. may have endeavored, in all good faith, to maintain the authority of their courts, the persistency with which they refused to release the vessel became a matter of wonder to the world, as, not only were the required papers relative to the expedition found in good order, but there was also on board an official agent of the French Government charged with the direction of the operations.

Nevertheless, the serious nature of the case became apparent from the diplomatic notes which were exchanged between France and Portugal, some characterized by their harshness, while others were offensive to the dignity of the respective Governments, and also from the fact that the former sent two ships-of-the-line, fully armed and equipped, to the capital of the latter, with strict executive orders, it being a noticeable fact that while the French Government took up this position all the London official journals unanimously advised Portugal not to yield, notwithstanding that the Government of Great Britain had volunteered to act as a peaceful mediator between the two nations.

Whether or not the Anti-slavery Society of London had anything to do with the aforesaid events, as was justly suspected, the fact is that the results were extremely favorable to its views—thanks to the political circumstances which strengthened for the time being the official union of France and England. For the latter, ever skilful in taking advantage of any opportunity which might be propitious to her interests, and having also at the time undertaken the settlement of the Italian question, with all its public changes, and its absolute tendencies, still unknown, thought it opportune to recommend to her ally (with all due precaution against offending her dignity), the abandonment of her successful undertaking for obtaining laborers on the African coast, and offered her in exchange a great number of them from the East Indies. And France, who by having limited the work of said laborers to the space of four years for some, and for others to six, found that her colonies were not much benefitted by the new system, declared herself willing to make a sacrifice of so little moment, knowing that it would be the means of giving her in time the right of demanding more abundant and valuable acquisitions.

It is for this reason, according to my understanding, that the mind of Napoleon III. underwent a complete change with regard to the labor of the negroes and the colonial requirements, which change was proclaimed to the public when it was least expected, in the following remarkable document:

"Fontainbleau, 1st of July, 1861:—Mr. le Ministre—Since the emancipation of slavery, our colonies have endeavored to obtain laborers from the coasts of Africa, by ransom and by means of the contract of *engagement* which secures a compensation to the negroes for their labor. These contracts are made good for five or six years, after which time the laborers are to be taken back gratuitously to their country, unless they should prefer to remain in the colony, in which case they will be allowed to reside there in the same manner as the other inhabitants.

"It must be observed that this species of *engagement* differs entirely from the slave trade, for in fact, while the one has slavery in view, the other on the contrary leads them to freedom. When the negro is once engaged as a laborer he is free and is not subject to any other obligation than those contained in his contract.

"Nevertheless, doubts have arisen with regard to the results which these *engagements* may have in African countries, and the question has been asked whether the price of the ransom does not constitute a premium in favor of slavery.

"In 1859 I had already ordered that all *engagements* should cease on the eastern coast of Africa, where any difficulty might have arisen. Later, I restricted still more these operations; and, lastly, I have expressed the wish that all the questions which the African emigration should give rise to, may be carefully examined.

"This day I have signed a treaty with her Majesty the Queen of Great Britain, in which her Britannic Majesty consents to authorize the *engagement* of laborers for our colonies, from her possessions in the East Indies, under the same conditions which are laid down for the English colonies.

"We will then find all the free laborers which we will need, in the East Indies, in the French possessions in Africa, and in the countries where slavery still exists. Under these circumstances I wish the traffic of Africans by means of the ransom to be entirely discontinued by the French traders, said change to take place from the day on which the treaty made with her Britannic Majesty shall be carried into effect, and to continue in force all the time of the duration of said treaty.

"If this treaty should be suspended, the ransom of Africans shall not be recommenced except under special authorization, and then only if it is found to be indispensable, and if there are no difficulties in the way.

"You will therefore take the necessary measures to carry this resolution into effect by the 1st of July, 1862, and all negroes who have been ransomed on the coast of Africa after this date shall be prohibited entering the colonies.

"NAPOLEON."

From the recent triumph which the emancipators of the blacks have obtained, we naturally come upon a new question, which it is necessary to analyze in order to discover whether the love of humanity or purely interested and selfish stubborness keeps a large number of slave owners in constant alarm, and causes an exterminating strife between two incompatible ideas, all on account of the black race.

The question to which I refer is that of the importation of Chinese laborers into the American colonies, in which project the English Government took very decided initiatary steps with the end of promoting it as a substitute for negro labor, as has been proved by numerous documents inserted in this work.

And since the abolition of one system and the adoption of the other exhibit an inconsistency which cannot be favorably explained, with due regard for the humane principles which counselled the liberation of the negroes; let us compare both institutions in their respective legislation, and see whether justice, as it is understood by the scrupulous English philantropists, is a strongly marked feature of the new idea, or whether it is merely a question of words serving as a basis for their violent attacks upon the former.

It is on this point I wish particularly to call the attention of my readers, since the argument will be facilitated by the remarkable data which it furnishes for the better understanding of the subject. The ransom of the negroes is not submitted to voluntarily by the ransomed individuals themselves, but is the consequence of right of coercion which is exercised over them by other negroes; while that of the Chinese on the contrary, has nothing compulsory about it, since it depends entirely on their own will whether they submit themselves to it or not. There is, however, a vast dissimilarity in this comparison, a dissimilarity which does not depend on the interest of the ransomers, but on the civil state of the respective countries where the negroes are bought, and those where the Chinese are contracted for.

If philanthrophy could establish in the former the civilization which exists in the latter, it could then with reason interrupt the redemption of Africans, and do away with the material disparity which exists between the two systems; but as it is at present, humanly speaking, impossible to place the civil state of those countries on a level, it is evident that the philanthropy which persistently interferes with the redemption of the negroes, and remains an impassive spectator of the revolting scenes of barbarity, such as the sacrifice of five hundred human beings on the coast of Madagascar, and the slaughter of two thousand in Dahomey, is absurd and even criminal in the eyes of the world, especially as at the same time it encourages the servitude of the Chinese under the same conditions and for the same labor, as will be presently demonstrated.

The personal interest of the contractors being the chief object in both systems, and the benefit of the colonies being only a secondary consideration, the engagement of the Chinese naturally degenerated into a system similar in every respect to the redemption of negroes—the ordinances for their introduction into the island of Cuba, for instance, being similar to those which existed for the introduction of Africans before the prohibition of the redemption—the regulations existing for the labor and management of the laborers under both of these institutions, as an integral part of the estates, being nearly alike.

For this reason the second article of the *Regulations for the introduction of Chinese laborers* decrees that every importer must have a consignee in the island of Cuba, who must be a well known and wealthy proprietor to be a responsible agent, this being also exacted in the respective epochs of the *Contracting Company* and of the private contractors who purchased the privilege of taking negroes to the Indies. And as it is further expressed in the fifteenth article of the same Regulations that said consignee shall deposit fifty dollars in the Spanish Bank of Havana for every Chinaman that is consigned to him, within twenty-four hours after the arrival of the vessel which brings them, it is evident that said deposit, although it is refunded, increases the expenses of the contracting parties, and consequently burdens still more the civil state of the Chinese in the countries where they are employed.

It is true, and it would be wrong to omit to mention the fact, that the Chinese go to the colonies as day laborers only, and that but for a limited period, while the negroes receive no remuneration for their labor further than the necessary provision for their material wants and their moral instruction, but at the same time this difference is counterbalanced by the fact that the engagement into which the Chinese enter is not always so profitable to them as would appear from the contract, this being the result, not of any omission or evasion on the part of the contractors, but of the regulations themselves, and the clauses which they contain.

The slowness or delay in the work of the journeymen, which are so many hours lost to the legitimate interests of the proprietors, is compensated by making a discount from their salary in proportion to the time lost; any breach of discipline committed by the Chinamen on the plantations is also punished by fines, which imperceptibly, but none the less certainly, diminish their wages, which are extremely small, so that the majority of these laborers are placed in precisely the same situation as the majority of the negroes—that is to say, that at the expiration of their contract the Chinese are in a state of complete destitution, without any resource but the renewal of their contract, thus being subjected to perpetual labor, in the same manner that the law perpetuates the servitude of the negroes who are incapable of obtaining their freedom through the means placed within the reach of the industrious and orderly by their owners.

The better to understand all the minor details in the comparison which I have made between these two systems, it will be necessary to bear in mind that the proprietors give small plots of land to the negroes on their plantations, that they may cultivate them for their own benefit, on feast days or during their hours of relaxation, excepting in harvest time, during which they have but little spare time; or else they have them instructed in some profitable trade or employment, so that the industrious and intelligent may have the chance of obtaining their freedom; from which fact we see that though the negroes are not paid for their labor by any settled wages, unlike the Chinese, who are contracted for stated sums, they nevertheless receive a voluntary remuneration, which has been established by the true philanthropy of the owners, and which has been sanctioned, by time, until it has become to be considered almost in the light of a legal obligation. Having called attention to this point with the purpose of making my comparison perfectly intelligible, I will here, with the reader's permission, append such articles of the Regulations for the Chinese laborers as may serve to corroborate the above statement.

The sixth article will, of itself, suffice to illustrate some points. I will, therefore, produce it, in its own words :

"Every contract shall contain the following particulars : First, the age, sex and birthplace of the Chinese laborers who shall be engaged. Second, the length of time that the contract is to last. Third, the salary and the quantity and quality of the food and clothing which they are to receive. Fourth, the obligation of the masters to give them medical assistance during their illness. Fifth, whether the salary is to be discontinued in case of the illness of the laborer, when said illness does not originate in his work, or whether the continuation of the wages is to be left at the option of the owner. Sixth, the number of hours which the laborers will be obliged to work, determining whether the owner shall have the right to increase them, in some days, so long as he compensates for this increase by a corresponding decrease in others. Seventh, the obligation of the contracted laborer to indemnify the owner the hours of labor which he loses through his own fault."

Then follows article seventh, from which the civil state of the voluntary Chinese laborers has every appearance of being perpetual and forced, since it is extremely difficult for any of these laborers to save a sum sufficient to enable them to return to their native country, as they receive very small wages, which are further diminished by the circumstances mentioned in the former article. And in order to show what good reason I have for thus expressing myself, I here copy from article seventh, word for word:

"In every contract made with the Chinese it is an essential condition which ought to be expressed in an additional clause, that, after the expiration of the term of the contract, the Chinese laborers shall not be permitted to remain in the island of Cuba unless they enter anew into a contract of the same nature, in the condition in which they were before, either as apprentices or journeymen under the supervision of a master, or else as field laborers or domestic servants, recommended by *their masters;* in default of which they shall be compelled to leave the island, *at their own expense,* within two months of the expiration of the contract."

After reading these regulations we cannot but see what course the Chinese are compelled to take, as it must be a difficult matter for them to return to their own country owing to the immense distance and the interrupted communications. For although the aforesaid article does not stipulate to what particular place such laborers shall go when their contract has expired, it is natural that they should be unwilling to venture into any strange country, of whose laws and customs they are entirely ignorant, perhaps to endure the same fate, or to expose themselves to the hardships which they have experienced in the island.

The eighth clause of article sixth identifies the contracted Chinese with the negro slaves in such a manner that both systems of labor are considered one and the same thing by the owners and overseers of the plantations, and in the workshops where they are employed. The sixth clause and several articles of this regulation, which will be inserted here, may be used to combat this assertion, but I insist that, from their very spirit, it will be easy to corroborate the declarations which I have made with regard to the similarity of the civil status of the Chinese and negro laborers.

The sixth clause, in fact, expresses that in every contract made with the Chinese it will be necessary to state the number of hours he is to work, daily; and also if the master is to have the privilege of increasing the number of working hours when he may deem it necessary, compensating said increase by a proportionate decrease whenever it may be practicable. My readers will understand that as the contractors are immediately interested in the matter, they naturally endeavor to draw up the contracts in such a manner that the greatest possible advantage may accrue to the proprietors, and this is the more natural as the contracting of these Chinese originated in the necessity of procuring laborers to substitute the negroes, or to make up for any deficiency in the number of the latter, and it would be useless and unprofitable to engage them under other conditions. For this reason the clauses concerning the hours of labor are drawn up in the contracts in ambiguous terms, generally specifying only that the hours of labor shall be arranged according to the custom prevailing with other laborers. Thus it is that article fifty-fourth of the *Regulations for the introduction of Chinese in the island of Cuba*, says as follows:

"When it is expressed in the contract that the master is to have the right of distributing, in the manner most conducive to his interests, the number of working hours agreed upon with the laborer according to what is prescribed in the sixth clause of article seventh, it is understood that said right is limited in such manner that the laborer " can never be compelled to work over fifteen hours a day, and is always entitled to at least six hours of uninterrupted rest, either by night or by day." This article, although it is not exactly ambiguous, proves most unmistakeably that the masters can, at their option, establish the distribution of the hours of labor, according to their own interests, and that the Chinese, with but a slight difference, are obliged to do the maximum of labor which is imposed on the negroes, according to article twelfth, in the regulations which have already been inserted in this work.

And this identity will be still more apparent even, if we allow that the hours of labor are distributed in a manner favorable to the Chinese, if we take into consideration what is expressed in the fifty-third article of the Slave Regulations; as the former assigns twelve hours daily as the average term of labor to the contracted Chinese, while in the latter, ten hours' work only can be exacted from the negroes, except during the harvest season or in case of urgent necessity.

When the contractors make over the Chinese to private individuals it is very evident that the latter have to pay a sum which will cover the expenses of the contractors, *i. e.*, the advances made to the Chinese in their country to induce them to enter into the engagement; the commissions paid to the agencies there established for this enterprize; the consular fees; the expenses of the fitting out of each ship in its outward and homeward voyage, and of the maintainance, clothing and attendance on the Chinese during the passage; the expenses of the consignees, who must be residents in Havana, according to the regulations ; the deposit of fifty dollars to be made in advance to the Spanish Bank of said city for each emigrant ; the percentage which shall accrue from the capital invested in all the undertakings; and lastly, the profits calculated to stimulate the carrying on of the enterprize.

From these antecedents we cannot but come to the conclusion that the Chinese are sold to the proprietors of the plantations and workshops by the parties who contract them as free laborers, in the identical manner that negroes are sold to these same proprietors by the traders who redeem them as slaves. And even supposing that the price of the Chinese differ much from that of the negroes, this does not do away with the positive fact that the Chinese are sold and that they have greater difficulty in obtaining their freedom than the negroes, as we will presently demonstrate.

In fact, the sale is legalized by the twenty-third article of the Regulations concerning the Chinese, which says :— " Those who introduce Chinese laborers will have the privilege of transferring them to other contractors, to landholders or any other individual, under whatever conditions they may deem proper, provided those persons pledge themselves to fulfil the contract made with said laborers, and to observe these regulations. The cessionaries of the Chinese will hold the same power, under the same conditions ; but if the stipulations expressed in the original contracts are altered, then the said transfer will be null and void." By which transmission of authority from one cessionary to another it is evident that the Chinese are legally sold in the island of Cuba in the same manner as the negroes, and without any restrictions.

That the Asiatics in the Spanish possessions may not oppose themselves to the workings of their disguised servitude, article thirty-fourth, of the Regulations, says as follows: " The laborers, be it understood, on signing or agreeing to the contracts with those who contract them, thereby lose all civil rights which are not consistent with the fulfilment of the obligations which they have contracted, unless it be some right expressly mentioned in the regulations." This article alone is sufficient to sum up the comparison which is now being drawn to prove that the philanthropy which labors for the introduction of Chinese in the colonies so as to destroy slavery, is entirely misdirected; but there are others which still further prove the opinion here expressed, as they refer to the children born in this condition.

The civil freedom of the Chinese laborers being a fact, according to the name of this institution, it would be natural that the law should not interfere with the children born on the Island of Cuba during their mothers' servitude, excepting to protect and sustain them in their helplessness during the first years of their life. This would appear from article thirty-six, which says: "Laborers can exercise their parental authority over their children, and their marital powers over their wives so long as they are consistent with the legal condition of the said children and wives."

But, in order to show what that legal condition is which limits parental authority, article thirty-seventh follows immediately, with these words: "The children of laborers, born during the term of the contract of their mothers, shall remain in the same condition as their mothers so long as said contract lasts; but on attaining the age of eighteen years they shall be entirely free, even though their mothers may still be contracted.

"The minor children, which the women may have at the time of entering into the contract, shall remain subject to the condition which the mothers may agree upon with the contractors. But if no stipulations are made beforehand, then the children will be entirely free; and shall be fed, lodged and clothed by the owners of their mothers, on the same conditions as those established for the latter, until they have accomplished their twelfth year."

Now, after carefully analyzing all that comprises the former chapter, we arrive at the conclusion that the law gives us to understand that the contract of an Asiatic laborer can last over eighteen years, that period having been assigned for declaring free the children of contracted females who may be born in the Island of Cuba during the servitude of their mothers, even should these continue in the condition of laborers; and this estimate does not refer to the number of years stipulated in the original contract, as none is ever made for a term of over eight or ten years, and many for a lesser period, but is founded on the supposition that the condition of these labors is perpetuated from the moment that they enter the island, since it is impossible for them to leave it at their own expense.

We can also draw another and more important conclusion, which is the most conclusive proof that the state of the Chinese laborers is assimilated to that of the negro slaves, viz : that the master takes possession of an individual over whom he has no natural right, and whom he cannot claim as his property, but by the laws of servitude, even though his authority over him be limited to a certain period.

We see also that, although the law declares these individuals to be free on arriving at the age of eighteen years, their freedom is merely nominal, as it is further decreed that all Chinese who are not contracted shall be expelled from the island of Cuba, within two months of their freedom, so that the so-called freedmen, not wishing to be sojourners out of their native land, have no option but to return to the state in which they lived when minors, according to the condition of their respective mothers, which cannot be other than that of servitude.

And now, in order to prove with what truth I have said that the redemption of the Chinese from their servitude, by their savings and by the fruit of their labor, is impossible or at least very difficult, I must call attention to article forty-third of said regulations, which says as follows: "Every laborer will have the right to liberate himself from the dominion of his master, by paying in advance, in ready money, first: the amount paid for him; second: the amount which the laborer may owe his master as an indemnification for loss of labor or any other cause; third: the highest value which, in the judgment of the appraiser, the services of the laborer has acquired since he entered into the service of his master; fourth: the amount of damages which may result to the master from the difficulty to replace him by another. The laborer cannot avail himself of this right during harvest time, nor at any other time when urgent work is required on feast days."

After the remarks and commentaries which have been made, the perusal of said article will convince any impartial mind that the law has designed to identify the two races of laborers, that the ostensible differences should not create any very serious obstacles to the regulations of the plantations nor to the interests of the landlords. And, as in matters which solely depended on a name, and nothing more, that assimilation would have been absolutely impossible; yet the law made it appear more easy for the negro slaves to acquire their freedom, than for the contracted Chinese to emancipate themselves from compulsory labor.

To accomplish this end there were, no doubt, as many obstacles raised against the latter as there were facilities granted to the former; and while the orderly and intelligent negroes are paying the price of their emancipation, by instalments, no right being left to the owner to raise the original value of the slave, or to retain him in bondage after the conditions of his emancipation are fulfilled, whether it be or not the busy season, all which conditions are inserted in the rules and ordinances which have been copied entire in this work; the most laborious and fortunate Chinese could only cease to be compulsory laborers by the voluntary generosity of their employers, who would be willing to liberate them and to give them, besides, their passage back to China.

A real and positive difference of much importance in the regulations exists between the condition of the negro slaves and the Chinese laborers, viz: that which relates to corporeal punishments, which are prohibited, as a general rule in the said regulations, to be inflicted on them.

This difference arises rather from the fundamental circumstances of the education of each class when they arrive in the island of Cuba than from their civil state. The Chinese springing from an enlightened society in their own way, and belonging to one of the great historical branches of the human family, among whom some think the art of printing had its birth, and that artillery was first invented as a pious modification of war, not as a destructive element which has been given to its use now-a-days by nations who suppose themselves infinitely more civilized; that race among whom philosophy and jurisprudence had already made so much progress in the remote times of Confucio, and where, at the present day, the arts exhibit themselves so wonderfully advanced, it would not have been just to establish them among us on the same footing as the negroes, who are born and live in a savage state until their redemption opens to them the doors of a civilization of which it is necessary to teach them the first rudiments.

The English themselves, on abolishing slavery in their colonies in a decided and definite manner, allowed the punishment by lashes to remain in their regulations of those who, from that time, were called apprentices; based, no doubt, on the facts just stated of their absolute want of culture and limited understanding. To act otherwise in a question so much discussed, would be as much as to condemn in parents the natural jurisdiction which makes them inflict corporeal punishment upon their children, without injuring them, of course; which is the way that the negroes are punished according to the regulations.

And yet, as in the same race all the individuals differ so much from one another, there are cases, and this is well known by all who are acquainted with the island of Cuba, in which corporeal punishment is inflicted on the Chinese, without the interference of the authorities, provided the punishment does not go beyond the limits of humanity which govern the negroes. This is done in the presence of everybody, and is blamed by no one, because the delinquency which causes the punishment is also made public, though it may have been committed privately.

Moreover, the regulations which prohibit the corporeal punishment of the Chinese for ordinary faults do not absolutely exclude them from correction; on the contrary, it is recommended for grave cases, and to be done with solemnity, the well behaved being obliged to witness the punishment of the bad, as may be read in the following article:

"78.—In case of insubordination or resistance by force to the orders of their superiors, on the part of the laborers collectively, the owner shall have the right to use force also to subdue them; giving immediate information to the delegate protector, that he may, should the gravity of the case require it, *direct that the culprits be punished in presence of the other laborers.*"

This rule, as is evident, cannot mean anything else but corporeal punishment by summary procedings, and not such as are customary to the administration of justice in conformity with the existing laws; as in that case the delegate protector could not impose it, nor could the delinquents be punished *in the presence of the other laborers*, except in case they were sentenced to death.

In short, analizing the jurisdiction and the state of being of the new institution of the contracted Chinese, it proves to be the same as that of the redeemed negroes, to labor in a conditional or temporal servitude, with slight modifications which do not exist in fact, but simply in name. And this being the case, as is evinced by the printed regulations which are officially circulated, and is practically carried out in the island of Cuba, in presence of both natives and foreigners, (the British government and the London Anti-Slavery Society may easily know the fact, and they do know it, and care nothing about it), we shall come to the conclusion which has already been arrived at in this chapter, viz: that the persistent persecution set up against the redemption of the negroes is an absurdity founded in human pride, which having been started through error, will not now confess they are wrong

How, otherwise, could this pertinent tendency against the redemption of negroes keep in constant action thousands of intellects fitted for other and much better and useful occupations, however insignificant they might be; by the advice emanating from those very persons, and always reproduced in favor of Chinese immigration, whose regulations they do not ignore, and whose practices they know?

To give another turn to this question it would be necessary to suppose that they are influenced by cunning; the labor of the Chinese not being as productive as that of the negroes, and degenerate so much in field labor as to become almost useless; for which reason some people have suspected that what they aim at is only to equalize all the colonies which Europe has in the New World, improving those which at present produce little or nothing, at the expense of those which are at the height of their prosperity.

I am not the one to give countenance to this uncharitable idea; prefering to attribute this palpable contradiction, which results from all that has been said, rather to a compromise entered into with rooted prejudices and with the exigencies resulting from them.

For the rest, it may well be considered that if the Chinese voluntarily accept of servitude, being civilized people who have a vast knowledge of natural rights and the general notions of civil rights, which are within the reach of all, it is very probable that the negroes would not reject it if in a state of civilization as forward as that of their coleagues in the colonial labor, they could understand it previously to and at the time of their voluntary contract.

For this reason I think that all attempts which tend to prohibit the redemption and civilization of the negroes, are at least as bad as those which tend to the propagation of an immigration which constitutes a real servitude to the Chinese, because, as to the former, it perpetuates their abominable state and renders them of no service to the civilization of the world, as they can only acquire it through forced labor; and the latter, because a people who are poor, perhaps, but already civilized, are degraded in foreign lands.

Let all thinking men of the nations interested weigh the subject I have just analyzed, and let them become accustomed to listen to the truth free from artful dissimulation, for I still have much to say to them.

CHAPTER X.

Calamities which the perverseness of the Abolitionists has occasioned in the world.—Civil war of the United States.—Origin and history of the revolt of the South.—Insurrection at Harper's Ferry.—Death of John Bown.—Excitement and blasphemies which it called forth in the North, and in the slave States.—Fruitless efforts to maintain peace.—Municipal elections.—Parliamentary commotions.—The election of Lincoln renders war inevitable.—Proclamations of the Executive abolishing slavery in the rebellious States and respecting it in the others.—The constitutional legality of said proclamations analyzed.—Their negative results towards the re-establisment of the Union.—Remarkable documents as to its contradictory sense.—Aspect taken by the civil war after the issuing of the said proclamations.—Calamities brought down on the people, on the National Treasury, and on the public credit.

IF the treaties now in force for the prohibition of the redemption of Africans, and the unceasing labors of those who desire to abolish the system of labor imposed upon said negroes by civilization, had been productive of no other evils than the decline of the colonies, the moral and physical degradation of Hayti, the indignity of having civil equality applied to an inferior race, in our midst, the continual violation of public law, besides all the international outrages to which they gave rise, and even the slaughter of wretched African captives by barbarians of their own race, who sacrifice their prisoners when unable to sell them, then we might even tolerate that fatal persistency of purpose which has proved the author and unwearied promoter of so much discord and has caused the ruin of so many communities.

But, in addition to the serious results which I have just mentioned, each of which is in itself of sufficient significance to silence sentiment and restore to reason her legitimate ascendency, another, an immense, terrific and irreparable calamity has been the consequence of that baneful fanaticism: the battlefield has been chosen as the bar at which to discuss the question which has arisen between mistaken philanthropy and the most important interests, and the thunder of cannon is heard while the voice of reason and philosophy is hushed.

In one of the most flourishing countries in the world, human blood now flows in torrents in a doubtful and ambiguous cause, which, whatever be the manner in which it may finally be settled, cannot have any but absolutely negative results; and this will appear evident to all if they will take into consideration the spirit in which the war has been conducted on both sides. I repeat, the cause will be defeated in any event, for, if the abolition sentiment triumphs, the future freedom of the negroes will prove worse than their present state of servitude, as has been the case in all parts of the world; and if, on the contrary, slavery is perpetuated by force of arms, it is highly probable that this institution will then be restored to its original form, that it may be less exposed to the attacks of modern interference.

I mean that, if the abolitionists triumph, the advent of peace will prove fatal to the South section of the great American federation; and, if they are defeated, Christianity and its civilizing influences will be made to recede eighteen and a half centuries. This is the present state of the question, and such will inevitably be its termination, if the obstinacy of the one party and the rancor of the other do not, for the common weal, adopt a different policy.

Twelve years have already elapsed since this antagonism began to assume a threatening aspect in the United States of North America, and this I do not affirm at random, for the antagonism already existed, though in a pacific form, for a very long time, owing to the difference in the local institutions and the counter tendencies of opposite interests.

In one of those slave States which are now defending their cause with the greatest ardor, tumultuous meetings, fiery discourses and propositions of disunion had already been presented to the consideration of impartial observers, whereby they were enabled to predict with certainty and without any great mental effort what was so soon to come to pass, if the impending evil were not averted.

In fact, two years after, the disruption of the Union was foretold, and even the time when the catastrophe was to take place was designated; [1] and, in spite of this natural conjecture which was expressed by an obscure individual, and which was undoubtedly held by some few politicians who, unlike the generality of their class, were not blinded by their own private interests, the indifference of some, the fanaticism of others, perhaps the crafty machinations of foreigners, and the impertinent self-conceit of the majority, resulted in the confusion in which we all now find ourselves.

Because, while the Northern States were making powerful efforts to overcome the Southern States in the Halls of Congress, this being a terrible threat against the manorial property of the wealthy planters, while the Southern States, knowing the danger which threatened their legitimate interests, were speaking of the disruption of the Union as the only means of saving themselves; while any one possessed of common sense could foresee what was about to happen; and the future filled all loyal minds with horror, the philanthropic abolition societies did not scruple openly to make known their exertions in their dicourses, making new exactions from all nations and preaching their doctrines, with the greatest solemnity, in places where the greatest harm would naturally ensue.

While the scenes which were plotted in darkness and terminated in bloodshed, were being enacted at Harper's Ferry, to be followed ere long by a far greater and more terrible drama, the efforts to increase the number of cruisers of the nations interested in the prohibition of the slave trade were redoubled, and the most vehement and injurious words were uttered by an English Minister in Parliament against slavery and against all nations which maintained the institution of organized labor. And as the South had been exasperated to an inconceivable extent by all these causes combined, each of which would in itself have sufficed to bring about the dreaded and already inevitable disruption, in a case where prudence should have been consulted, passion, upheld by legality, held its

---

(1) I here refer to several publications of mine on the American question, in all of which will be found that, in 1851, I foretold that in ten years the great collision between the North and South would take place, resulting in the political separation of the two sections.

sway; and where the expulsion or imprisonment of some turbulent individuals would have sufficed, the life of an aged man was unhesitatingly and wantonly sacrificed. A lamentable circumstance by which false philanthropy was enabled to influence the feelings of truly benevolent persons, and which was solemnized by excited multitudes with funeral pomp and sacrilegious comparisons!

A periodical of New York, *La Cronica*, in its issue of the 9th of December, 1859, contains the following:

"*The Consequences of the Death of Brown.*

"Our readers are already aware that on the 2d instant, John Brown, the unfortunate leader of the insurrection at Harper's Ferry, suffered the penalty of death by hanging. We think it expedient to say something upon the effects which have been produced in all the country, and more especially in the Northern States, by the severe penalty imposed upon a man who personified, as it were, the political ideas and social aspirations of a great portion of the Union. And we think it all the more opportune, as society at large has agreed not to consider this as an isolated and unimportant act, but rather as one of those events of great political significance, which serves to forward a cause in one day more than it would otherwise have been forwarded in several years unmarked by such extraordinary occurrences.

"Hardly had the telegraph announced the death of Brown to all the cities of the North, than public demonstrations of sorrow and even indignation began to be evinced on all sides. In this city some of the churches were kept open from ten to twelve (the hour of execution) with the purpose of celebrating solemn religious services for the soul of Brown. Sermons were preached in which comparisons were repeatedly drawn between Brown and the apostle and martyr St. Stephen, and God was fervently prayed to cause the death of this *new martyr* to redound in favor of the slaves. In Philadelphia, Boston, Manchester, Syracuse, etc., etc., meetings were held, in which some Protestant ministers and distinguished men pronounced discourses upon the events of the day. The bells of the City Hall, and of several churches were tolled for the space of two hours. In both assemblies of the Legislature in Massachusetts it was resolved not to hold the session upon that day, and it can be said that all the North unanimously agreed in solemnly protesting against the death of the man whom they qualified as a *martyr to liberty*, and against the conduct of Mr. Wise, Governor of Virginia, whom a Boston orator styled the modern *Pontius Pilate*.

"The cry of indignation sent forth by the North, has loudly resounded in the South, adding fresh motives for the excitement of the inhabitants who can no longer restrain the rage with which they are inspired by what they call the aggression against their legitimate rights. As usual, they have already threatened to dissolve the Confederation, peremptorily informing the North that the time of the dreaded crisis has arrived ; *that the fate of the Union hangs, so to say, upon a single thread, and that to prevent its breaking, the co-operation of all the different parties in the Union, both in the North and in the South, is needed.*

"The North, on its part, is cognizant of the imminence of the danger, and seems to be disposed now, as upon other occasions, to make new concessions, in order to save that Union from which is derived the strength of both sections of the country. The most sensible portion of this population prudently endeavors to calm the irritation of the Southern slaveholders ; hence the fact that a meeting has been called in this city, at which it may be publicly declared that the inhabitants of the North sympathise with those of the South in the present circumstances, and that they openly condemn the conduct of John Brown and his accomplices, as well as the dangerous theories which some persons are endeavoring to inculcate in the minds of the populace. All this shows that the danger has been acknowledged, and that efforts will be made to avert it ; but moderate men have to battle at every step against the inconsiderate tendencies of the abolitionists, who, being attacked in the person of John Brown, and threatened, for the future, by the Southern publications, are anxious to revenge the outrage already suffered, and to avoid any others that may be attempted. In the meantime, exasperation and rancor are ever on the increase, the spirit of sectionalism is daily more and more aroused, and as the idea of an approaching political disruption becomes more and more familiar the greater also is the probability of its taking place.

"The far-seeing prudence and good sense of a portion of the Northern people, will, no doubt, greatly contribute to the lulling of the storm ; but, can such an anamalous situation be indefinitely prolonged ? Will a remedy be at length found for so strong and threatening an antagonism ? This is the great problem, upon the solution of which depends the existence of this Republic."

It is very rarely that we find expressed, in so brief and lucid a manner, the preamble to such extraordinary and transcendental events as have since come to pass; and which were foreseen and pointed out in the preceding article.

The solution of the problem was only deferred long enough to enable the minds already divided, and respectively confirmed in their antithetical opinions, to form their plans of action, in order to meet on the field of battle.

And what else could be expected when sophistry had made every effort to stifle the voice of reason, before which the immense interests which had been called in question might plead their legitimate rights ?

At the time when *La Cronica*, of New York, expressed itself in the above mentioned terms, in all the territories in which property was menaced, the most violent passions were laboring towards the accomplishment of disruption. And that these passions may be better estimated by their own demonstrations, as they really were, rather than through a defective description, my readers will allow me to insert a few paragraphs from several speeches made by the Governors in the South before the Legislative assemblies of their respective States, relative to the events which had occurred until the death of Brown, and to those which were preparing to follow.

In Virginia, within the jurisdiction of which the insurrectionists of Harper's Ferry were sentenced, Mr. Wise, who was called by the Northerners the modern Pontius Pilate, because as Governor of the State he punctually and faithfully fulfilled the painful duty, which the general interests of the people imposed upon him, was the one who most energetically set forth the difficult state of affairs during those awful moments. His message gave a detailed account of all the facts relative to the insurrection ; and in speaking of the fanaticism which swayed the abolitionists, he said that it was by it that the judgment of a considerable portion of the inhabitants of the Republic had been perverted, to such an extent that it became the basis of their religion, of their political principles, of their administration of justice, of their public and private actions, and, in fine, of their whole existence, this fanaticism being the result of the education of three successive generations.

He then went on to say: "If the majority does not cease violating the good faith sworn to the Confederation, disturbing our peace, destroying our lives and our property, and depriving us of the protection to which we have a right, by perverting the form and opposing the manner in which the Union should be preserved, *we must resort to arms*. The question is so essential, that we ought not to leave it endangered any longer. We cannot allow outrages similar to that at Harper's Ferry without suffering a fate worse than death, as citizens, and the dishonor of perishing, as a State.

"It cannot be denied that we have a great many good and sincere friends in the States where there is no slavery, but the conservative elements are passive, while those of the fanatics are active, and whilst the former are decreasing the latter are daily increasing in number and in strength.

"We must depend solely upon ourselves: we must fight for peace, we must arm and organize ourselves, we must demand that each State shall declare its intentions, for the future, with respect to slavery, and what the Constitution and the laws of the United States in general and of each State in particular, have established for its protection in our federal relations; and we must, proceed in accordance to the answer given. We are now in arms...... Let us defend our position or else abandon it at once. Let us act at once and endeavor to effect a definite arrangement. No more temporization with the Constitution. No more compromises. The rest of the convicted insurgents are sentenced and shall be executed, unless the General Assembly resolve to the contrary."

The same spirit of resistance and disunion was evident in the speech of the Governor of South Carolina: of that State which many years previously had taken the initiative for the disruption which has now taken place.

"In order to be prepared for any emergency," he said, "I would recommend you to adopt at once such measures, as in your opinion, may be neccessary in order to procure that the Southern States may act in concert for the defense of our institutions, should they be endangered at any time by our government departments falling into the hands of the enemy. The election of a *Black Republican* President, will decide the question of our security in the Union; and even though the forms of the Constitution should be observed, its vital principle, will nevertheless be extinguished, and the South will have to consent to occupy an inferior and degrading position, or it will have to seek a new safeguard for the future. Let South Carolina make all possible efforts to obtain the co-operation of the Southern States in this movement which is evidently of such vital importance; let her sacrifice everything except principle, for this purpose, and prepare herself to oppose a determined resistance at all events; without for a moment forgetting that she is a sovereign State which of her own free will entered into relations with the Federal Union, and has an unquestionable right to resume her independent position in the family of nations."

And, finally, that we may not have to waste time in examining other local manifestations when a single instance will serve fully as well to show the universal spirit which prevailed in the South, let the reader give his attention to the statement of an American traveller, given in the New York *Express*, after a tour through nearly all the Southern States.

"The more I hear and see in these parts, the greater becomes my dismay respecting our future, and the fear that we shall not be able to avoid what would be the greatest possible calamity for our country. I have just met with a strong conservative, one of the most strenuous partizans of the Union, who holds high position in the country, and has just arrived from New Orleans, via Alabama, Georgia and South Carolina, stopping at Montgomery and Columbus where the Legislature is congregated. He tells me that in the entire route he has not met with a single individual who is not in favor of the immediate separation of the two great sections of the Republic and the formation of a separate Confederacy among the slave States; that all efforts to argue on the subject with the inhabitants are useless, as they turn a deaf ear to all reasoning or argument, and that for the first time, he almost despairs of a peaceable arrangement of the matter The excitement here is very great, and if perchance we succeed in passing this crisis in safety, it will be due only to the prudence and the immense efforts of the moderate and conservative party. As a proof of the effects produced here by this state of affairs I must tell you that the present value of landed property is only thirty-two per cent of what it was six months since, and this is only in anticipation of coming events."

Not only was this alarm and this settled and universal antagonism constantly increased by the demonstrations at Harper's Ferry, the meetings in the Northern States, the untiring efforts of foreign diplomacy and, in fact, all the elements that have been pointed out as raging previous to and since the death of Brown, but fresh fuel was added to the flame by the publication of an abolitionist work. Whether this book was written with premeditated intentions of provocation we know not, but this we can positively affirm: that it helped to bring about the dissolution of the Union; for the author taking advantage of the great excitement among the enemies of slavery, either acting on his honest conviction, as we should like to beliéve in honor of the press, or with the purpose of rapidly making a fortune, as was conjectured by some, in which case he certainly succeeded, not only described the servitude of the negroes as being the worst institution to be found in ancient or modern history but he also succeeded in having an official motion made by the representatives of both Houses, at Washington, recomending the work to the attention of the public, in the same manner as if it had contained the sacred words of a new Evangelist.

For this reason, on the 5th of December 1859, when the Congress for 1860 had not yet been legally constituted, Mr. Clark, a zealous representative of the slave States, entirely devoted to the Federal Constitution, presented a proposal that all the Representatives who had made the motion in favor of Mr. Helper's book should, for that act, be excluded from eligibility to office. As was to be expected from the spirit which pervaded that assembly, owing to the events which were at that time taking place in the Republic, this proposal produced the contrary effect, which soon became seriously evident at the presidential election which followed.

The provocative sentiment of the abolitionists who, in the exclusiveness of their doubtful exigencies, aimed a death-blow at the material and immense interests of vast territories, was by no means universal in the North, being in a positive minority in some of the States. The State of New York, for example, wishing to be free from any responsibility of the coming events which now plainly appeared inevitable, organized those sympathising meetings alluded to in La Crónica, in the article herein inserted ; and afterwards, in order to give a fuller proof of its attitude, in the election of its rulers which was to take place about that time, by nominating Mr. Fernando Wood, the greatest friend in the North to the institutions of the South, and carried his election by an immense majority of votes.

In fact, the returns of this election prove that it could not have been more adverse to the abolitionists, nor more favorable towards an amicable adjustment between the two opposite tendencies which were on the point of rushing to arms. For, as Mr. Wood had, on account of his energetic and enterprising character, a great many enemies as well as friends, the cause of the sympathizers in that election was divided into two parts, each one having a different candidate ; whereas that of the abolitionists was united in the unanimous vote for one single individual. Notwithstanding all this Mr. Wood obtained thirty thousand and ninety-four votes. His colleague in opinions, though his opponent in the aspirations for office, obtained twenty-six thousand eight hundred and thirty-three, and Mr. Opdyke, the abolitionist candidate, only succeeded in securing twenty-one thousand eight hundred and eighteen. Thus, it is evident that the conservative party in the State of New York had a majority of over two-thirds.

But all these conciliatory demonstrations, all the efforts of a better judgment which condemned with great justice, everything in which an aggressive and ruling idea served as an obstacle to peace, were defeated in the final results; because, as Mr. Wise correctly said in his message to the Legislature of Virginia, the conservative elements are passive, whilst those of the agitators are constantly kept in motion by the impulse of their fanaticism.

In short, the election of Mr. Lincoln as President of the Republic, was the signal for the commencement of a war of extermination between the two sections ; for the South having been accustomed to have the ascendancy in the administration, had not the patience to suffer, even in anticipation, its first electoral defeat, but considered it in the light of an official summing up of all the former aggressions, from the time of Brown's insurrection, and hastened to take up arms against it, demanding a separation ; and the North through its imprudence being now obliged to make war in order to maintain the integrity of the federal Constitution according to the laws in force in all the States, instead of appeasing the excitement and dissipating the alarm of its antagonists by means of conciliatory measures that should above all have respected the interests which had been threatened, it continued to attack these interests in their basis, at first only occasionally and unofficially, though always under the influence of abolitionist tendencies, but afterwards with the full sanction of the Government, thus destroying every chance of a peaceable arrangement.

The 22d of September, 1862, will always stand as one of the most calamitous days in the annals of the great federal Republic ; for although the events of that day had been foreseen and did not surprise any one, owing to the symptoms which always precede any important measure, its official character, nevertheless, produced the effect which was to be expected, closing the doors on all legitimate adjustments between the two ideas which were being sustained with such fury by force of arms.

It is useless to disguise the fact that the proclamation issued by President Lincoln on the 22d of September, 1862, against the slavery of the negroes, or rather, we should say, against the legitimate property of the rebellious provinces (for the slaves of the other States, which were faithful to the federal Constitution, were not included in the said proclamation), instead of suppressing the rebellion, as the author, with evident inexperience, had intended, was the means of infusing into it additional vigor. But before we go on with our comments, it will be well here to insert the aforesaid documents.

The first says thus :

"WASHINGTON, September 22, 1862.

"I, Abraham Lincoln, President of the United States of America, and Commander-in-Chief of the army and navy thereof, do hereby proclaim and declare that hereafter, as heretofore, the war will be prosecuted for the object of practically restoring the constitutional relation between the United States and the people thereof in which States that relation is, or may be, suspended or disturbed; that it is my purpose, upon the next meeting of Congress, to again recommend the adoption of a practical measure tendering pecuniary aid to the free acceptance or rejection of all the slave States, so-called, the people whereof may not then be in rebellion against the United States, and which States may then have voluntarily adopted or thereafter may voluntarily adopt the immediate or gradual abolishment of slavery within their respective limits; and that the efforts to colonize persons of African descent, with their consent, upon the continent or elsewhere, with the previously obtained consent of the governments existing there, will be continued; that *on the first day of January, in the year of our Lord one thousand eight hundred and sixty-three, all persons held as slaves within any State, or any designated part of a State, the people whereof shall then be in rebellion against the United States, shall be thenceforward and forever free*, and the executive government of the United States, including the military and naval authority thereof, will recognize and maintain the freedom of such persons, and will do no act or acts to repress such persons, or any of them, in any efforts they may make for their actual freedom; that the Executive will, on the first day of January aforesaid, by proclamation, designate the States and parts of States, if any, in which the people thereof respectively shall then be in rebellion against the United States; and the fact that any State, or the people thereof, shall on that day be in good faith represented in the Congress of the United States by members chosen thereto at elections wherein a majority of the qualified voters of such State shall have participated, shall, in the absence of strong countervailing testimony, be deemed conclusive evidence that such State and the people thereof have not been in rebellion against the United States.

"That attention is hereby called to an act of Congress,

entitled 'An act to make an additional Article of War,' approved March 13, 1862, and which act is in the words and figures following :

"Be it enacted by the Senate and House of Representatives of the United States of America in Congress assembled, That hereafter the following shall be promulgated as an additional article of war for the government of the army of the United States, and shall be obeyed and observed as such :

"ARTICLE.—All officers or persons in the military or naval service of the United States are prohibited from employing any of the forces under their respective commands for the purpose of returning fugitives from service or labor who may have escaped from any persons to whom such service or labor is claimed to be due, and any officer who shall be found guilty by a court martial of violating this article shall be dismissed from the service.

SECTION 2.—And be it further enacted, That this act shall take effect from and after its passage.

"Also to the ninth and tenth sections of an act entitled 'An Act to suppress insurrection, to punish treason and rebellion, to seize and confiscate property of rebels, and for other purposes,' approved July 17, 1862, and which sections are in the words and figure following :

"SEC. 9.—And be it further enacted, That all slaves of persons who shall hereafter be engaged in rebellion against the Government of the United States, or who shall in any way give aid or comfort thereto, escaping from such persons and taking refuge within the lines of the army, and all slaves captured from such persons, or deserted by them and coming under the control of the Government of the United States, and all slaves of such persons found on (or being within) any place occupied by rebel forces and afterwards occupied by the forces of the United States, shall be deemed captures of war, and shall be forever free of their servitude, and not again held as slaves.

"SEC. 10.—And be it further enacted, That no slave escaping into any State, Territory, or the District of Columbia, from any of the States, shall be delivered up, or in any way impeded or hindered of his liberty, except for crime or some offence against the laws, unless the person claiming said fugitive shall first make oath that the person to whom the labor or service of such fugitive is alleged to be due is his lawful owner, and has not been in arms against the United States in the present rebellion, nor in any way given aid and comfort thereto; and no person engaged in the military or naval service of the United States shall, under any pretence whatever, assume to decide on the validity of the claim of any person to the service or labor of any other person, or surrender up any such person to the claimant, on pain of being dismissed from the service.

"And I do hereby enjoin upon and order all persons engaged in the military and naval service of the United States to observe, obey and enforce within their respective spheres of service the act and sections above recited.

"And the Executive will in due time recommend that all citizens of the United States who shall have remained loyal thereto throughout the rebellion shall (upon the restoration of the constitutional relation between the United States and their respective States and people, if the relation shall have been suspended or disturbed) be compensated for all losses by the acts of the United States, including the loss of slaves.

"In witness whereof I have hereunto set my hand and caused the seal of the United States to be affixed.

"ABRAHAM LINCOLN.

"Done at the city of Washington, this twenty-second day of September, in the year of our Lord one thousand eight hundred and sixty-two, and of the independence of the United States the eighty-seventh.

"By the President:
"WILLIAM H. SEWARD,
"Secretary of State."

After this proclamation, the first day of the following year arrived, and as the promise had been given in a solemn manner, and the rebellion, instead of ceasing as had been hoped, had increased in extent and power, endangering the constitutional existence of the loyal States, in order not to undo what had already been done in its aggressive procedures, the supreme magistrate of the nation issued his second proclamation, in the following terms:

"Whereas, on the twenty-second day of September, in the year of our Lord one thousand eight hundred and sixty-two, a proclamation was issued by the President of the United States, containing, among other things, the following, to wit:

"That on the first day of January, in the year of our Lord one thousand eight hundred and sixty-three, all persons held as slaves within any State or designated part of a State, the people whereof shall then be in rebellion against the United States, shall be then, thenceforth and forever free, and the Executive Government of the United States, including the military and naval authority thereof, will recognize and maintain the freedom of such persons, and will do no act or acts to repress such persons or any of them in any effort they may make for their actual freedom.

"That the Executive will, on the first day of January aforesaid, by proclamation, designate the States and parts of States, if any, in which the people therein respectively shall then be in rebellion against the United States; and the fact that any State or the people thereof shall on that day be in good faith represented in the Congress of the United States by members chosen thereto at elections wherein a majority of the qualified voters of such State shall have participated, shall, in the absence of strong countervailing testimony, be deemed conclusive evidence that such State and the people thereof are not then in rebellion against the United States.

"Now, therefore, I Abraham Lincoln, President of the United States, by virtue of the power in me vested as Commander-in-Chief of the army and navy of the United States, in time of actual armed rebellion against the authority and government of the United States, and as a fit and necessary war measure for suppressing said rebellion, do, on this first day of January, in the year of our Lord one thousand eight hundred and sixty-three, and in accordance with my purpose so to do publicly proclaimed for the full period of one hundred days from the day of the first above mentioned order, and designate as the States and parts of States wherein the people thereof respectively are this day in rebellion against the United States the following, to wit:

"Arkansas.
"Texas.
"Louisiana—except the parishes of St. Bernard, Plac-

quemines, Jefferson, St. John, St. Charles, St. James, Ascension, Assumption, Terre Bonne, Lafourche, St. Mary, St. Martin and Orleans. including the city of New Orleans.

" Mississippi.
" Alabama.
" Florida.
" Georgia.
" South Carolina.
" North Carolina and
" Virginia—except the forty-eight counties, designated as West Virginia, and also the counties of Berkeley, Accomac, Northampton, Elizabeth City, York, Princess Ann and Norfolk, including the cities of Norfolk and Portsmouth, and which excepted parts are, for the present, left precisely as if this proclamation were not issued.

" And, by virtue of the power and for the purpose aforesaid, I do order and declare that all persons held as slaves within said designated States and parts of States are and henceforward shall be free ; and that the Executive Government of the United States, including the military and naval authorities thereof, will recognize and maintain the freedom of said persons.

" And I hereby enjoin upon the people so declared to be free to abstain from all violence, unless in necessary self-defence ; and I recommend to them that in all cases, when allowed, they labor faithfully for reasonable wages.

" And I further declare and make known that such persons, of suitable condition, will be received into the armed service of the United States, to garrison forts, positions, stations and other places, and to man vessels of all sorts in said service.

" And upon this, sincerely believed to be an act of justice, warranted by the Constitution, upon military necessity, I invoke the considerate judgment of mankind and the gracious favor of Almighty God.

" In witness whereof I have hereunto set my hand and caused the seal of the United States to be affixed.

" Done at the city of Washington, this first day of January, in the year of our Lord one thousand eight hundred and sixty-three, and of the independence of the United States of America the eighty-seventh.

"ABRAHAM LINCOLN.

" By the President :

" WILLIAM H. SEWARD,
" Secretary of State."

The importance which these documents have towards the end which I propose to myself in writing this work, obliges me to carefully analyse them in their legal foundations, and in all the points of real transcendency which are therein contained or which may result from them. And since it was for the sake of the inviolability of the federal Constitution that they were issued, let us examine how far they are in conformity with the law which they invoke.

The political federation of several sovereign States, for such is the real nature of the Union constituted among the thirteen States which declared their independence of England, and those which, afterwards, joined the said Federation, does not destroy nor injure the special laws of each, as these are absolutely independent of the Constitution which serves to bind them together, guaranteeing their respective rights. This principle gains two-fold strength when it is considered that all attacks made against the institution of slavery in the slave States, which is protected by their respective constitutions, are not only attempts against the integrality of that bond which regulates the harmony of the Federation, but also aim a deadly blow at the interests of said slave States. In this estimation, the measure proclaimed by the executive of the Republic, on the 22d of September, 1862, and confirmed on the 1st of January, 1863, which was adopted to punish the attempt made against the federal Constitution by those who proclaimed themselves independent of it, is, to say the least, as unconstitutional as the very act which it attempts to punish, and therefore lacks the moral strength which would be necessary to render it a salutary measure.

The suppositions that it is an act of justice, authorized by the Constitution as a *military necessity*, will not be held by any reasonable mind, since, with this act, the material strength of the federal army was not increased, nor was that of the secessionists diminished; the situation of the ranks in the former was not bettered, and the resources of war of the latter were not destroyed. Such measures as a military necessity might constitutionally authorize, might have been instituted, such as, for instance, the enrolment of negroes as soldiers, wherever the authority of the President could be enforced, a war tax levied upon the property which these negroes represent, or their removal to other posts, according as expediency might demand for the furtherance of military operations.

And since it was with no such intentions that these proclamations were issued, their tendencies ought to be considered purely political, and, consequently, contrary to the federal Constitution, in defense of which they were dictated.

With equal and even more forcible arguments might this measure be censured, in a legal point, showing inconsistencies in each of its phases, and an unlawful procedure in the whole. However, as this is not a part of my design, let me proceed at once to consider its effects.

What were the intentions of the Federal Government, upon issuing the first proclamation?

This question brings up a thousand others, which have been decided by actual events in the most unsatisfactory manner.

Some people believed that the South would become discouraged by the proclamation; as if the history of the world had ever presented a single case where a rebellion has been put down by a mere threat which could not possibly be carried out! On the contrary, it merely gave an additional proof, to the wealthy planters of the South, of the pernicious influence which the abolitionists exercised over the executive power of the Republic; and, as this dangerous influence destroyed, in the South, all desires and even all hopes of a constitutional reconciliation, the said document served only to strenthen them in their spirit of disunion and in their determination to organize a still greater resistance. For this reason the operations of the war, from that time, took a still more disastrous aspect, the army of the South having been reinforced in such a manner as to enable them to make powerful invasions into the North, and to make protracted defenses in their fortifications as well as on the battlefield; for this reason the flattering expectations which had been entertained by those who hoped, in good faith and with feelings of fraternity, for the submission of the South, have since then been utterly abandoned, notwithstanding the brilliant triumphs achieved in Pennsylvania by the Northern army.

These proclamations did not even serve to satisfy public opinion among the Federals, for I have already shown that the majority of these were not abolitionists.

Thus it was that, on the appearance of the first proclamation, so much was said against the government, in almost all the papers in the Union, that in similar circumstances the sentiments of opposite factions have rarely agreed so unanimously; and this was owing to the fact that the proclamation which abolished slavery in those regions where its power did not reach, allowed it to exist where it might have been enforced; thus the conservatives attacked it as radical; the radicals condemned it as conservative, and everybody considered it imprudent and useless, with the exception of a few interested officials.

Even if, as some have suspected, and I believe, these proclamations had been issued with an international political end, they would still appear unreasonable, since they did not resolve anything in decided terms, and consequently were not admitted as useful by the government of Great Britain, as they might otherwise have been. And the opinion which has been expressed as to the intention of the said proclamation, viz.: the prevention of the national recognition of the South by the European powers, by flattering England through its abolitionist exigencies, is not founded upon slight grounds, being confirmed by the English ministry, that is to say, by a dispatch of Lord Russell to the representative of that nation at Washington, which is written in the following terms:

"EARL RUSSELL TO LORD LYONS.

"Foreign Office, January 17, 1863.

"My Lord—The proclamation of the President of the United States, enclosed in your lordship's despatch of the 2d inst., appears to be of a very strange nature.

"It professes to emancipate all slaves in places where the United States authorities cannot exercise any jurisdiction nor make emancipation a reality; but it does not decree emancipation of slaves in any, States or parts of States occupied by federal troops, and subject to United

States jurisdiction, and where, therefore, emancipation, if decreed, might have been carried into effect.

"It would seem to follow that in the border States, and also in New Orleans, a slave owner may recover his fugitive slave by the ordinary process of law, but that in the ten States in which the proclamation decrees emancipation, a fugitive slave arrested by legal warrant may resist, and his resistance, if successful, is to be upheld and aided by the United States authorities and the United States armed forces.

"The proclamation, therefore, makes slavery at once legal and illegal, and makes slaves either punishable for running away from their masters, or entitled to be supported and encouraged in so doing, according to the locality of the plantation to which they belong, and the loyalty of the State in which they may happen to be.

"There seems to be no declaration of a principle adverse to slavery in this proclamation. It is a measure of war, and a measure of war of a very questionable kind.

"As President Lincoln has twice appealed to the judgment of mankind in his proclamation, I venture to say I do not think it can or ought to satisfy the friends of abolition, who look for total and impartial freedom for the slave, and not for vengeance on the slave owner.

"I am, etc. RUSSELL."

In order to demonstrate how unanimous were the sentiments entertained by everybody with respect to the inconsistency contained in the proclamations, and exposed in the foregoing dispatch of Lord John Russell, I ought to mention that one of the most eminent men in the South, universally renowned for his great talents and public character, said in answer to various consultations of mine upon the subject, what I here copy:

"As to the antagonism manifested between the Southern and Northern States, allow me to observe that slavery has nothing whatever to do with the disagreements which have given place to the furious contest resulting from it.

"It is well known that the rapid progress made in the Northern States, in their population and industry, are due only to the extraordinary ingress of foreigners, who are attracted to its soil by the advantages afforded by its political institutions and the prospects afforded by its boundless territories. Nevertheless, while these States were thus increasing in power and influence in the councils of the nation, they also began to unfold a tendency to oppress the weaker States, and to monopolize, exclusively, the advantages accrueing from the federal mechanism, entirely disregarding the interests and rights of the latter, while their arrogance and oppression ever increased, until the abuses and exactions arising from them became so intolerable, that the only resource left to the Southern States was to revolt against them, claiming a separation from, and an independence of, a Union which denied them an equal participation in the common advantages.

"The violence done to the federal Constitution by the Northern States is what has sundered the links which bound them to the South. Let it not be said that the slave question is at all involved in the gigantic struggle carried on between the South and the North.

"As a proof against this supposition, see how the South willingly sacrifices slavery and slaves, rather than submit to the Northern yoke, when the latter guarantees both to them, in case of their submission; whilst the North, which is so ready to liberate the slaves who are not in their dominion, encourages with the prospect of continued slavery the loyalty of the States where the federal authority still prevails."

I think that the illustrious republican, whose name I withhold, very much against my will, as I am not authorized to publish it, is mistaken in his idea that the slave question is not connected with the war, as this idea might be triumphantly combated with what has already been said relative to the mechanism of the Federation, by which each State makes its own laws, independent of the rest, and with facts and antecedents which are publicly and universally known. Perhaps, since the issuing of the proclamations, which, instead of reconciling, have been the means of further disuniting the two sections, which were engaged in a furious struggle owing to the slave question, the South has decided to give to their cause a force and an aspect quite foreign to the original question; as was correctly explained by Lord Lyons to Lord Russell in a despatch dated Washington the 13th of January, saying: "The emancipation proclamation has disgusted many, has made still more doubtful the possibility of any other result to the war, whenever it may end, than separation." It is evident that we cannot avoid the slave question if we wish to bring up the antecedents of the war, or to establish the foundation of a solid, just and lasting peace.

For the rest, I may add that the aforesaid letter was written in Havana on the 25th of January 1863, that is to say, eight days after the despatch of Lord John Russell to the English Minister at Washington; and, consequently, the ideas expressed in one could not have been copied from the other, unless we might suppose a suspicious understanding to exist between the most influential persons of the South and the Government of Great Britain.

If some regard be had to these explanations, which justify the responsibility attributed to the abolitionists, of being the promoters of the civil war which is destroying this nation, and also a brief analysis of the great disasters suffered by this same nation in all its public phases, since the unfortunate insurrection at Harper's Ferry, the great statesmen and potentates of the world will have to be very careful to ultimately resolve the negro question with deeper reflection and greater caution than they have yet employed.

Upon this very ground, now the bloody theater of the most horrible tragedy ever presented to the political world with the attributes of war, I am analyzing this question, the fatal legacy bequeathed to the New World by civilization, I know not whether through the obstinate philanthropy of a celebrated friar, now almost deified in the estimation of the unthinking, who undertook to secure the indolent repose of the Indians at the cost of the slavery of the negroes; or on account of the climate in the tropics of the Western hemisphere, which renders the cultivation of the soil impossible to any laboring agents less robust than the Africans. I am hardly able to enter more circumstancially into this analysis, although I am not naturally faint hearted; and were I to give the results of the analysis with mathematical exactness, they would undoubtedly overwhelm the mind of the reader, and cause him to shun the sight of these lines with horror.

It is undoubtedly for this cause, which is in itself justifiable owing to the respect due to public sentiment, even though it may be prejudicial to historical exactness, that all writers who have wished briefly to demonstrate the injuries caused by this great question, have touched upon the subject very lightly and with faint coloring. It is also for this reason that I, concealing all violent emotions in order not to transmit them to others, will avail myself, firstly, of other expositions which are certainly worthy of credit, coming, as we will presently show, from interested parties; after which I will, with the promised circumspection, give some numerical data which I have myself collected.

"THE AWFUL CONDITION OF THE COUNTRY.—WHO ARE RESPONSIBLE?

" Three years ago this country was the envy of the world. Thirty millions of people of all classes, conditions, religions and nativities were living happily together under the freest government upon the face of the earth. The poor and the oppressed of all nations found a refuge upon our shores. Our flag was known and respected in every land and on every sea. Our commerce bore to distant climes the products of our soil and of our manufactures, and brought us in exchange all the comforts and luxuries we could desire. To be an American citizen was so great an honor that even the aristocrats of Europe showed us especial favors and treated our representatives with distinguished consideration. We had just sent France her Emperor, and Italy her Liberator, after having received and protected these illustrious exiles. The future King of England had visited us to see for himself the supreme greatness and happiness of a free people under a government of their own choice. Peace, contentment and prosperity at home—admiration, envy and honor abroad—in these words is pictured the condition of the United States three years ago.

" To-day one half the country is in rebellion against the government. Three hundred thousand American soldiers are arrayed against each other around the national capital. The loyal armies are destroying public and private property at the South, and the rebel armies are invading and devastating the North. The flames of burning towns and villages are answered by the red glare of burning ships. Our commerce is almost totally destroyed, and what is left of it has abandoned our flag and sought safety beneath the British ensign. Rebel pirates infest the seas, ravage our coasts and dare to enter our harbors. Fifty millions of dollars worth of property was destroyed or captured in Maryland and Pennsylvania last week, and our losses elsewhere are double that sum. Thousands of brethren who lived in amity and peace three years ago have since been slain by fratricidal hands and now sleep beneath the sod. The national currency has depreciated until gold is at an enormous premium. The necessaries of life command extravagant prices. Our manufactures have ceased almost entirely in some sections of the country, and in others are kept in feverish activity only by the demands of the war. In one of our largest cities business is suspended that the citizens may arm to meet the rebel invasion. Peculation, embezzlement and corruption are rioting in official circles. A few hundred of men without souls are becoming amazingly rich, while the masses of the people suffer. Our statesmen have degenerated into scheming, thieving politicians. The national debt, already large, is daily and hourly increased by war expenditures, and knavish hands are diligently engaged in robbing the Treasury in a thousand ways. Such is the awful condition of the Republic. Who are responsible?

"Thirty years ago a few fanatics began the agitation about the negro. It is now a matter of history that, if this agitation had not occurred, slavery would have died a natural death in most of the Southern States, as it did in New York, New Jersey and elsewhere. These fanatics came originally from New England. It was believed in olden times that Boston and its vicinity was under the curse of God for its Puritanical persecutions. With this curse the New England fanatics have infected the nation. After preparing the way by tracts, lectures and sermons, the abolition faction dragged the negro into politics. The Southern slaveholders resented this attempt to deprive them of their property. The extremists of both sections joined hands in the infamous work of dividing and destroying the country. Through its successive stages, like some foul disease, this abolition conspiracy against the Union can be traced by the impartial historian. All sorts of remedies were attempted; but all failed, because they were merely temporary and did not aim at the extermination of the disorder. The great men of the nation passed away, uttering fearful warnings of impending danger. At last the crisis came. A set of unscrupulous politicians gave the abolitionists the opportunity they desired, and a sectional party seized the reins of government. Goaded to madness by the inflammatory appeals of Southern fire-eaters, one slave State after another left the Union. The abolitionists encouraged and applauded this movement and trampled under foot all proposals for reunion. Awed by the patriotic outburst of the people when Sumter was attacked, the fanatics at first acquiesced in the war for the Union; but, having control of the government, they soon managed to transform the contest into a war against slavery. Led on by Sumner, Wade, Wilson, Chandler, Greely, Cheever, Garrison, Wendell Phillips and other such madmen, the abolitionists rejected all means of conciliation and endeavored to crush out every spark of Union sentiment at the South. Their threats, speeches, resolutions and acts of Congress at last culminated in emancipation proclamations. The Constitution of the United States was torn to tatters. The South was united, and the North divided. Our best generals were removed because they would not subscribe to the abolition creed. Victory then left our banners and perched upon the rebel standard. The war is no longer a war to subdue the secessionists or to annihilate the slaveholders, but a bitter struggle for the existence of the nation. For all this the abolitionists are responsible. Their leaders still walk in high places and fill their pockets from the national Treasury, and their journals are still supported by official patronage and government contracts; but the end of these things is at hand. Cowed by the infernal storm they have raised, these fanatics now cry out for help against the rebel invasion, and preach that the duty of the hour is to forget the past and save the country. This delusive call has been heard once too often. The duty of the hour is to remember and to punish. First, let the rebels be defeated and driven back, and then, without hesitation or delay, let those Northern abolition traitors, who are responsible for the rebellion and for the success it has achieved, be held to a strict and final account."

Thus did one of the most widely circulated papers in the United States, the New York *Herald*, express itself a short time ago, when the result of the sanguinary encounter which took place in Pennsylvania, in July 1863, between the belligerent armies, had not yet transpired. With the exception of the references to political parties, the same could have been said by all the other papers in the Republic, since such is the true state of affairs, in whatever manner it may be related.

And now, entering into some details which the Herald purposely omitted, I can further add, with official data, that the war in the United States, at the aforesaid date, had already cost the Republic a loss of nearly six hundred thousand men, who died on the battle field and in the hospitals, to which number, which is truly awful when we consider that it consists of the flower of the land, the youths, who are most needed for the reproduction of future generations and the requirements of labor, we must add two hundred thousand men who have been totally disabled by wounds.

Well then: estimating the population of both sections of the former Confederation at thirty millions, without taking into account the floating population, separating one half, which are females, and dividing the other half into three equal parts, the result will be five millions of men between the ages of twenty and forty, which are the best years of life; and, moreover, supposing that, from the beginning of July, from which time the computation is made, until March 1864, which will complete the third year of the war, two hundred thousand men will have been killed and disabled, that is to say, in three years a decrease of a million of men, it will become evident that in so short a period the war has destroyed twenty per cent of the best citizens. Add to this the decrease in the population from the fact that foreigners no longer come here to be naturalized, and many of those who had already settled here have repented the step and left the country, as also from the natural diminution of births, the number of widows being already very great, and this fifth part, of relative losses, may be considered as positive losses so soon as the estimates shall be completed.

As man is the originator of all prosperity, from the estimates made of the population, it would be easy to deduct, in a proportionate scale, the damage to public and private wealth, if it were not that the immense devastations of the war do not allow us to form any correct estimate.

In the North American Republic the wealth would have decreased one fifth, at the same rate as the working population, for the want of these last in the productive labors; if it were not that to the million of men killed and disabled, we ought to add another million, at least, of men employed in the war and who consequently cannot work. That is to say, the productive forces of the country have lost, in the space of three years, forty per cent of their original importance, there having been no standing military force before the war, and the army being now entirely composed of the working classes. Besides this, let us add the cities which are in ruins, the ships laden with merchandize which have been burned at sea by the privateers, the railroads and magnificent bridges which have been destroyed through the stratagetic necessity of the belligerent armies, the enormous quantities of the agricultural produce which have been destroyed in order to prevent their falling into the hands of the invaders, and all the accumulation of horrors and extermination brought on by war, and then we will see how bitterly humanity may lament over the ruins of a fertile land and of a civilized nation, the short-sightedness of some statesmen and the infamous exactions made by the philanthropical ideas of a criminally fanatical sect.

From the slight sketch which I have just drawn, (slight indeed in comparison with reality), no one will wonder that the official revenues of the Government treasury at Washington should have decreased in an incredible manner. And as when the war is aggressive it cannot be maintained without money; though it is very different when it is in the defensive, for then privations and valor vie with each other with strange emulation, which effects wonders, it will not appear surprising, but on the contrary very natural that the country which until within three years enjoyed unexampled prosperity, should now find itself on the brink of absolute discredit.

The debt of the Federal Government amounted to seventy six millions and one hundred thousand dollars, on the 7th of March 1861, a date to be deplored by all human sentiment, not on account of Lincoln's election as President of the Republic having then take place, but because it is analogous with the rupture between the North and South of the Confederation in the midst of the clash of arms. From that date until the 30th of June 1863, which is the termination of the fiscal year acording to the laws of the United States, that debt was increased to one thousand two hundred millions of dollars, making it sixteen times greater than it was before; and as the estimates of expenditures as well as the receipts for taxation and other sources have been pretty well conjectured for the present year, the *minimum* of the federal debt at the end of this fiscal year can be ascertained in a positive manner, to be no less than two thousand two hundred millions, or twenty nine times greater than when the war broke out. From these figures, which represent a great part of the entire wealth of the country, arose, as might well be expected, the discredit of the Government funds, and although the paper money which represents them, has fluctuated from eighteen to seventy-two per cent discount on the value of gold, it may now be said, to have settle down to about half or a little more of its nominal value, which is what the official credit of the United States now represents in its home and foreign commerce.

I will end this chapter by repeating to my readers the opinion which I have emitted and will sustain, that the principal cause of this devastation is the negro question and that all others are only secondary.

On the 22nd of September 1862, when the civil war in North America, had lasted a year and a half, the paper money of the Federal Government was at two per cent discount for gold. The first proclamation of Mr. Lincoln against slavery was published on that day, and from that time until January 1863, which was when the second proclamation was published, the paper money suffered an extraordinary depreciation of *forty two per cent!*........

CHAPTER XI.

Anarchy begins to manifest itself in the Northen States.—Political parties into which the federals are divided, and the principles that each profess.—Brief sketch of their respective political history.—Their characters in the present war.—Dangerous changes produced by the war on the public customs of the country.—Supremacy of the military over the political institutions of the Republic.—Famous outrage of General Burnside against Representative Vallandigham.—Commotion produced by the deed in all the States.—Demonstrations in favor of peace made by the democrats to check the progress of military despotism.—Famous meeting in New York on the 18th of May 1863.—Attitude of the Governor of the State in favor of said meeting.—Demonstrations in opposition by the dominant party.—Means of which the government avails itself to annul the combinations of the partisans of peace.—New treaty with England concerning the negroes.—The invasion of Maryland and Pensylvania by the confederates coincides with all that has been said.—The exasperation of the political parties of the North in presence of the common danger.—Triumphs of the federals in the war.—Republican meeting in opposition to the democrats.—Some emisaries of the London Abolitionists take part in these irritating demonstrations.—The conscription of three hundred thousand men.—Reasons why it was decreed, and manner in which the interested parties explain it.—Riot in New York.—Horrors of anarchy.—Horrible persecution and murder of negroes as a natural result of so many aberrations.

As if sufficient disgrace and confusion had not already been brought upon the moral and physical elements of the world by this question, into the mysterious intricacies of which I dare not at times penetrate, wondering if it has not been providentially so ordained, to perplex our minds, confuse our judgment, involve truth in darkness when it ought to shine with the greatest splendor, and in fact, to turn light into shadow, harmony into discord, peace into strife, and public prosperity into ruins. I repeat, as if these dreadful mistakes, the correction of which has been submitted to the logic of arms, thus robbing human reason of one of its highest attributes, had not been sufficiently calamitous, another evil still more disastrous than any of the preceding, worse than war, and infinitely greater than any scourge which God has inflicted upon his creatures since the deluge, anarchy with all its horrors has lifted its head, in these regions of North America, eager for extermination, and originating in the same cause—the negro question. . . .

Titus Libius said some centuries ago :—"*Nulla magna civitas dinquiescere potest*"—no popular city can long preserve its tranquility.[1]

For this cause Rome perished, and Carthage was annihilated ; Tyre and Sydon disappeared from the face of the earth ; Greece fell into insignificance, and of Sparta scarcely a recollection remains in history. For this cause the people of Israel became Deicides, lost the homes of their fathers, and were scattered as wanderers among the nations of the world ; they have lost their original faith, and shall never be reunited as a nation. Also, for the same cause, in modern times, the importance of the emporiums of commerce—the Levant, Pisa, Geneva and Venice, lost their glory, and from the summit of greatness fell into slavery. And scientific Portugal and conquering Spain, who distributed empires east and west, bounded by conventional lines, were in their turn dismembered and almost divided ; for such in this world is the natural law of things among nations as well as among individuals. But, although the same was to be expected, some say, in this gigantic Republic of North America, because ambitious and eager to extend its dominions it wished to renew the times of Atila on this continent, invading, like the Scythians, nations of other races towards the South, who differ from them in their customs and their laws, still no one could have imagined that the hour of desolation had already arrived, nor could the most experienced persons conceive the idea of such a dreadful chaos, though they may have anticipated the approach of a local disruption which was liable to be brought about on account of the negroes.

I might here take up the relation of the calamities which the abolitionists have brought upon magnificent centres of prosperity and upon this great nation, in direct

---

(1) Lib. Eod.

opposition to the sentiment by which they are actuated, but I will not offend my readers by supposing that they have already consigned to oblivion the facts already advanced, which undoubtedly are vividly impressed in their memory. Having premised this explanation I shall proceed to give the history of new misfortunes which succeeded those already mentioned, and venture on prophecies of future and greater calamities if peace does not speedily heal the dangerous wounds which threaten to destroy the existence of the social body, and prevent its complete dissolution.

And as such a narration would not be comprehensive without some illustrative digressions, the reader will permit me to explain several antecedents of the new phase of this momentous question, in order that he may know to whom to attribute the responsibility of the events that are now transpiring, and draw correct inferences therefrom.

The Federal Republic has been divided for a long time into two parties, each one being composed of various opinions, which were also subdivided among themselves; and it is said that this difference of opinion is necessary to secure the perfect harmony of the system. One is called the Radical Republican, and is opposed to slavery; the other is the Democratic party, which has reasonably conservative tendencies, and to the latter belonged all the political men of the slave States.

For many years the Democratic party controlled the Administration, selecting at will, the Presidents of the Republic, and having always a majority in both Houses of Congress in their interest. Foreseeing that the time might come when the official preponderance would be transferred to the other party, as it did not depend upon material but upon purely political interests, which are proverbially unstable, the Southern States, following up the absorbing ideas of the Democratic party, conquered Texas, carrying slavery into it, attacked Cuba with the intention of annexing that island, because slavery existed there also; gained over the good will of a portion of the Mexican people who were anxious to be identified with the United States, and even desirous of giving up to them some of their large territories; and lastly, attempted by a clever but badly executed stroke, to implant their power in Central America, in order that their supremacy might remain unimpeached and that their control over the administrative power might be perpetuated.

This project, as was to be expected, failed in its greater part and brought upon the Republic open censure and international enmities, which were more or less concealed. And as the conscience of honorable people ever condemns the calculations of aggressive ambition when it affects the fame of a country, especially if said combinations prove unsuccessful, the Republican party had at length the prospect of seizing the executive power as a matter of conscience, in order to put a limit to the aggressive tendencies which caused so much harm to the external credit of the country.

I will not say that insidious counsels were permitted to regulate the course of the new Administration, for as human nature is ever inclined to extremes it rarely uses prudent foresight in the most important and difficult circumstances; but it can truly be assured that while the electoral triumph of the Republicans favored the tendencies of foreign abolitionists, their proceedings also contributed in an immense degree towards the expansion of the principles they advocated, and to the fears of all true Americans.

Had prudence presided over the acts of the new Administration, nothing would have been easier than to establish itself favorably in public opinion and consolidate its power, disapproving the external enterprises for which the Democratic party had obtained so much disfavor. But whether the electoral triumphs elated the Republicans more than was reasonable, or whether some secret enemies wished to give the death blow to the Republic by encouraging its anti-slavery tendencies, the fact is that menacing demonstrations were immediately made against the defeated party, and that from them resulted not only civil war, but the most inveterate hatred between the two factions, while all peaceable and loyal Republicans sided with the Democrats.

These feelings of inveterate aversion were nevertheless suppressed for a long time, for the safety of the Republic within the bounds of the Federal Constitution was the common aim of both parties. But the war which commenced with a fury which could not possibly have been foreseen, (for according to theories which have now proved falacious, the greatest amount of public liberties produce a proportionably sound civilization which makes itself known by its humanizing instincts), the war, I repeat, which was commenced in such a cruel manner was carried on with unceasing vigor until it became intolerable to humanity and to policy.

In the preceding chapter, in statistics which overwhelm the mind with horror, there are corroborative proofs of this truth, although they are not the only ones that exist in official documents and in private accounts which will some day figure in history.

When it is said that during three years of civil war, one million of men perished, besides more than a hundred generals on both sides,[1] when it is known that defenceless cities have been reduced to ruins, not because they resisted the invaders, for such was not the case, but because they belonged to the enemy; when itis read, with scandal to all moral sentiment, that *the conquerors stamped the wives and daughters of the vanquished with the seal of prostitution, in their private acts of brutality, and in their proclamations which they issued at the sound of the beating drums,[2] when the names of those tyrants who, disgracing the noble insignia of military authority, took the life of peaceful citizens in reprisals, and admitted substitutes for execution, drowning in blood the holiest family affections, are brought to light and held up to universal execration ; when all this is circumstantially published and true Americans blush at the degrading

---

(1) According to the data taken from the archives at Washington, before the invasion and the great battle fought in Pennsylvania iA July, 1863, the federal army had lost, since the commencement of the war, thirty-seven generals killed in battle, or who died from wounds therin received. In the subsequent engagements, eight more generals, also of the North, have been killed. Supposing the Confederate army to have suffered equal losses since the beginning of the war, and that by the completion of the third year others will have been killed, I do not think the computation of one hundred generals, killed in battle, will appear exaggerated.

(2) Not long since, in September of 1863, an enactment for the enrolment of soldiers was published in Arkansas, in the following form :

No compromise with the rebels ! No quarter for the bushwhackers ! Desolation shall tread in the steps of treason wheresoever the regiment may march. *Up to the work of death !* Wat Willis, of Louisiana, wants one hundred men who can live on half rations, and are willing to die before pay day ! . .

charges which they know cannot be denied, then it will be seen that we had reason in denouncing the military spirit which has been fostered by this war, and to call the civil war of the United States of America an intolerable evil to humanity.[1]

And that it is not less intolerable from a political point of view in a country that has ever been jealous of its liberties, cannot be denied, when we remember the history of all republican nations and observe the course of events under a philosophical aspect.

I can speak from experience, for I have seen in the United States of North America, individual free-will which heretofore has been so perfectly unrestrained and so absolutely independent of any other, repressed by the narrow limits of military ordinances. I have seen the strict enforcement of the principle of passive obedience to the voice of command, which however indispensable it may be to maintain discipline in armies, is extremely dangerous to the liberty of nations. I have seen manufactories converted into barracks; workshops into parks of artillery; public squares and markets into encampments, and the most elegant private residences into guard rooms, with full consent of the owners. From these transformations in a society which was once pacific, essentially laborious and industrious, where an army was not to be found on this side of the frontiers, and even there in very insignificant proportions, it may be that no real and positive dangers will redound against the institutions, whether the war be protracted or whether it be terminated before the end of the fourth year. But besides the facts which I have already enumerated, each of which is in itself a political threat, while combined they constitute an evil which cannot but have terrible consequences. I have seen the organs of public opinion demanding that their oponents shall be silenced—here, where the liberty of the press has been free from any restraint. . . .

Military glory, that dazzling delusion which serves to conceal the real horrors of war, and derives its lustre from the blood of its victims; the scourge of mankind, be-

---

(1) The author of this book was born in Spain when the civil war broke out between the liberals and royalists in 1820; and having entered the military profession in 1835, he enlisted in the Queen's troops and made a campaign of five years.

queathed to us by Cain, the opposer of science and progress, and the mortal foe of Christianity—military glory, I repeat, is now rapidly invading, at the sound of drums, the noble hearts of free men, to reduce them to the condition of slaves. I have also seen in the most populous cities of the United States, ovations such as were offered to Cæsar made to generals who had been but moderately successful. McClellan has been, and will always be considered of transcendental importance for the political good of the Republic only, because he has ably commanded the military hosts. Meade, who a short time since was scarcely known, except in his brigade, has already been openly designated for the presidency; not because he has distinguished himself as a legislator,or proved himself an excellent Republican, but because he has triumphed over his enemies in a tremendous battle, on three successive days.

And thus, considering men and things in relation to this danger, which has altered the appearance of so many great cities preparatory to their destruction by tyranny, it will not be wondered at that when the despotism of camps openly proclaimed itself and endeavored to subdue the spirit of the citizens, the one being represented in the memorable outrage by General Burnside, and the other in the eloquent words of Senator Vallandigham,[1] when he

---

(1) In order that these facts may be known with more accuracy without accumulating them in the body of this work, I will here insert the narration of the case, as it was given by *La Cronica de Nueva York* in the following paragraphs;

"Public attention is now concentrated upon an event of considerable importance, the result of which it is impossible to foresee, although almost all our cotemporaries are of opinion that it may well be the cause of civil war in the North itself. It is known that General Burnside after being recalled from the chief command of the army of the Potomac, was appointed Commanding General of the State of Ohio, where he soon made himself notorious for the rigor of his measures. One of them was a definite prohibition to write, speak or express any ideas contrary to the course taken by the Government or the acts of the abolitionists, under penalty of transportation, imprisonment or death, according to the circumstances of the case.

"A representative of Ohio, Mr. Clement L. Vallandigham, a strong democrat, one of the most strenuous champions of the peace faction, and a candidate for the office of governor of his native state, delivered a speech at Mount Vernon, on the 30th of April, attacking with the greatest vehemence the acts of General Burnside, qualifying them as arbitrary and impolitic. This was violating with premeditation, the above order, and said General, exercising his authority, ordered the arrest of the offender,

spoke in favor of the peace of the Republic, the most far seeing men (I will not say the best, for fear of giving offence to the less clear sighted), rose up at once and unanimously joined in protesting against that outrage, as a forerunner of greater ones, being as it was a declaration of military despotism, the legitimate consequence of war, the logic of camps and the inevitable result of an authority constituted upon the principle of blind obedience. While this was happening, after two dreadful years of exterminating gloom, during which any word in favor of peace would have been useless, and not one among the contending parties had as yet dared to utter it, with what glorious satisfaction did I consider on my own grounds, the practical unfolding of the budding idea which had controlled me for some time past, which I emitted in conferences of almost a public character, defending it from incredulous prejudices, presenting it to the consideration of men of power among the belligerents, and discussing its basis in private conferences.

Oh! then I would not have exchanged, for all the wealth in the world, the happy anticipation of the realization of my hopes ; because, as a heavenly reward, ward, the words of the prophet, "How beautiful upon the mountains are the feet of him that bringeth good tidings, that publisheth peace ; that bringeth good tidings of good, that publisheth salvation," [1] resounded in my ears.

And then, considering that the manifestation of a portion of the public sentiment was practicable, I also believed that sooner or later we should certainly see the fulfilment of the prophecy, "And they shall beat their swords into plowshares, and their spears into pruning

---

which was surreptitiously carried into effect on the morning of the 5th instant, Mr. Vallandigham being at the time in his house at Dayton. No sooner did the friends of the prisoner become aware of it than they gathered *en masse*, made an attack, and endeavored to carry him off from the midst of the troops but were unsuccessful, and Mr. Vallandigham was conducted to Cincinnati as a criminal. The inhabitants of Dayton then rose up in revolt, cut the telegraph wires, set fire to the office of the abolitionist paper of that city and other buildings, the value of which is calculated to be $40,000, and destroyed the railroad bridge of Xenia. General Burnside, on his part, sent troops to Cincinnati and Columbus, declaring the counties of Dayton and Montgomery in a state of siege, by which measures, together with the arrest of thirty of the ringleaders, peace was at last re-established."

(1.) Isaiah, chap. lii., ver. 7.

hooks; nation shall not lift up sword against nation, neither shall they learn war any more." [1]

But let us return to the narration of facts, interrupted by this digression caused by my own enthusiasm, which, I am sure, the reader will understand and excuse; the outrage made by Burnside, was the forerunner of serious tumults which were then inaugurated on a small scale, and which broke out later with unmistakable symptoms of social dissolution, productive, nevertheless, of inestimable good, by making the idea of peace prevail unanimously in the different sentiments which had been variously held by the people, for want of some cause which should harmonize them, that cause being presented by the above mentioned outrage. For in most of the Northern States distant from the seat of war, and especially in that of New York, which being the most populous, is also the most influential in the course of events, large meetings of the democratic party were organized, not so much to protest against the oppressions of General Burnside, as to demand peace at all hazards.

The meeting which was held in the city of New York, on the 18th, of May, 1863, is of immense importance for the cause which is vindicated in this book ; but as a minute narration of its features would be foreign to the ends to which the present chapter leads, I shall confine myself for the present to stating that more than thirty thousand citizens were present, who adopted the following resolutions :

"Resolved, That the electors and people of the State of New York, who have hitherto professed the name and held to the principles known as democratic, desire to declare their unalterable attachment as well to those truths as to the constitution and amendments thereto, forming the supreme law of the land; that they regard obedience to the constitution as alike the duty of the citizen and the magistrate, and regard such obedience as the only means of perpetuating the Union, and by it the only hope of restoring the same.

"Resolved, That the sovereignty of the States and the sovereignty of the people, as laid down in the Virginia and Kentucky resolutions, of which Jefferson and Madison

---

(1.) Isaiah, chap. ii., ver. 4.

were the authors, are the fundamental principles of the democratic party; that they are the vital essence of the constitution, pervading every line and provision of that instrument, and to deny them would reduce our political federative system to anarchy or despotism. (Cheers.)

" Resolved, That under the constitution there is no power in the Federal Government to coerce the States, or any number of them, by military force. If power of coercion exists at all, it is a legal power and not military. That the democratic party, if true to its own time honored principles, cannot sustain a war against sovereign States ; that we believe it to be the duty of the party to proclaim these sentiments boldly, that the people may feel there is at least one political organization which will deal honestly, independently and truthfully with them.

" Resolved, That the war, in its inception and further continuance, being contrary to the constitution, must necessarily fast consume all the elements of union; and hence, that our duty as citizens, our obligations as men, and our relations to our common father, alike demand that an end should be put to what is repugnant to the law, abhorrent to the humanity and civilization of this enlightened era, and inconsistent with the benignant spirit of morality and religion. (Cheers.)

" Resolved, That attempts to do away with the provisions of the constitution, which point out the mode in which all crimes are to be punished, are high-handed violations of the sworn duties of our rulers, and that the participants in such a policy are guilty of aiming a blow at the very life of the supreme law.

" Resolved, That the claim of dictatorial and unlimited power, under the pretext of military necessity, and the trial of citizens not in the land or naval forces, or in the militia in actual service, by courts martial, are monstrous in theory and execrable in practice. (Applause.) That it is equivalent to an entire abrogation of the constitution and the erection in its place of a military despotism.

" Resolved, That the dogma of unlimited submission to the executive branch of the government is unworthy an American citizen, and inconsistent with the principles of constitutional liberty,—(cheers,)—that such a concession is rather suited to the dark and sullen era of feudal despotism than to a time when the rights of man are regarded even by monarchs, and we attribute this exhibition of abject servility as dictated by a spirit of fanaticism bent on effecting its object even at the sacrifice of personal liberty. (Hurrah.)

"Resolved, That we should be unworthy of the name of American citizens of this free and independent State, claiming the first rank among the sovereign components of the American Confederacy, if we did not protest against the cowardly, despotic, inhuman and accursed act which has consigned to banishment the noble tribune of the people—the Hon. Clement L. Vallandigham—(Cheers, the audience again rising in the utmost enthusiasm, 'Three cheers for Vallandigham,' and 'Three groans for Burnside,')—we protest against it in the name of liberty, in the name of humanity, and in the name of Washington. We hope the people of Ohio will have the opportunity of passing condemnation of this act by the election of Mr. Vallandigham as the next governor of the State. (Cheers.)

"Resolved, That thus believing, there can be no reliable security to persons or property pending this war, and that by its continuance the government itself will be utterly and irrovocably subverted, and that the South as well as the North must alike crumble into general ruin and devastation, we recommend, in the name of the people, that there be a suspension of hostilities between the contending armies of the divided sections of our country, and that a convention of the States composing the Confederate States, and a separate convention of the States still adhering to Union, be held to finally settle and determine in what manner and by what mode the contending sections shall be reconciled, and appealing to the Ruler of all for the rectitude of our intentions, we implore those in authority to listen to the voice of reason, of patriotism, and of justice. (Cheers.)

"Resolved, That to the end that our principles thus publicly avowed may be practically carried out, and that a State authority emanating directly from the people may exist, to call any future conventions of the peace democracy, if it shall become expedient or necessary, and disclaiming any intention to distract the democratic organization in this State so long as it shall reflect the sentiments of the masses, the following named gentlemen, representing each Congressional district, are appointed as a State Committee for that purpose, with full power to take such action in behalf of the success of our principles as may seem to them just and proper."

In this meeting were read a great many letters of adherence, written by persons of distinction belonging to the democratic party, but among them all none were so significant as that of the Governor of the State, Horatio Seymour, addressed to a previous meeting held in Albany, not only on account of the official position of that gentleman, but for the energetic and menacing frankness with which it was written, as the reader can judge for himself:

"EXECUTIVE DEPARTMENT, May 16, 1863.

"I cannot attend the meeting at the Capitol this evening, but I wish to state my opinion in regard to the arrest of Mr. Vallandigham. It is an act which has brought dishonor upon our country. It is full of danger to our persons and our homes. It bears upon its front a conscious violation of law and justice. Acting upon the evidence of detailed informers, shrinking from the light of day, in the darkness of night, armed men violated the home of an American citizen and furtively bore him away to military trial, conducted without those safeguards known in the proceedings of our judicial tribunals. The transaction involves a series of offences against our most sacred rights. It interfered with the freedom of speech; violated our rights to be secure in our homes against unreasonable searches and seizures; it pronounced sentence without trial, save one which was a mockery, which insulted as well as wronged. The perpetrators now seek to impose punishment, not for an offense against law, but for the disregard of an invalid order, put forth in utter disregard of the principles of civil liberty. If this proceeding is approved by the government and sanctioned by the people, it is not merely a step towards revolution—it is revolution; it will not only lead to military despotism—it establishes military despotism. In this aspect it must be accepted, or in this aspect rejected. If it is upheld, our liberties are overthrown, the safety of our persons, security of our property will hereafter depend upon the arbitrary will of such military rulers as may be placed over us, while our constitutional guarantees will be broken down. Even now the Governors and Courts of some of our Western States have sunk into insignificance before the despotic powers claimed and exercised by military men who have been sent into their borders. It is a fearful thing to increase the danger which now overhangs us by treating the law, the judiciary and the State authorities with contempt. The people of this country now wait with the deepest anxiety the decisions of the administration upon these acts. Having given it a generous support in the conduct of the war, we pause to see what kind of government it is for which we are asked to pour out our blood and our treasure. The action of the administration will determine in the minds of more than one-half of the people of the loyal States whether this war is waged to put down the rebellion at the South or to destroy free institutions at the North. We look for its decision with most solemn solicitude. " HORATIO SEYMOUR."

The great excitement and commotion with which the democratic party inaugurated the most significant of its political evolutions, against military despotism engendered by war, and then in favor of peace, as a natural consequence, caused the republicans to display equal activity in opposing their adversaries, by pursuing a contrary course. And, as the existence of this last party depends entirely on the principle of the abolition of slavery, it immediately hastened, through official, though indirect means, to promote the adoption of most violent measures against the South, by means of new international treaties which should be binding on the entire Republic; in which manner the republicans would not only effectually destroy the pacific manifestations of their adversaries, but, by rendering the basis, until then existing, for a decorous adjustment between the North and South impossible, they would make themselves all powerful in authority with the resources of war.

Owing to this, the *London Telegraph* announced to all the world, on the 2d of June, that a project was being discussed in both Houses, to demand for the Royal Navy the right of search under the flags of all nations on the coasts of Madagascar; and for this reason also, ten days after, this same ministerial organ, becoming the interpreter of Lord Palmerston, added: that a treaty had just been signed, between the United States and Great Britain, to establish mutually between the two nations the aforesaid right; from which it appears that the radical party of the federals had divested their immunity of its haughtiness, with the double object of placing an obstacle in the way of any peace project which should be proposed by the opposite party, and of preventing the Southern States from being acknowledged as a belligerent nation by the European powers.

Such was the state of things when some defeats suffered by the federal troops on the Potomac, and the urgent necessity for provisions and other resources which those of Lee's command were suffering, induced this general to make a powerful invasion into the Northern States; this he actually effected, resolutely and victoriously marching, with over one hundred thousand men, through Maryland and Pennsylvania, putting Philadelphia in peril and menacing the Capitol.

This event gave hopes to a great many, and filled the majorities with serious apprehensions, spreading universal alarm, which, although in some was but apparent, was visibly manifest to all. The fate of the Republic depended on the issue of a battle; and, as in situations of extreme danger, the least favored party never fail to reap advantages, the democratic party, owing to the ill success which had attended the efforts of a favorite of the radicals, made tumultuous demonstrations in favor of a renowned general, by whom they were to effect a reaction in the confidence of the government. And then, weighing the danger of the country and invoking a remedy as of extreme necessity, the opponents of the radical administration were not content with demanding in a menacing tone such measures as should contribute to their party aims, but, placing themselves on strategic grounds, in order to accommodate their position to subsequent results, they also gave vent to menaces, which they determined to carry out as soon as the common enemy should be repulsed.

"Let us rout and defeat the rebels first," said the *New York Herald* in an article which has been inserted in chapter X, "and then, without delay, let us exact a rigid and final account from the abolitionist traitors of the North, who are answerable for the rebellion and the triumps it obtained."

An officer who was then scarcely known, and who was chosen at a venture from among the subaltern generals, to take the chief command against the invading army, displayed the activity which is so important in military operations, and caused a terrible dissappointment to Lee; he sacrificed many victims to his country, it is true, but he also gave three days of victory to the federal army. Over an extension of thirty-three miles, are still heaped the bodies of those killed on the celebration of the anniversary of the national independence, and in that bloody field, which stretches to an almost boundless expanse, where not a tree has been left to lift its sheltering branches, every one having been uprooted by the iron which was belched forth from three hundred cannons of immense calibre, inconsolable mothers wander about, instinctively gathering up pieces of human flesh with the purpose of carrying home the remains of their sons!

The success of that dreadful day greatly encouraged the republicans. Who knows but what the democrats did not hope for adverse results, so as to overwhelm their enemies and make peace with the South!

But, happening as it did, the abolitionists had · their meetings also, and the churches were profaned by having the exclusiveness of parties and the passions of men discussed in them.

I have myself been a witness of this. How many sarcasms have been uttered there against the meetings held by the partizans of peace, how often has the epithet of traitor been hurled at them! And with what unparalled arrogance did they proclaim the unconditional submission of the South as obtainable solely through a war of extermination! Whilst these opinions were being developed, I can do no less than confess that my eyes have often dilated with wonder on looking on the place in which we were, as the subjects discussed by these clergymen were entirely inappropriate to the sanctity of a church.

There were no exaggerations that were not proclaimed, no folies that were not committed. In a church of Jersey City, I heard a venerable man, with white and flowing hair, his face showing the marks of more than seventy years, dressed as if for a feast, finish his discourse, after several jokes, with a very objectionable song. The audience applauded the wittiest parts, as if they were in a theatre, and when he concluded the last stanza, the air was rent with bravos, hurrahs, thunderings of canes, whistling and obstreperous bursts of laughter.

The sinister intentions of a disguised enmity was also heard in another church, under friendly appearances. The English abolitionists did not fail to take their places wherever the idea was discussed of inundating with blood the property which was founded on the labor of the negrees. And that I may convince my readers that I am not mistaken, let them see what the *New York Herald* of the 7th of July 1863 says, in giving the details of one of these meetings.

"On Sunday evening the Broadway Tabernacle (Rev. Dr. Thompson's) was well filled, to listen to an address upon English sympathy with anti-slavery in the United States, by Rev. Dr. Massie, of London, who comes as the representative of four thousand British ministers, with their protest against recognizing the slaveholders' confederacy, and their appeal for emancipation. Dr. Thompson briefly introduced Dr. Massie, who proceeded in a lengthy discourse to establish the sovereignty of God, the brotherhood of man, and the designs of Providence in making America the home of liberty, religion, and learning. He said he was ashamed that only four thousand British ministers signed the paper sympathizing with the United States in its conflict with slavery; but he affirmed that thousands withheld their signatures from misrepresentation, acting under the conviction that the American war had nothing to do with slavery. He showed that the interests of England and America were identical, and pointed out the difficulties under which the British people labored, among which was ignorance of the geography of the United States. Ministers had actually asked him to explain the difference between the terms "republican" and "democrat." He had addressed large audiences in Scotland and England, especially in Lancashire, and although some of the audience were working men, who had just come from the dockyards where piratical ships were being constructed, and hissed anti-slavery sentiments, not one accepted the challenge to defend the cause of the South. The vast majority of the people of England were in favor of the North, and earnestly looked for the abolition of slavery. Dr. Massie gave a detailed account of the great conference held in Manchester, where an address was adopted expressive of sympathy with the cause of the emancipation of the slave, which he read. It congratulated the United States on the abolition of slavery in the District of Columbia, the extinction of the slave trade, and the issuing of the President's proclamation.

"In conclusion, the address deprecated any retrograde action in reference to emancipation. Dr. Massie said he came to this country to plead the cause of justice to the negro citizen of the United States, and also as the friend of the slaveholder, that he might be delivered from the curse of power. He wished to gain the co-operation of America with England in diffusing the principles of the religion of Jesus Christ.

"After prayer the congregation was dismissed."

In short, and since the recent triumphs of the Federal arms, encouraged freedom of speech, all the accusations and threats which had been heard in the Democratic peace meetings against the other party were now flung back at them word for word.

From all this ill-disguised and ill-repressed anger, it was easy to guess the true state of their minds, and to forsee the disturbances which would break out on the first appearance of any real or imaginary offence. And as the spirit of evil is never idle, when not restrained with a strong hand, a prudent measure of a national character was taken as a pretext to fan into flames the destructive fire which had so long been smouldering within the Republic.

The arms of the French empire had just triumphed over the Republic of Mexico; re-establishing order in the interior by a new form of politics, well known to be a saving policy among the Latin race, though making the national independence very problematical. This European intervention introduced in the New World for the first time since its present nations became independent, so contrary to the famous Monroe doctrine, which is the creed of the Americans, and so contrary also to its official practices in respect to the countries of the other continent, did not have the best effect on the Federal administration, nor was it possible to let it pass unnoticed.[1] And as simulta-

---

[1] The American Government was so much on its guard with respect to the European intervention in Mexico, that in order to preserve its acions free from all casualties, it took special care not to compromise itself in other interventions, not even through diplomatic measures. The min-

neously with this intervention more direct, if not greater evils were threatened, (for the Emperor Napoleon did not disguise his intentions of recognizing the Confederacy of the South, and in England both Houses, and the other centres of public opinion, were making strenuous efforts to do likewise,) it was necessary for the Government at Wash-

istry of the other nations would have wished to take this strategic position by surprise, in order to form a precedent; and for this end, France, Spain and England, when they signed the compact, called upon the United States to join them, saying it was a matter of great importance to the Republic of the North. The compromise was evaded in Washington, as was to be expected; and afterwards the conflict with Poland having commenced, in a seemingly generous spirit which, it was said, sympathized with all liberal ideas, France, on her account, again invited the United States to join in strengthening with her powerful adhesion, the message agreed upon with England and Austria, to be sent to St. Petersburgh. The answer of the Federal Government is a model of its kind and says as follows:

"WASHINGTON, May 11, 1863.—M. Mercier has read to me and at my request has left me a copy of a dispatch, dated April 23, which he has received from M. Drouyn de Lhuys, and which refers to the important events now taking place in Poland and engaging the serious attention of the principal States of Western Europe. M. Mercier at the same time has communicated to me a copy of a dispatch relative to the same events, which has been addressed by M. Drouyn de Lhuys to the Embassador of France at St. Petersburg.

"By the first of these documents we learn that the step taken by the Cabinet of Paris with a view to exercising a moral influence upon his Majesty the Emperor of Russia, has received the approbation and the concurrence of the Cabinets of Vienna and London, and that the Emperor of the French, appreciating the value of our traditional sympathy for Poland on the one hand, and our ancient friendship for Russia on the other, would be happy to obtain the co-operation of the Government of the United States in this important question.

"Having taken counsel with the President, I am now able to communicate to you our views on this subject, for the information of M. Drouyn de Lhuys.

"The American Government is deeply sensible of this proof of the friendship of the Emperor of the French in asking its co-operation upon a subject doubly important in its relations to order and to humanity. It has been no less favorably impressed with the sentiments which the Emperor Napoleon has expressed in so delicate a manner at St. Petersburg, and with the appeal which he has made to the noblest of human sympathies. The enlightened and humane character of the Emperor of Russia, which has recently shown itself in the liberation of so large a number of serfs in his domains, gives us the assurance that this appeal will be accepted, and that it will meet at St. Petersburg with all the good will compatible with the general well-being of the vast States which the Emperor of Russia governs with so much wisdom and moderation.

"Nevertheless, notwithstanding the so favorable reception which we are disposed to give to the suggestion of the Emperor of the French, the American Government finds an insurmountable difficulty in associating itself, by any active co-operation, with the Cabinets of Paris, London and Vienna, as it requested.

ington either to neglect by a criminal indifference the importance of these events, or to take a decided attitude in the midst of its civil troubles, to prevent the consumation of the one and to remedy the effects of the other. Choosing the second extreme, as was natural, and taking advantage of those movements of sublime enthusiasm, in

---

"Having founded our institutions upon the rights of man, the founders of our Republic have always been regarded as political reformers, and it soon became evident that the revolutionists of all countries counted upon the effective sympathy of the United States, if not upon their active assistance and protection. Our noble Constitution had hardly been established when it became indispensable for the Government of the United States to examine to what degree it was compatible with our security and well-being to interfere in the political affairs of foreign States, whether by an alliance or any concerted action with other Powers, or otherwise. An urgent appeal of this kind was addressed to us with regard to France. This appeal was sanctioned by and acquired new strength from the treaty of alliance and mutual defence which then existed, and without which, it must be confessed to the honor of France, our sovereignty and independence would not have been so promptly secured.

"This appeal touched so profoundly the heart of the American people, that it was only the deference felt for the Father of his Country, then at the apogee of his moral greatness, that compelled it to declare that, in view of the condition of the Republic, of the character of its constituent parts, and especially the nature of its exceptional Constitution, the American people must confine itself to advancing the cause of progress in the world by exercising at home a wise power of self-government, but keeping aloof from all foreign alliance, intervention, or interference.

"It is true that Washington believed that a time would come when, our institutions being firmly consolidated and working harmoniously, we might safely take part in the deliberations of foreign Powers, to the general advantage of all nations. Since that time many occasions have arisen for departing from a rule which, at the first glance, might seem to be an inevitable cause of isolation. One was an invitation to join the Congress of the Spanish States of America, then just liberated. Another was the urgent appeal of Hungary to aid her in the recovery of her ancient and illustrious independence. Still another, the project to guarantee Cuba to Spain, conjointly with France and Great Britain. More recently, the invitation to co-operate with Spain, France and Great Britain in Mexico; and later still, the proposition of some of the Spanish American States to establish an international council for the Republican States of this continent. All these suggestions were, in succession, declined by our Government, and this decision was each time approved by the judgment of the American people. Our policy of non-intervention, however rigorous and absolute it may appear to others, has thus become a traditional policy, which ought not to be abandoned, except upon urgent occasions of a manifest necessity. It would be still less wise to deviate from it when a local, though we hope transitory insurrection deprives our Government of the advice of one part of the American people, to which so grave a deviation from the established policy would be far from being indifferent.

"The President does not doubt a moment that the Emperor Napoleon will see a proof of the deference for him and the French people as well as a desire to co-operate for the maintenance of peace and the progress of

which the triumphs of Meade, the fall of Vicksburg, the precarious state of Port Hudson, which at last surrendered to the beseigers, and the taking of some forts outside of Charleston, were being celebrated, the Federal Government ordered and commenced to carry out a draft of three hundred thousand men. The occasion was propitious it cannot be denied, if on the part of the opposing faction a pretext had not been made to deminish the preponderance acquired in so short a time by the Republicans, and if the economical necessities of the administration had not introduced into the official decree which I have just cited, some clauses, contrary to the perfect equality of all the citizens. For in fact, if Mr. Lincoln believed one hundred and fifty thousand men, added to three hundred thousand who are now under arms, would be sufficient to continue a series of the recent triumphs until the submission of the Southern States to the Federal Constitution was effected, and to be well prepared against the internal complications, he also calculated that this mass of consuming and unproductive people, enlisted under a certain character of perpetuity would need, for their maintainance, equipment, and armament, much greater sums than those existing, or likely to exist, in the public treasury.

---

humanity in Europe, in this fidelity to our traditional policy, the observance of which has contributed to our security, and, we hope, also to the interests of humanity."

I think that in the document which has just been inserted there is less of sincerity than of political tact, because the principle of non-intervention, so much applauded in theory and trampled upon in practice, has been as little binding on the Americans, when it has been to their interests to infringe it, as on the European nations who have endeavored to propagate it the most eagerly. In the Mexican question, against the results of which, the Ministry of Washington, in its diplomatic notes has prepared itself, there is a recent case which shows the justice of these remarks; I allude to the case of Anton Lizardo, the official documents of which are well known; and as to Europe which displays so many scruples about other interventions, on account of the supposed sanctity of that false principle, how can it logically reconcile this idea with the war in the East, the war in Italy, and its present attitude towards Russia on account of the revolt of Poland? Leaving aside all these considerations and giving our whole attention to the case which now occupies us, there is no doubt, that the answer of American diplomacy to the French Ministry was given in anticipation of the events which have transpired, nor is it foreign to the object which has occasioned this note; so that if the war of the French in Mexico degenerates into a permanent intervention in the interior policy of the country, which can no longer be doubted, the Federal Republic, on account of its antecedents and doctrines is in a position to take an active part in the affairs.

For this reason, doubling the number of men needed, in his order for the draft, he said, that all citizens who should wish to commute their personal service, could do so by paying three hundred dollars, with which sums the Government would procure substitutes.

As I have already stated, the Democrats only awaited a favorable opportunity to overthrow, by a single stroke, all the advantages of their adversaries, and although we cannot affirm that they took this opportunity to instil into the minds of the people the spirit of opposition which immediately broke out against the draft, still it is very evident that the rioters participated in the designs of the Democrats.

This resistance was organized upon two foundations, both equally dangerous to social order; one arose from the eternal question of the poor *versus* the rich; the other was of a purely political nature, and pronounced itself against the original cause of the war.

On the former point the rioters expressed themselves in these terms: If the country is really in need of re-inforcements, let us have the draft, we have nothing to say against that, but must the entire burden of military service be borne by the poor alone? What is meant by making only those who have not three hundred dollars wherewith to redeem themselves become soldiers? Let there be no distinctions made between free citizens, and let the laws be carried out without the slightest restraint on individual liberty. Whoever can procure a substitute with his own money may do so, and none will complain; but let the Government beware of assuming the power of controlling our actions and our will, establishing arbitrary quotas, and setting a price on men's lives.

And then, from the other point of this tumultous clamor they proceeded in this strain: Enough of war! All the negroes in the world are not worth one drop of the blood which is being spilt for them. This struggle is carried on not in the cause of humanity, but for base interests, and we must at once and forever rid ourselves of those who thus despoil us. Death to the Abolitionists! Death to the niggers, and destruction to everything that opposes the establishment of peace, the first and greatest necessity of a free and industrious people!

The events which immediately followed these demonstrations oppress memory and fill the imagination with horror. Bloodshed, fire and desolation rapidly spread through the city and reigned supreme, meeting with little resistance, and much to satisfy their cravings. Charitable institutions, public buildings, private residences, churches, stores, and manufactories, all were invaded by the mob, sacked and reduced to cinders. The offices of the Abolition periodicals, and the dwellings of the most prominent Republicans were attacked with frightful impetuosity, a few owing their safety solely to the extensive preparations for defense made before the attack.

And the negroes, those unfortunate beings, the innocent and even unconscious cause of the civil war and so many disorders, who are well satisfied with their mode of life, and never ask to be raised to a higher state, not even those who are free and have received an education adapted to their faculties, and who know the civil condition in which the rest are kept; the negroes, I repeat, whom everybody tries to mould into white men, and who are raised to that condition by some, through a philanthropy which has now degenerated into a malignant pertinacity to overthrow the peace of the world, the laws of nature and even the happiness of their protegés: and by others, from a sanguinary rancor, which drags them from their agricultural labors to send them to the war; the latter in their severity, in order to insure them against the contagion of a disastrous and criminal emancipation: the former in their anarchial paroxysms, against the authorized ordinances: the unfortunate negroes, I repeat, were hunted down in New York as if they had been wild beasts, they were beaten to death like mad dogs, and thrown into the flames, or hung alive, on the lamp-posts, to be tortured or thrown into the sea with feet and hands bound, to make their death more painful.

During those dreadful days of death and desolation, in which they saw the flames devour their homes, their wives and children, without any signs which might denote a cessation of these horrors, perhaps even without a thought of a better life, they, who were free in the North, would have willingly exchanged places with the slaves of the South, if only their peaceful labors were not interrupted by the malignant echoes of abolitionism, which ever effects the destruction of whatever it intends to make subservient to its philanthropic dreams or the hidden avarice of its speculations! * * * *

Such is the summing up of the evils brought upon this world by the fatal idea which, though sprung from Heaven-born charity, was perverted by interest, that most successful of Satan's works. Anarchy has not ceased to reign, for the draft had to be suspended in order to put an end to the devastation ; and the principle of authority, with difficulty restored with the presence of forty thousand soldiers in a State where the law has heretofore been self-supporting, was rent by the hands of the incendiaries, perhaps overthrown forever; for evils are easily renewed if the elements which caused them are again put in motion by wrongly interpreted measures or by any malignant suggestion.

And in the meantime, commerce flees terrified from one of its greatest and most lucrative centres, and all the industrial pursuits which do not depend on the war, will soon cease because the funds are being carried into other countries where they may rest on a security which is no longer to be found here.

Add to all this accumulation of calamities, the fate of the unhappy negroes, at sea, when the vessels that bear them are closely pursued and the captains that command them are devoid of conscience. I have heard of a great many of these cases, so dreadful that I will not relate them, but will say only that the death of at least four hundred negroes was caused solely that about fifty white sailors might not be obliged to go to Sierra Leone!

And are things to continue in such a state much longer ? Is this the way that the most important labors of philanthropy are to be carried out ? Is public right to go on in this manner, is the peace of the world to be held so cheaply, and is it thus that whole nations shall be allowed to destroy themselves ?

Oh ! this cannot be, unless the mighty powers of the earth are inspired by the Evil One !

CHAPTER XII.

The necessity of making peace, and on what basis it should be made.—Obstacles which the question presents on account of the international rights in reference to the negroes.—Various combinations which are announced for the purpose of putting an end to the war.—They are analized and the results are unfavorable.—The peace cannot be solid and lasting unless the existing treaties on the redemption are revised.—With this fundamental improvement the peace would be indestructible between the North and the South.—Project of a treaty to arrive at that object.—The great question whether the two sections should unite or separate politically at the time of making peace.—Authoritative opinions which have been given and still exist in favor of and against both objects or ends.

From all that has been said in the preceding chapters, an incontestible, absolute and urgent truth results, namely: that it is necessary to make peace in such a manner as shall be acceptable to all.

This proposition, however simple it may appear in its form, is, in fact, exceedingly complicated, when we consider the history of slavery, the existence of the international treaties, and the motives which have caused the war.

The end which I will aim at in this important part of my work, and to which I will devote my entire energies, is: To grant to the negroes a new civil state, almost superior to their natural comprehension, which shall differ entirely from the condition in which they have lived, for three and a half centuries, among civilized nations, and from the barbarous and untutored existence which they lead in their own country. To satisfy the all pervading sentiment of holy charity proceeding from the Christian religion which was given to the world when the blood of the Savior was shed on Calvary, which was defended by the martyrs, and has finally spread throughout the world, the idea of human liberty. To insure safety and respect to the interests of labor, which has made vast territories of waste lands productive to commerce, and has raised above the horrors of paganism eighteen nations of civilized people. In fact, to unite in the bond of unity two jarring tendencies, which now seek their mutual destruction, either by re-establishing a constitution which has been overthrown by the exaggerations of both parties, or else by recognizing two distinct nations, which once formed but one, without in any manner lessening their original greatness.

As I shall have to contend with inveterate prejudices, secular abuses, erroneous ideas, with apparent injustice, with fraudulent interests, with local views of an unfriendly character, with arrogant pretensions, with exclusive tendencies, deep rancor, and perhaps also with the vanity of some wealthy parties, who, having settled on some other plan less important, will not be willing to replace it by a better one which is not of their own contrivance. My task is as arduous as the ability with which I undertake it is limited.

But I have justice, which is the infallible result of absolute truth for my beacon in my moral speculations; and although I am aware that evil passions and wicked interests generally prevail over it, still I believe that by being equitable and having truth for a base, everything that depends upon the will of man is possible.

"Truth," said a philosopher, "is the motive power of modern nations to which the dominion of the world has been promised; and if for the love of country we have seen a nation of heroes rise, from the love of truth which is greater and more sublime still, the civilization of the whole human race will at last be seen to emanate."[1]

And as to the present question, the truth is, that while the arrangements that may be made to settle it keep the doors of scandal open to selfishness, and to legitimate interests, founded fears; whilst in the name of humanity and within the law, which neither emanates from justice nor has been founded upon the principles of true charity, the civilization which is maintained by labor is menaced;

---

(1) Aimé Martin: *Education des meres de famille.* Lib. 1, chap. xii.

as long as odious exceptions are made in the divine sentence which condemns all men equally to live by the sweat of their brow, and this, not for the purpose of improving in a civil sense a degraded race, but to perpetuate its ignorance by excluding it from all intercourse ; as long as in said arrangement, I repeat, the interests created within the limits of social morality, of common advantage and practical history by all the nations by them affected, are not kept in view, the peace which may therefrom result will not rest upon a solid foundation, and the clashing of arms will still continue.

In order that peace may be a fact, it is necessary that the treaties should also be facts, and this will not be the case as long as one of the contracting parties can be injured, and whilst by an equivocal interpretation of the law there are means of eluding its fulfilment.

Let us not deceive nor attempt to fortify ourselves with absurdities, to maintain, with vain pride, an agreement which is not only imperfect but full of defects. It is now forty-five years since 1818, that the philanthropy of the abolitionists began to obtain legal concessions against the redemption of the negroes, and since that time the redemption of the negroes has not only failed to be extinguished but it has prospered ; the prohibition far from realizing the idea of its efficiency, has clearly demonstrated the manner in which it could be frustrated, openly and secretly, by the very nations by which it has been proclaimed. Add to this the desasters which this fatal agreement has produced ; the lands it has ruined, the blood it has caused to be shed, instead of the fruitful sweat which it desired to spare, and the frightful chaos with which it threatens the world ; and after that no one will hesitate to abandon the path which has been followed during those forty-five years ; or we shall be obliged to proclaim frankly that the pertinacity of the abolitionists is an infamous conspiracy against the property of the nations who, in behalf of true humanity, avail themselves of the labor of the negroes.

If, as an ancient philosopher very well said, " even idiots are taught by experience,"[1] and if it is true, besides, " that circumstances occur every day which may make us

---

(1) Titus Livious; Hist. lib. xxii.

modify the most rooted opinions," as a modern statesman has also stated,[1] for experience presents itself to the sight bespattered with blood and pregnant with horrors, and the necessity of a radical transformation of the treaties cannot be more urgent, owing to the circumstances which have occurred and are notorious, it is clear that the repetition of the evil which it has caused up to this time and which threatens so many others for the future; could not be attributed to stupidity but to malice; it would not be attributed to the offuscation of some ignorant minds, but as a preconcerted plan of miscreants against society.

But the fact is, that with the present civilization, however much it may tend to the deification of interest by the natural effects of rationalism, the idea of slavery is not only in opposition to human liberty but is looked upon as an anachronism in the nineteenth century.

But as after a conscientious and rigorous analysis on the character and origin of this institution and on its present application, sufficient explanations have been given to show, by exact comparisons, that at present the nomenclature only is preserved, with the want of foresight, of charity and good judgment; labor being the law of God for all men, and that by its means only the negroes can liberate themselves from the ignominious state in which they live in their own native country, it is high time to give to each thing its precise interpretation and true name in behalf of the peace of the world, and in favor of the same civilization which we all proclaim and all desire.

If this be done, a conciliatory plan may be frankly adopted by all the nations interested in this question, which besides would have the advantage of stability; because by assimilating it to common right, without injuring this or any other country, but rather favoring all, would close to litigation the smallest opening.

I would explain my views at once, just as I have conceived them, on the basis of justice, looking to the quiet of nations, were reports of peace which deserve to be commented upon in circulation. They have no official character, but, to a certain extent, they are probable; and as

---

(1) Llorente, Spanish Minister of Finance, Parliamentary speech in the Cortes, April 5, 1858.

the people are getting tired of the war, though this cannot be suspected from what is going on in the battle-field, it might so happen, in consequence of a revolution of public sentiment, or by some peremptory necessity of high policy, that upon the said basis the arms should at once fall from the hands of the combatants; resulting therefrom that an armistice rather than a peace would be concluded; because by leaving the former causes of the war in existence, their effects would again reproduce themselves sooner or later.

One of said reports, and I have seen several of a similar nature, coinciding in date, place of writing and spirit, is found in a recent letter from Paris, written by a person who is generally well informed, which, following in the wake of the European diplomacy in this question, and having reference to the evolutions of the representatives of the two American sections at that Court, said as follows: "The possibility of a speedy arrangement between the Northern and the Southern States is again spoken of. It appears that the Southern States *propose the abolition of the slave trade*, and accept the arbitral intervention of France for the adoption of the measure to be used in the meantime, in order not to affect too suddenly the rights of the slave owners."

The other report, though not directly from Paris, is of very great importance, infinitely more than the other; and it has already been so considered by every respectable organ of public opinion, having been published in the papers and greatly discussed; and it is even stated that on its account the Federal Government will change its interior policy.

It is nothing less than a letter from Washington, published in the *Herald*, making revelations of great importance on the policy of England and France as to the two beligerant sections of the United States. My readers will allow me to insert it entire in this place, in order that with more knowledge of the matter they may be the better able to judge the commentaries which I shall write after it.

"WASHINGTON, July 24, 1863.

"The movement under the leadership of Mr. Seward, having for its object the offer of liberal concessions to the insurgents and the ending of the present war, has received an impetus from the news which has just reached us from our foreign ministers in London and Paris. It is now admitted by the most sanguine members of the administration that never were our foreign affairs in so menacing a state. England—so the official advices indicate—has determined to furnish the South with an iron-clad navy, including ships, guns and seamen. It is equally certain that the emperor of France has made up his mind definitely to interfere in our domestic affairs. It is true that at the date of the last advices from abroad the impression was general in Europe that Lee would defeat Meade's army, Washington be captured, and Baltimore and Philadelphia seized, while the Northern States seemed apathetic and indisposed to continue the war; but this condition of things only finally determined the English and French governments to pursue a policy which they had all along been prepared to pursue, and which comported with their interests and sympathies.

"The changed condition of affairs due to the fall of Vicksburg and Port Hudson, and the rebel defeat at Gettysburg will not, it is believed by the most sagacious of the friends of the administration, alter the character of the action which France and England have finally determined to adopt. The appearance of a fleet of French vessels at New Orleans, to protect the interests of the Creole population at that point, and the sailing of a very large iron-clad fleet from the English ports, are certain to take place. Indeed, it is understood here that the real peril to the North will come when it is apparent to the Emperor Napoleon and the British Cabinet that there is a strong probability of the overthrow of the South as a military power.

"So long as the contest was an even one, they could afford to be neutral and let the matter be fought out; but the moment there is a danger of the North overpowering the South, then intervention will be tried to compel a separation upon which both England and France are determined—England to cripple the power of this great republic, and France to preserve her dominion in Mexico. There is no doubt that if the North and South were to come together, France would immediately be compelled to relinquish her hold upon Mexico, and this Louis Napoleon is determined shall not happen. Hence, it is argued, he will take time by the forelock, aid the South against the

North, earn a title to its gratitude, and thus retain his hold upon Mexico, and pursue his schemes in Central America. England also is aware that should the Union be restored, it will find both North and South embittered against her and ready for war. It is a matter of certainty—and the English understand it well—that the American Republic will follow the example of the old Roman Republic, which always embarked upon a foreign war after a civil convulsion so as to induce a unity of national spirit.

"With these indications before them, and with the unofficial dispatches of our ministers and consuls abroad, Mr. Seward and the President are convinced that this is the most critical time, so far as regards our relations with foreign Powers, that we have had since the commencement of the war. We cannot afford to permit England to destroy our commerce, nor allow France to pursue her designs on New Orleans. This state of affairs made the President and Secretary of State anxious to settle up our present quarrel. They see very clearly the straits of Jeff. Davis and the rebel government—indeed, their absolute despair—as is shown by the call for a levy *en masse* of the fighting population of the whole South; and they believe that proper measures taken now would restore the Union and put an end to the present unhappy war. From what I hear I am inclined to believe that measures are now on foot looking to this end, and that it is not impossible that we may see a sudden change of parties in the United States within the next month—that Governor Seymour, Vallandigham, and the odds and ends of the democratic party, and the conservative republicans, may be found to be warm supporters of President Lincoln and his able Secretary of State; while the republican presses and orators— the Sumners, Phillipses, Wilsons, Wades, Chandlers, with the *Tribune, Times, Post*, and all the agency of the radicals, will be brought to bear in an opposition party against the reunion that will be proposed by the President. Of course the whole shoddy interest in the war, and the enormous sums interested in the moving of armies, will be bitterly opposed to any adjustment. But the prospect of peace North and South, will, it is believed, rally the bulk of the people of the North to the standard of the administration, provided it will decide upon some such course.

"The letter of the Solicitor General (Whiting), asserting that the administration must continue in its negro policy, no matter what emergency arises, is understood to be the occasion of that gentleman being sent abroad. His letter was a move on the part of the radicals to commit the government unofficially to the negro policy. His being set aside at this time is an indication that different counsels are beginning to prevail in the White House, and there is a hope that the whole abolition gang will soon be thrown out.

"Of course, reunion at this stage of the war will involve the necessity of the administration changing its abolition policy. The programme is, that the Territories, as decided in the recent Congress, shall remain free forever, thus preventing the extension of slavery. Slaves freed by the march of the armies will remain free. Missouri is to become a free State, as she has chosen to be, and Maryland and Delaware may also be free if they should so decide. But the other slave States are to retain such of their slaves as will be under the actual control of the masters at the end of the war. Mr. Seward argues that slavery has received a blow in this country from which it can never recover, and that it would be better to leave the natural causes at work to end it than to convert the South into a desert by depriving it of its laboring population. It is understood that this plan will not suit the radicals, and the embarassment of Mr. Lincoln now is, not to bring about a reunion so much as to know what to do with this party in case he should consent to a peace. The situation is a perplexing one, and will call out all the sagacity and administrative ability of the people in power."

This book is not written with so transitory a character that it will lose its importance before its doctrines be accepted in councils ; or another, that like this, shall dispel all the ulterior difficulties to establish a permanent agreement on the question of the negroes, shall be found. I make this statement, in order that an intention of exclusiveness opposed to all other arrangements, such as might control any spirit less philosophical, may not be attributed to my arguments.

I have known by experience these many years, and by

the lessons of the world I have constantly known, that he who does everything by his own suggestions is more daring than wise. This being premised, let us enter upon the analysis of the data which we have just inserted.

The first says, "That the Southern States propose the abolition of the slave trade, and that they accept the arbitration of France for the arrangement of the measures to be adopted in the meantime, in order not to affect too suddenly the rights of slave owners." And it seems to me that this assertion in its true sense is susceptible of two interpretations, the one absurd, and the other unlikely. Because, if the abolition of the slave trade is taken as meaning the abolition of the importation of *Bozales*, the Southern States cannot propose the abolition of that which is already legally abolished by all the international treaties, and this is the sense in which the proposition has appeared to me to be absurd; and if the object referred to is not to traffic with the Creole negroes born in the United States, and in the condition of slaves, which is a private business that greatly facilitates agricultural labor in the districts that are short of hands for its labors, this would be the same as to limit property, contrary to all right, both in its extension as in its speculations, for which reason I think it unlikely.

What is sought, therefore, is not to abolish the trade, but to pursue it with efficient results; stipulating, no doubt, extraordinary compromises in new arrangements to be made. Unless by calculations hitherto unknown, the means have been found in the Southern States to lay aside slavery, which is the only agent of labor which constitutes its wealth. In such a case the report we are analyzing should be interpreted differently, and then the arbitration of France would come in play.

If it is not so, as it certainly cannot be, admitting the prohibition of the clandestine trade to be still in force, there must result from the new international compromises which the Confederacy may contract, one of two things, viz : that in order to comply scrupulously with her engagements she should infringe upon the rights of territorial property with abuses and other tyrannical and dangerous encroachments ; or else leave things in the same state as they are now, with no other advantage than an additional protocol, offering the same inducements as heretofore to the cupidity of traders and an inexhaustible fund of dissatisfaction and recrimination to the governments.

In the first case there would happen to the land owners in the Southern States what happened a few years since to those of Brazil; and, indeed, with still more disastrous consequences, considering the necessity to replace upon the estates the great losses of hands caused by the war, and by the abolitionist proclamations of the Federal Government. That is to say, that supposing that the Confederate Government should act in the same manner as the Brazilians, banishing at once from the country, in a tyrannical manner and without the least trial, all those suspected to be carrying on or to have carried on the same trade, and encouraging denunciations to the prejudice of morality and at the expense of the public treasury, (since forty dollars were offered for each *bozal* negro of any expedition who might be discovered, even after the individual had reached the States in which he then constitutes a property until then inviolate,) the Southern planters would see their estates irretrievably ruined, as many of the estates of the Brazilian planters have been; and what now is an abundant supply for local consumption and exportation, they would have to obtain to-morrow at the expense of great crifices in other more happy countries.

In the second instance, that is, in case of making a pro-formulary protocol, entrusting its execution to the cruisers, with more or less good faith, which is the most that any Government of a productive country who does not wish knowingly to ruin the interests of its subjects can do, to serve foreign intrusions, the question would remain in its present state: and sooner or later, when it would suit the views of another more powerful nation to create a crisis such as are only settled by arms, viz: some insulting words implying supposed or real bad faith in the fulfillment of existing treaties against the slave trade; half a dozen inconsiderate and notoriously aggressive notes; two or three cases of outrages on the flag upon the high seas, for which the odious right of search offers so many opportunities, and which until now the Anglo-Americans have rejected with much propriety, but to which they now seem to have acceded, with less regard to honor than thirst for revenge: all these means together, or any one of them separately would suffice to break the peace that might now be made upon such foundations, and oblige them to enter into a war infinitely more dangerous than the one now carried on.

For the Confederate States not to run upon this rock it would be necessary that the required supply of hands on the plantations should not have been so much diminished by the war, which still continues to destroy them; this is in the supposition that in the normal state of things the creole negroes are in sufficient number to fill the complement of laborers indispensable in the entire Republic.

Besides, the question of negro labor is no longer a question of locality, but a general one, which if settled here to-day without sufficient solidity, may, to-morrow, after having produced so much injury to the commerce of the world, spring up in another place with a more alarming character and greater danger to all.

To comment on the second report of peace, I should have to repeat much of what the first suggested to me, as both in their hypothetic conditions leave the important question of which we treat pending on a definite treaty.

I will not take into account those exaggerated international dangers to which the Washington letter alludes, as we have no facts sufficiently significant, aside from the proclamation of the Empire in Mexico, to warrant them to be of such gigantic proportions as the said letter represents them. This is not to say that they are not true to some extent, and that the belligerent parties of North America should not measure and weigh well their ulterior resolutions of war in accordance thereof.

Confining ourselves therefore to the basis contained in said document to bring about a peace, I will frankly say that they are not acceptable by the Southern States, unless driven to it by despair, and in order to give this opinion more comprehensiveness in the minds of others, I beg to be allowed to view the question according to the analysis of the said basis.

"That the *Territories* shall forever remain free, as sanctioned by the Federal Congress, avoiding in this manner the propagation of Slavery." Here we have a precept which, if it does not affect the States, at least renders useless, unless large tracts of land which aspire to become members of the Union, and which by being deprived of the means of labor, coerces liberty in its most legitimate desires.

If those *Territories* can exist and progress in proportion to their geographical extent and their natural wealth, without the aid of foreign hands, there is no reason why those impediments against the importation of laboring people into them should be recommended; as it is clear that no one seeks what he does not require, nor do laborers go where they cannot be employed. But on the other hand if the said *Territories* require, and this is the fact, a great impulse of material strength for their development, is it not lamentable that their present well-being and their future prosperity should be sacrificed to a noble, but evidently mistaken sentiment?

The same holds good with regard to the States of Missouri, Maryland, and Delaware, whatever may have been the resolutions which exceptional circumstances have made them adopt under the pressure of events: and on extending these considerations to the countries that have availed themselves of the labor of the negroes as slave countries, be it understood that I hold the same opinions towards the rest of the world, as no laboring negroes should be taken forcibly and by redemption where they were not needed.

In any case, their usefulness or convenience can be estimated by no one better than by each country within itself, and subservient, of course, to the political and economical views of its own administration; without taking into account foreign interest, so long as no injury is done, within the laws of nature which are binding to all the world.

The Washington letter further says: "that the remaining States where there are slaves, shall retain those they may have at the termination of the war; and as if human nature in its combinations which tend to evil, knew not how to express the satisfaction it feels at its own success"; Mr. Seward adds, that slavery has received in this country a blow from which it will never recover; and it is therefore better to leave to natural causes the completion of the work of emancipation, than to convert the country into a desert, by depriving it of the laboring population. According to this, the Southern States will, on the termination of the war, retain the slaves which may remain to them; and this they did not require that any one should tell them, as it is for their own interests to do so. As to the emancipation of those whom the soldiers of the North have taken to a military life, or to any other work as free people, it would not do to consent to their reinstatement in their former condition, without very great danger to property, as based upon morality and discipline. Add to the number thus rendered useless for labor, those who have perished in the field, who are many, and we shall not only arrive at the confirmation of this promise, but it will prove the truth of the fatal prediction of Mr. Seward, admitting that he has really made it, if in the treaties of peace a remedy is not provided.

This being so, we shall always have to come to the nenecessity of making peace in a manner that will satisfy the interests of all : let each side sacrifice to the good faith of its wishes and to the moral of public law a reasonable amount of its aspirations ; and let the statesmen prove that they are worthy of the name, not by the position they occupy, but by the consistency of their acts.

To arrive at this point, which is the climax of my aspiration, and which is the conclusive evidence of the question we are discussing, some with arms and others with arguments, it is necessary also that some one should take the initiatory step to establish a preliminary agreement, upon which the operations of war could be suspended.

If those international fears expressed in the Washington letter were true, we can readily understand how difficult it would be to trust for peace to a previous revision of the existing treaties respecting what is called slavery, because the two most powerful nations among all those who would have to consent to the revision, being interested in the continuance of the war, it is not likely that they would agree to so very important a measure, if peace should be the necessary result.

For that reason, therefore, and as if in reality such an unlikely international conspiracy existed, I think that the Federal States and the Southern Confederacy, who are now belligerents, should commit its solution to themselves alone, suspending at once the effects of all contracts made by either party to the prejudice of the other, and absolutely resisting all foreign exactions of similar character.

This fundamental resolution once taken, I also think it indispensable to enter upon the path of moral promises and real indemnifications ; and then, to strengthen what now may be agreed upon, with due regard to local rights and to the justice due all parties, I am fully of the opinion that the government of the United States, if the Union is re-established, or the true governments which may result from the peace, if the independence of the South should be consummated, should formally and absolutely compromise themselves to urge upon all the interested nations the propriety of revising said treaties relative to the negroes, that there may be a true, solid, reasonable and moral compact of positive execution agreed upon, that will not be opposed to the spirit of Christian civilization, and be propitious to the interests of all.

Without imagining that I have discovered the right method to accomplish this purpose, but with the commendable pretension of having approached it as near as possible, I consider that it will be easy to realize the views contained in both documents, and having already sufficiently shown the necessity of framing them, I shall now proceed to explain the first, such as I have conceived it is.

The basis of a peace independent of the international treaty by which the present jurisprudence respecting the negroes is to be altered, should rest upon the following three principles:

First.—To recognize on both sides the liberty of action to individuals and to localities, each to regulate their interests in conformity to their respective requirements. In this wise the States that now have the institution of compulsory labor by the negroes, would have the right to abolish it, if they should think it proper, either collectively or individually; and those States who do not make use of the compulsory labor of the negroes, as well as the Territories, might establish it with the same freedom, if their views, their customs and their natural laws and policy counseled it.

The morality of this principle will be better understood when the project of the treaty which is to substitute all those which have been hitherto made by the interested nations in reference to the negroes; because in said project the civil condition of the laboring negro is modified, without the slightest prejudice to social order or the discipline of the labor, and this change is made acceptable in all its parts, even to the most exquisite moral susceptibility.

Second.—Should the Union be re-established, the Federal Government would have to raise funds to indemnify, on a proportional and equitable scale, the planters whose negroes may have been emancipated by the troops of the North or escaped by their connivance ; but if the independence of the South should be consolidated, it will be the duty of the Confederate Government or to each particular State to settle this matter with absolute independence of the Northern States ; and always bearing in mind the sacrifices imposed by the war on the general mass of the citizens.

This second principle which might be dispensed with, taking the question of slavery in the abstract, is not so important but as it might be connected with the material reestablishment of the plantations by the acquisition of other laboring negroes. And as it is not probable that any planter will be willing to deprive himself of his own to supply the wants of another, it may be anticipated that the third principle on which the basis of peace must rest, consists in rejecting all foreign proposition which may tend to strengthen the existing treaties against the redemption of African negroes : since the revision is the point to which all Northern and Southern efforts must be concentrated in an entirely opposed sense to that which until now has with such ill success prevailed for the last forty-five years.

The question of limits and the natural regulations of political relations between the two republics, if in reality there are to be two, or the particular relations between the States if the Union is restored, would also be essential matter for some of the articles of the treaty which might be proposed. But as the character of these local matters are unconnected with the general intention of this book respecting the negroes, I do not think it necessary, but rather out of place to enter into details for a definite settlement, when the better knowledge of the Americans, looking to their own interest and to their own rights might advantageously replace the greatest combinations which might be proposed here.

I say the same thing with respect to the main question as to there being one or two nations constituted by means of the peace; for being a foreigner and absolutely impartial to either aspirations, it would be out of place to express my wish or even to give my advice.

This fact, however, will not prevent me from discussing the possibility of adopting without difficulty either of the two resolutions ; and to the analysis of so delicate a matter

I shall devote myself, not from a vain desire of handling it, but because they also are contributive to the ends of this book.

I have, before now, stated that there are international dangers in the separation, which would already have been made evident, if there was any truth in the disclosure of the Washington letter. According to these disclosures and by reason of the greatness imparted to a country by the number of its inhabitants and the extent of its territory, it may easily be suspected that the marked tendencies of the Southern States to constitute their national independence is incompatible with peace. But those dangers and the diminution which would result from the dismemberment of both sections would be more apparent than real, when we consider that the greatness of nations is shown rather by the affinity of their internal elements with their international relations, than by the numerical scale of their inhabitants and the number of square miles.

Let us suppose that in the anxiety of preserving the Union, the sacred fire of independence would be but partially extinguished in the heart of the Southern States, and that from this cause their efforts would be multiplied to perpetuate themselves in power, with great detriment to the policy of the North; or that its antagonism to the men of that section who might constitutionally remain in power, would weaken the acts of the Administration, appearing always as a dangerous threat. In this case, which is more than probable, there is no doubt that the restoration of the Union would be a calamity, since while making a show of strength it would really possess none, owing to the absence of harmony between its elements; and it is evident that this being the case, it would be better for the nation to be divided into two administrative nationalities, each being the arbiter of its own laws, but united for its common existence by indissoluble treaties of offensive and defensive alliance and commercial relations.

The idiosyncrasy of the respective interest of both the North and the South would admirably contribute to this solution; the complexion of their political and economical laws and their geographical conditions. But I must add that the considerations expressed in favor of said solution are not absolute, inasmuch as there exist others equally possible which recommend above all things the re-establishment of the federal greatness in a conciliatory and permanent manner.

Considerations on both plans have already been suggested to the minds of all thinking men both in the North and in the South ; so that the exclusivism against a decorous and useful settlement cannot be apprehended on laying the foundations for peace, there being many respectable statesmen in the South who advocate the restoration of the Union, and in the North those who favor the consolidation of the Southern Confederacy.

Among the former the venerable Mr. Johnson deserves special mention, whose letter, addressed to a New York paper on the 13th of May, 1863, will always hold a conspicuous place in the history of the efforts made by true patriotism in favor of the re-establishment of peace on the basis of the old Constitution of the Republic. At the same time, as well as previously and subsequently, many others expressed the same opinion, as did also Guthries, Wickilffes, Jones, Rodney, Bates, Rives, Sumner, Ruffin, Morehead, and so many other enlightened patriots of the Confederation who spoke and wrote upon the excellence of the Federal Union with a view to its restoration.

There are also many in the North who have spoken and written in favor of separation, especially in those large meetings which not long since have taken place for the purpose of putting an end to the war. The three cheers addressed to Jefferson Davis by the Democrats of New York at the opening of the great meeting in Union square still harmoniously ring in my ears ; and not because the political symbol which that name represents is more or less sympathetic to me, but because such a demonstration in favor of the President of the Southern Confederacy, made in the most powerful State of the North gives an idea of the conciliatory tendencies which exist in the entire Republic.

In order that such an idea should spread to all its extent, giving an immense force to my opinions relative to peace, it would be necessary to insert entire the speeches made at that meeting. I will not do so, that I may not deviate too much from the object to which these investigations lead me ; nevertheless, I will not omit some passages which are to the purpose, and which, of themselves, are very significant.

The honor of that meeting is due to Dr. Bradford, although another gentleman no less competent, citizen Dinning, presided over it; as after the latter had introduced the former, as the expounder of the principles of the party who had called the meeting, the said Doctor not only established those principles on all the constitutional theories consigned by the most eminent men from Washington down to the present day, but demonstrated in an legal, and I may almost say in an absolute manner, that the war was being carried on contrary to all law, according to the Constitution of the Republic:

"No independent State at any period of the world ever voluntarily relinquished sovereign power, much less created a master and conferred upon him the absolute authority to coerce it or to subjugate it. Chief Justice Dana, in the Massachusetts Convention for the ratification of the Constitution, said that 'the Federal Government springs out of and can alone be brought into existence by the State Governments: demolish the latter and there is an end of the former.' (Cheers.) The Union was founded on the great principles of mutual protection, mutual interest, and equal rights in whatever concerns our persons, privileges and property. The least discrimination in the Constitution in favor of or against the enjoyment of any one of these would have been fatal to its adoption, and so long as the principles upon which it was adopted shall be preserved, not only by the parties to it, but by the Government created by it, so long can the Union exist and no longer. As was truly said by a distinguished gentleman of this State, 'Successful coercion is as much revolution as successful secession.'" (Cheers.)

He afterwards spoke of the qualification of each of the parties into which the republic is divided respecting the war; and to explain it, set down the following proposition:

"HOW CAN DEMOCRATS SUSTAIN THIS WAR?

"Having thus thown that it is the duty of the democratic party to return to its own principles and to reiterate them; that the chief of them is, that the States are sovereign and independent, and that the general government is feeble and dependent, and has not, therefore, military power by which to coerce the States into compliance against their own idea of law, right and justice, we declare that, admitting that the power exists, its exercise in inconsistent with union. If civil war is inconsistent with federative union, so is union inconsistent with war.

"But suppose none of these objections existed to the present war, how can the democratic party sustain it? Its objects are not left to supposition. They have been proclaimed by the President, by the action of the late Congress, and by the practice of the army itself. It is not to sustain or to restore the Federal Union, but to destroy and uproot the domestic institution of States, to destroy private property, and to subvert the form and theory of the Federal Government itself. (Cheers.)

"To support the war is to support the policies of the war. This proposition is too plain to be disputed; from it there is no escape. To support the war is to support confiscation—not by the Courts under the Constitution, but by acts of Congress contrary to the constitution; emancipation and arbitrary arrests, not by any lawful authority, but by the monstrous and frightful usurpations of the President—(hisses)—subjugation not to bring the South back into the Union, but to reduce it to the condition of Territories and convert it into one vast San Domingo. These are the policies of the war, and if the war should be successful these policies will be accomplished.

"The professed democrat, therefore, who is deliberately for the war, is not a democrat in fact, but an abolitionist of the most radical, violent and destructive kind. It is useless for a person to say that he is for the war for one set of purposes, when the war is not prosecuted for any of those purposes, but for the opposite and antagonistic purposes. This is to stultify himself. The abolitionists do not care on what pretences or professions people support the war; they only ask that they will support it on some pretence; for, the policies of the war being fixed, support of it, on whatever pretence, enures to the aid of those politicians just as certainly and effectively as support of it on the positive ground of these policies. How can democrats endorse such a war? How can the democratic party as a party sustain such a war? By endorsing the war we of necessity endorse the policy of those who prosecute it in chief command. To support the former, and at the same time oppose the latter, is an absurdity. To do the one we necessarily do the other. The President's emancipation proclamation and the war go hand in hand together. It is pusillanimous to carp at the moral pigmies of the crisis while we cringe to its giant. This war is the curse of the age in which we live. (Cheers.) Without it we would have retained all the liberties now lost. Without war there had been no abridgment of liberty of person, or speech, of the press, or onerous taxes to pay, or issuance of negro proclamations. True, these are not necessarily concomitants of war, but only so when it is managed by negro philanthropists. (Hisses.) They have had the management of it thus far, and will continue so to manage it as long as it lasts. This war has been the pretext for all the wrongs against which the democratic party protest, and the 'war power,' the instrument of their accomplishment. (Cries of 'peace, peace,' and cheers, the people rising in a body, waving hats, handkerchiefs, &c., &c.")

After which, setting forth his theories in regard to peace, with great applause from the meeting, he said :

"Then if the democracy would work a reformation they must strike at the cause of the evil. The continuance of the war will be fatal to our liberties. Suppose that this war be continued for two years more by the assistance of democrats, would there be a vestige of civil liberty left ? Of what use would democratic victories be then ? It would be out of the power of any party to restore the government to the old order of things. But in that event we could get no victories. The whole legitimate and usurped power of the government, wielded by the unscrupulous demagogues who now control it, would be more than a match for any political combination that might be formed against them. The only road to democratic victories is through peace. Why should politicians fear that a peace party may prove unpopular. If the war has damned the republican party, is it not logical to suppose that a peace policy might prosper the opposition. (Cheers.) Do the people love war more than peace ? (No ! no !) Do they prefer the hardships of the camp, the dangers of the battle field, the onus of taxation, to the comforts, the pleasures, the prosperity of peaceful homes ? (No ! no !) But this matter is beyond the control of politicians. The great body of the people are tired of the war, and demand peace on the basis of existing facts, and politicians cannot change their views in this respect. If the men who now occupy the position of leaders do not see and recognize this fact, they will be forced to give place to men who do see it. The people have been traded and trucked about so much during the war, by old political hacks, that they have become suspicious and restive, and refuse to be sold any more.

"Again, in addition to these irresistible and sufficient reasons why the democratic party should declare for peace, is the palpable common sense and hard-headed fact that the war cannot succeed. We have been beaten. We cannot conquer the South. (Tremendous cheering.) A glance at all history would have told this before it was undertaken, had we read it aright. No purely agricultural people in a state of revolt, contending for their domestic rights, have ever yet been subjugated; and no revolted people who have been able to maintain an independent government for a twelvemonth have been conquered or put down. The last twelvemonth has united the South, and though we had twice our power they could successfully resist us. As invaders we are impotent. To equalize the chances of war the invaders should possess ten times the power, and every advantage of position. That is not the case. All the power of the then colossal Spanish Empire under Charle V., and the succeeding Phillips, failed to conquer two or three miserable Dutch provinces, almost Lilliputian in extent (Cries of 'bravo!') Even petty and contiguous Portugal expelled victoriously from its soil all the hosts of the same still greater Power. Not in vain stands recorded in more ancient history the imperishable record of Marathon; and in our own day we have seen the miserable Mexican rabble soldiery driving the best disciplined army of Europe from their soil, because the latter were invaders.

"God did not intend that we should succeed in this war. Had he intended it he would not have placed in command a Lincoln—(groans for several minutes, and cries of 'Boo! boo! boo!')—with such coadjutors as a Butler or a Burnside. (Renewed groans and hisses, and cheers for Vallandigham.) We will not compare these men to a Davis, or a Lee, or a Stonewall Jackson. It is not necessary. Mind, character and capacity will always evince, declare and maintain their superiority. These qualities will triumph sooner or later, it matters not how far greater the physical resources in the hands of the opposite qualities. The Roman Commonwealth, in spite of territory, population, armies and resources, was destroyed from wanting any mind by which the mind of Cæsar could be balanced and encountered. Holland was lost to Spain when the Prince of Orange and Prince Maurice were superior to all the viceroys and the captains the mother country could oppose to them. The South American dependencies were gone when she had no opponent of Bolivar. The civil wars of France, after every kind of trial and of vicissitude, all closed in the pre-eminence of Henry IV., in head and heart the master of his epoch. The Carlists had not any match for Espartero. The Sardinians had not any equal of Radetsky. The same lesson is impressed on us by the collision of Washington and George III.; of Charles I. and Cromwell. It is true that history need not repeat itself, and that events are neither bound by theories or precedents.

"In this connection, we must refer to the ludicrous attempts that are made upon every military reverse to attribute the result to every other than the true cause. (Ha! ha!) When a battle is fought it is generally lost, and then come the reasons. Sometimes the commanding general has omitted to obey the orders of his superiors, or an obedience to their orders was the cause; or, again, he has moved too slow, or has not been properly supported— now he has had an inferior force, then an adverse position; and, in turn, all the various causes to which military defeats are attributable are served up to the credulous people. We never hear the truth. (Cry of 'Never.') If any know it none dare tell it. The hand of God is lifted against us. His illimitable power overturns all our designs and subverts all our plans. (Cry of 'We want peace.'")

Finally, it cannot be denied that there are in the North many and very powerful partisans of peace, even at the cost of separation from the South; and that among the Confederates there are also many who entertain the opinion, on fundamental principles, that the Union be re-established.

These precedents being given, and the basis on which a decorous arrangement might be commenced between the two sections being stated, I shall terminate these remarks with the project of the general treaty which, in my opinion, would re-establish the good international relations throughout the world respecting the question of the negroes.

CHAPTER XIII.

Features which the international treaties should have in order that they may be inviolate.—It is shown that these features do not exist in the treaties which have been made for the prohibition of the redemption.—General summary of all the propositions demonstrated in this work.—Doctrines which result from them, and natural applications indicated by the same.—Project of a general treaty to restore public right in the matter relating to negroes, satisfying true morality, protecting all interests created since the discovery of America and improving civilization in African soil.—Considerations which arise out of the said project of treaty.—End of the work.

To maintain the inviolability of any international compact, whether it be founded on abstract ideas, or affects the material interests of the contracting parties, it is necessary that the experience of all the time which has elapsed since its ratification should produce the absolute conviction of its usefulness ; or that the legitimate benefits which one of the contracting parties obtains from it, be of such importance as will oblige it to oppose all manner of reforms instigated by the other parties.

Such conditions, it is clear, do not exist, nor have they existed for forty years back, in the treaties concerning the question of slaves, whatever be the standing point from which they are examined. For having first ruined the British colonies in the Western hemisphere, and subsequently all the others where slavery was abolished, without improving in the least the condition of the free laborers. The stipulations concerning the negroes in their respective countries, the vain gratification of some theories already proved fallacious, can no longer overrule the eloquence of facts, nor is it possible that the idea of human infalibility, of itself so arrogant, should perpetuate the errors of some statesmen, regardless of social morality, the interests of the world, and the peace of those countries.

In the preceding chapters I have endeavored to solve the various propositions of great importance to the purposes which have urged me to this work ; and to the philanthropic task, sustained by my perseverance, I think I have succeeded in establishing, on immutable principles, a sound basis for an equitable settlement of the negro question, with the following data :

First.—The historical demonstration of the savage, desolate state of the Africans, before the discovery of America.

Second.—The historical demonstration of the great modification produced in their unhappy state, by the introduction of the redemption, without increasing their warlike spirit, which had always been, and still is, their natural propensity, in common with all barbarous nations.

Third.—The historical, philosophical and legal demonstration that the civil state of the negroes in the colonies is not that of slavery, which name has been erroneously applied to it, and is in all respects false.

Fourth.—The legal demonstration that the Chinese contracts to provide laborers for the colonies, place those individuals in the same position as the negroes whom they are intended to substitute, with but very few conditions in their favor, which are scarcely ever fulfilled, whilst many that are against them are strictly enforced and carried out, are calculated to perpetuate their state of servitude and bondage. A more glaring inconsistency with the' views of the English philanthrophists, can hardly be imagined, who recommended the acquisition of Chinese for the purpose of enslaving them, though a civilized and peaceable people ; whilst they prohibit the redemption of the blacks and oppose the organization of their labor, though through the former they are liberated.

Fifth.—The practical and evident demonstration that the freedom of the negroes has ruined great productive districts, by affecting the social condition of said individuals ; and that the organized labor, which is improperly called slavery, is the source of prosperity in the districts where it exists, and keeps the negroes who constitute it, in a real state of civilization.

Sixth.—The demonstrations, in various shapes, that the

code of international laws with which it has been agreed to abolish the redemption, is demoralized and perverted in a manner which reflects little credit on the foresight of the great statesmen by whom it has been framed ; constituting all civilized nations as persecutors of each other, by means of their cruisers ; authorizing the humiliating and degrading right of search, so opposed to the dignity of the flags, so exposed to great abuses, and so liable to bring about ruptures ; whilst showing their absolute inefficiency to carry out the purpose for which they are intended.

Seventh.—Another demonstration, also general, with accurate estimates showing that the disastrous war which is now carried on in North America has been caused by the evidently mistaken turn which nations have given to the negro question, willing to ruin immense interests solely because of certain ill sounding words.

Eighth and last.—An exposition of the symptoms of anarchy which has shown itself in the principal cities of the Federal Republic, where the grossest outrages were committed against free negroes, and a demonstration of the dangers to that Republic, resulting from the continuance of the war, or from the re-establishment of peace if founded on the former laws in reference to slavery, which dangers will not only be converted into positive and disastrous realities, but will be common to all the colonies where there are negroes to destroy them, unless the nations, who are so deeply interested in the question, and who suffer themselves to be borne away by the turbid current of false philanthropy, do not at once resist its incessant exigencies with that energy which is recommended by the sad experience of the last forty-five years.

Having premised these demonstrations, which, considered as facts, not as theories, form a regular, perfect, clear and convincing body of documents, we can now enter at once into the exposition of the project of treaty, or rather, general agreement which it would be advisable for all nations to adopt who have an interest in the civilization of the world, and who for its sake have been wandering in their resolutions respecting the negroes ; for the purpose of establishing a jurisprudence which shall be as harmonizing as the intention which guides them in their speculations, and as useful to the moral and material interests of said nations and of the negroes themselves, as is demanded by necessity and counselled by experience.

A two-fold humanitarian sentiment counselled the redemption of the negroes when the New World was discovered; although the transfer of these individuals to the plantations established in America at the beginning of the sixteenth century was not altogether equitable. By the practice established by said sentiment, many thousands of unfortunate beings were benefitted. The Indians, not having the power of endurance to bear all the new obligations imposed upon them by the civilization introduced by their conquerors, were relieved of the most arduous tasks, these being laid upon the negroes; and these Africans, being always engaged in an inhuman and cannibal warfare in their own country, would have perished in their fiendish sacrifices had not the system of redemption been established. In the course of time, with the desire to perfect the basis of our civilization, another equally humane sentiment, which sprang from an exaggerated levelling principle, advised the abandonment of those speculations of three centuries back, which were based on the principles of charity and of the salvation of man by means of labor. The realization of this new sentiment also produced its natural fruits; and whereas those of the former were to economize human blood, until then lavished without stint in horrible hecatombs, and the improvement of immense districts, which by the mysterious providence of God had until then been unprofitable to the civilized world; those of the latter, in opposition to the former, restored things to their former state, which proved detrimental to the negroes both in America and Africa, and sowed among the whites the seeds of so much discord and devastation, that the mind cannot dwell on them without horror and dismay.

This being stated not at random but on the demonstrations already made, it will now be necessary to reconcile the extreme opinions, in order that they may all meet upon a common centre, to realize the generous idea from which both sprung. And as the initiation of any good measure is the patrimony of none, individuals and communities having the right to take it whenever experience justifies their resolutions, the United States of America, now since they are under the necessity of settling their difficulties in a general treaty respecting the institution of compulsory labor, or any other nation more or less interested in the question, should hasten to adopt the project which I here propose, in order to make it available to all; not absolutely, as it is written here, for I make no pretensions to infallibility, nor do I imagine that it is perfect either in the whole or in its details ; but such as it emanates from the fundamental idea by which it was inspired, and with such improvements as others, better versed in social morals and public rights, may judge proper and efficient.

And since, as a preamble to said project, I have already said enough for the readers of good faith and all sensible people to know and sustain the basis on which mine rests, it is now time that I should give it without further delay or other arguments, in the following terms :

ARTICLE 1.—Experience having demonstrated in an unquestionable manner that the institution of compulsory labor of the negroes, which is called slavery, is eminently christian and civilizing, with the exception of the errors of its nomenclature, which is of pagan origin and should disappear forever from among enlightened nations, as also those vices or abuses of said institution which, to a certain extent, justify the exertions made for many years to abolish it, the Powers who have signed this common pact agree, willingly and with perfect harmony, in declaring the institution of organized labor of the negroes to be legal in all nations, states, colonies, provinces, territories, districts, or plantations which may require it, or desire to use it; the effects of this declaration being subject only and exclusively to the administrative authority of the respective localities which may avail themselves of it, or to the supreme authority of the countries or states respectively, in accordance with the political organization of said localities.

ART. 2.—It being contrary to the common law of nations for any Power to exert any authority or influence, to which it has no recognized right, which shall in any manner interfere with the individual liberty, the customs, or the laws of an independent nation which has not solicited from it such direction or interference, the subscribing Powers recognize, collectively and individually, the right of the others to establish, in their political and mercantile relations with other independent Powers, such rules and proceedings as they may deem most expedient, provided always, that the lawful interests of civilized nations be not thereby injured. The subscribing Powers having also agreed in declaring that the prohibition of the redemption of negroes on the African coasts was the result of a grievous error, said redemption being, in fact, a truly humane and merciful system which affords the only means of introducing the light of christian civilization in those unhappy countries where darkness has so long reigned, the aforesaid Powers also declare that the negroes of Africa, Asia and Oceanica, shall be at full liberty to sell their slaves to the contractors who may desire to redeem them ; and all the free individuals of the places above mentioned shall enjoy the privilege of placing themselves, and all such persons of their families as may be dependent on them, under the system of organized labor, such as it will be explained in the following articles.

ART. 3.—Whereas the falsity of the present nomenclature applied to the institution of the organized labor of the negroes, will become evident to all by a comparison between any treatise of ancient law, and the regulations of the present times, or those which have ruled in any of the colonies wherein such labor has been practiced from the discovery of America down to the present day, the subscribing nations agree to prohibit, and do hereby forbid that in future the laboring negroes be called *slaves;* and they agree also in declaring that the so-called *slave trade* is nothing more nor less than the *redemption* of slaves and prisoners, who, from the moment that they are saved by this merciful and humane measure, enter at once into a state of civilization far superior to their former free condition, before they lost it through the tyranny of their rulers or their conquerors.

On this account, the negroes destined to labor, as the foundation of the civilization they are to acquire, shall be designated by the name of *redeemed laborers;* and so it shall be written in all documents of *cession* or *transmission,* which hitherto have been denominated *inheritance* and *sale ;* in the requisitions of *cimmarones* (runaway slaves,) whose name shall hereafter be *fugitives ;* in the citations and summonses of the Courts, and in all the legal acts in which the preservation of the former nomenclature might be offensive to humanity, or render the effects of this treaty inefficient.

ART. 4.—The redemption of negroes will be carried on in those districts where it was formerly done, without restrictions or hindrance which may result to the injury of the redeemers of good faith, whether they belong to a known company or carry on the undertaking on their own account. Of course in such districts of said localities as shall have been organized into a state of civilization, so that the redemption should be contrary to its local legislature, it shall be considered illegal to re-establish in the same the former customs of desolation and tyranny ; and in such cases, (which will not be likely to occur, as the interests of the speculators would suffice to keep them away from such places, when it would be so much easier to obtain their laborers at other points,) the interested nations might establish an absolute or relative prohibition, as might seem best in agreement with the native authorities of the said districts, and under the vigilance of all the Consuls. The Consuls shall also see to the enforcement of the regulations which shall be established for the internal order of the contracting vessels, which regulations shall stipulate the number of negroes that each vessel may carry, according to its tonnage, and the economical and medical attendance which shall be given to the negroes during the passage from their country to the port to which the vessel is consigned.

ART. 5.—In order that selfish personal interest may in no case interfere with the eminently Christian end which the contracting nations propose to obtain in declaring the redemption of negroes to be free, and taking into account at the same time the meritorious act which the masters perform in educating, by means of labor and in behalf of the civilization of the world, people who are so notoriously ignorant and in many places cannibals, the redemption is to be made in the countries of the negroes under the following conditions :—

First.—That the new civil state of the redeemed negroes be permanent, until by means of instalments, or by paying the whole amount at once, they shall refund to their employers the price of their redemption, in the same amount which the redeemers shall have received and no more ; as the instruction which the negroes have acquired to be useful to themselves and to society in the future, is to be considered compensated by the return of their labor until they shall have emancipated themselves from it. With the perpetuity of forced labor until the laborer shall restore the amount of his redemption, not only does the master recover the capital invested to acquire said laborer without any interest, but having the certainty of redeeming another, without additional disbursements, in exchange for the one who emancipates himself, he will not inhumanly overwork him, as he might be inclined to do if it was intended to liberate the laborers unconditionally after a certain number of years. And bearing in mind that the civilization of the Africans could not be effected, for the purposes which will be mentioned hereafter, unless they continue in this state for a certain number of years, even if by their good fortune they could emancipate themselves before the expiration of that time; and considering also that the frequent renovation of laborers on the plantations might cause to the owners great losses, both on account of the dangers to which the negroes are exposed by the change of climate, and for the loss of labor incurred by the first rudiments of their instruction, it will be optional with the master to consent or not to the emancipation of his laborers, before the expiration of ten years from the time of their redemption.

Second.—The emancipated negroes shall not be able to exact, as an absolute right, the privilege of remaining in the country wherein they have served; this right shall always be subservient to the political or administrative local authorities of said territories. But they will have the right to be conveyed back to their native land, at the expense of the respective Governments, and on the conditions which will be hereinafter mentioned; and this right shall not be limited nor deferred on any account, unless it be by war, declared epidemic, absolute impossibility through temporary want of means, or other unforeseen cause.

Third.—The negroes shall submit to the work imposed upon them in conformity to the regulations established to that effect in the countries to which they shall go; but the labor shall not last more than twelve hours each day, with the corresponding time of rest, in ordinary times, and sixteen hours during the harvest or other urgent work in which it is customary to reduce the hours of rest to one-third of the astronomical day. They will also be subject to the penalties established in the special ordinances of their institution for the offenses therein specified, and, in conformity with common right, shall be subject to the penal laws of the country for all transgressions which do not come under that head.

Fourth.—Considering that the white laborers of civilized nations work at least as many hours as are fixed for the redeemed negroes, for a trifling remuneration, which hardly suffices to supply the most urgent necessaries of life, as with it they have to support themselves and their families, pay house rent, clothing, and the expenses of sickness, besides laying aside wherewith to provide for their sustainance when they are out of employment, which in field work frequently occurs in the winter season, and taking into consideration also that the redeemed negroes are exempt from similar straits, because their masters, besides advancing a large capital for their moral and material improvement, furnish them with lodging and clothing, support their families, take care of their wives and children, attend them in their sickness ; and, in fine, provide for all their wants. The said negroes during all the time that they remain in the institution of organized labor shall not receive any wages for their services. But considering also that the institution is to be truly charitable and useful for the civilization of the negroes—firstly, in the countries wherein the labor is organized, and subsequently in their native lands, as will be stated hereafter; considering also that the return of the price of their redemption, besides being just to the masters, will be a stimulus to the negroes, and an encouragement to their industry and love of mechanical labors; and as, without said return, the negro could not emancipate himself, both the masters and the local authorities shall endeavor to facilitate to the redeemed laborers the means of acquiring the price of their emancipation; the former by teaching them some profitable employement in the extra hours of rest, when the work is limited to twelve hours per day, or by giving them plots of land, wherein to raise vegetables or live stock, the proceeds of which shall be their own property; and the latter by establishing municipal measures to raise a redemption fund destined to the efficient assistance of the well behaved and notoriously industrious negroes. For the same reasons which were given for fixing the minimum of the time of the forced labor of negroes at ten years, the laborers will not be allowed to begin to ransom themselves until after five years' service; but, in order to facilitate the ransoming, after the lapse of said five years, the negroes shall be at liberty to begin to deposit in a savings bank, which may be established in each estate, with the intervention of the local syndic, any sum they may be able to spare, however small or large it may be, from the first day of their redemption until the ransom is allowed them; which ransom they can pay in instalments of twenty-five dollars. From the many facilities offered for self-emancipation, it will be very evident that those who, at a certain time, have not emancipated themselves from forced labor, by returning the amount of their redemption money, are not competent to enter the condition of free laborers, owing to some organic defect in their nature.

ART. 6.—With the view of making the redemption useful, not only to the negroes whom an inhuman pratice sacrifices to the barbarity of their own rulers, if the charity of the enlightened nations did not come to their rescue, but also to the lands where they may live as forced laborers, and those they may inhabit after being emancipated, in all the plantations' where there are redeemed negroes, certain alternate hours shall be fixed on feast days, to give them oral instruction, both civil and religious, suitable to their capacity and nature. Said instruction shall refer more particularly to the principles of social morality embodied in the Christian religion, each nation according to their catholic or protestant faith, as all those who may sign this compact agree in the common spirit of the Holy Gospel. And, as there are, besides the laborers of the plantations, others, destined to domestic service, or to the trades in which their respective masters are engaged, the authorities of each country will see that the masters of the said workmen oblige them to attend church, even before they know the language; making them understand the principles of religion and the meaning of the ceremonies which they see performed in the church they attend.

ART. 7.—It being a commendable purpose and an esentially moral duty of the contracting nations to modify the ignominious state of men in a savage state in the districts where the redemption is carried on, they take upon themselves, now and forever, while it shall be necessary, the obligation of forming civilizing establishments, by way of experiment, on the borders of the said districts. With this end, and taking into consideration the situation of the respective colonies, and also the geographical interests of the possessions which each civilized country may have contiguous to the country of the negroes, all the aforesaid nations will agree for the purpose of designating the districts where the experiment of each shall be made. This fundamental operation being carried out with the most perfect harmony between said contracting parties, each one will take to the district which it intends to civilize a sufficient number of laborers already emancipated from forced labor; endeavoring that the sexes shall be in equal number, or, at least, that one third shall be female; which laborers, after laying out the locality of the colony to be established and settled, under the scientific direction of their protectors, will endeavor to draw to them, by means of commerce and a prudent behavior, the friendship of the inhabitants of the vicinity who may frequent the colony. In order that this experiment may not be useless, much care and a special knowledge of the land selected will be needed; endeavoring to have them near the more quiet and less warlike tribes, and prefering the localities which offer natural means of communication with the interior of the country, such as navigable rivers, open valleys, easily accessible mountains, and, above all, a healthy climate and commodious harbors. The civilizing colonies being thus founded in the countries of the negroes, in such a manner that their redemption by labor may produce the fruit which the civilized world must expect, and which no doubt it has all this time wished in vain to reap from the absolute prohibition of the redemption, we shall arrive at last, sooner or later, at the desired end, which is to open to commerce and to social intercourse with the world, that race which now gives rise to serious physiological doubts, owing to their continued state of barbarism; and the most susceptible philanthropy, if it be in good faith, will find nothing to object to, and much to applaud, in the new attitude of the subscribing parties to this compact.

ART. 8.—As the discipline and good order, as well as the material existence of said colonies, might frequently by endangered if left unguarded, each nation or people which have founded such settlements, according to the preceding article, shall keep a naval station to protect their respective colonies, and shall take an active part in the administration of the colonial government, should they deem it proper, if all the contracting parties agree to it. As the cruisers will be utterly useless when this treaty is established as an international law, it-will be easy to establish said stations without additional expenses to the respective nations. In the event of war between any of the contracting nations, the said colonies will be considered neutral ground, and their naval stations, on proving that they are such, will be exempt from all armed aggression, even should those respectively belonging to the belligerent parties happen to meet. The nations which thus protect the colonies shall furthermore send to them religious missions, to strengthen and encourage the Christian faith among the negroes who have acquired it during their term of forced labor.

ART. 9.—Both for the purpose of confining the colored population within the limits of the political and economical views of the respective Governments, and to encourage and extend civilization in Africa, it will be the right of said Governments to continue sending periodically on their own account to the civilizing colonies the negroes emancipated from forced labor in their respective jurisdictions. And in order that this may not be burdensome to the public revenue, said Governments may establish and collect a moderate contribution, not to exceed eight dollars, for each redeemed negro that shall enter their dominions, to form a fund to defray the expenses of those voyages, and all the charitable demands which will naturally arise, wherever use shall be made of the institution of forced labor of the negroes in exchange for their redemption.

ART. 10.—Each country shall be free in accordance with its customs, its laws and organization, to make the regulations by which the negroes are to be governed in their labor ; submitting them, however, to the rules already established in this project of a general treaty, which are binding upon all. As the object which is aimed at in this compact is eminently Christian and civilizing, it would be absurd to suppose that any of the contracting parties will so far abuse its authority as to make said ordinances contrary to the humane spirit of enlightened nations, therefore the discipline and penalties which are to be imposed on the negroes will also be left to the conscience of each people, respectively.

Experience has already shown that the change of name, and the prospect of an absolute freedom, more·or less remote, in places where their gradual emancipation has been attempted, has suddenly inspired the negroes with exaggerated ideas respecting their future rights, making them at once arrogant and presumptuous, and unfitting them for all systematic labor. For this reason, and because the re-establishment of justice and truth in the name of the institution and in the objects of the redemption can in nowise alter or diminish the gratitude and obedience which the negroes owe to their benefactors, nor their obligations as to labor, the local authorities of the places where said institution exists, as well as the owners of estates and all masters in general, will have the right to avail themselves of all the rigor authorized by this compact and by the local municipal ordinances, to remove and repress the effects of that false interpretation of their new civil state, among the negroes who hitherto have been called slaves, and shall hereafter be called redeemed laborers, in conformity to what has been expressed in article 3.

ART. 11.—The children which may be born to the negroes, in the countries where the institution of organized labor exists, will remain in the same condition as their mothers, and in all respects subject to the effects of this compact. Marriage shall be indissoluble, and the children shall not be separated from their parents against their will before the males have attained fourteen years and the females twelve. When the mother emancipates herself from forced labor, her children under four years will also be emancipated without any compensation, provided that their mother takes them with her, whether to the civilizing colony or to her new residence, if she is allowed to remain in the place where she was civilized. The emancipation of the minors may be effected at any time, after they have attained the age above stated, of fourteen and twelve years, provided they pay their master an amount equal to the average cost of the redemption of an African, and shall set out for the civilizing colony in the same manner as the other emancipated negroes. No disposition is made at present as to the freedom of unborn children, as the unreflecting might expect, because the knowledge of the human heart and of the workings of self-interest shows plainly that such a measure would involve, perhaps irremediably, in some places, serious dangers for the mothers when pregnant, as well as for the infants during their period of nursing and before they are in a fit state to do service.

If, owing to some extraordinary cause, either of the Governments should be unable to send to the model colony, the laborers emancipated from forced labor in their jurisdiction, it shall, in lieu thereof, adopt the necessary measures, which are to be previously consigned in the local regulations, in order that said emancipated negroes shall not live in idleness, but work by the day or establish some known and useful business. Vagrancy and idleness must be absolutely proscribed from all countries which are to be the schools of civilization for the redeemed laborers, who will, in their turn, convey to their native land the ideas and habits of labor, as a commencement and end of their future state, which will be infinitely superior to their present condition.

I think that the points on which I have touched will prove sufficient to lay as foundation, as good faith is to preside over the treaties which are proposed. The interests of moral civilization are herein consulted, as slavery legally and virtually disappears, and the labor imposed on the negroes through their redemption is easily redeemable, as the price of self-emancipation is greatly reduced by the increased facility of procuring other laborers, and the masters and overseers can place great facilities for that object within reach of the honest and industrious negroes.

The material interests of the lands which indispensably require the labor of the negroes are likewise secured—the act of emancipation being in no manner prejudicial to the necessities of labor, as the free and uninterrupted redemption will always supply an abundance of laborers from Africa, to take the place of those who emancipate themselves; and the remuneration which the masters receive from the emancipated laborers will enable them to procure others.

The idea of establishing civilizing colonies, which has

been proved practicable by the model colony in Liberia, would, of itself, suffice to incline the Governments interested, to favor the speedy realization of the idea herein set forth. From the creation of the world, down to the present day, the countries where the redemption is carried on have not taken a single step towards civilization; therefore, if the moral end which humanity proposes to itself is the perfection of all the human race, we cannot see why any opposition should be offered to the realization of this generous idea in those unfortunate countries.

This project of treaty presents still another phase by which it will specially recommend itself to the nations: it is useful to all parties, it interferes with no one's rights; on the contrary, it protects and encourages the interests of all; and, furthermore, as there is no reason nor inducement to violate its strict execution, it will re-establish, in this branch of public law, the dignity and inviolability of which it now needs; and will secure peace where it has been perturbed, and where it is now imperilled by the negro question.

It lacks an essential condition, and that is—sufficient importance in the author to secure for it a favorable reception; but God frequently makes use of insignificant instruments to accomplish great works; and, although I am not so presumptuous as to imagine that I am one of the favored ones chosen to work a radical transformation in the human mind with regard to these matters, who can tell how far my counsel may not be productive of good if it is received in a kindly spirit and honored with a careful consideration?

THE END.

INDEX.

PAGE.

CHAPTER I.—The origin of do slavery in primitive times.—Its various characters among the heathens.—Its successive features from the first appearance of Christianity in the countries of the negroes, as those countries were successively discovered.—Cause for redeeming in those countries, and the reason justifying the forced labor exacted from the redeemed negroes in America.—The existence of cannibalism among the people of that race and among the greater portion of savage nations shown by abundant historical facts and other proofs as regards Asia, Africa and America, from the most remote times down to the present day........................

CHAPTER II.—Respective condition of the nations of Eastern Europe when discoveries in Africa and Asia were made towards the South and East.—Why the civilization of said countries was not atempted by means of conquest, and why the enslaving of their inhabitants, for the purpose of civilizing them, by cultivating the New World, was peferred.—First privileges granted to introduce african slaves into America.—These privileges were obtained by the Flemish and the Genoese, anda fterwards by the Portugueso, the Dutch, the French, and the English, until the famous contract of ASIENTO was ma le.—Losses suffered in this undertaking by some Spanish companies and private individuals, arising from their humanity.—Beginning of Spanish legislation in reference to black slaves.—Its eminently moral and protective character.—Obstacles which were opposed to the introduction of slaves in the New World, and for what object 35

CHAPTER III.—The ideas of the ancient laws in matter of slaves excite puclic sentiment against modern slavery.—Radical difference which exist between the legislation of the heathens and that of our times respecting said institution.—Manner in which the Spaniards practically exhibited this difference, from the time that they introduced slavery into their colonies.—Religious principles which predominated in the formation of their laws.—Royal letters patent and circular instructions to the Indies dated 31st May, 1789, respecting the education, treatment and occupation of the slaves.—Comments made on the preceding document for the purpose of doing away errors of great magnitude 45

CHAPTER IV.—The change which took place in the political circumstances of the New World in the beginning of the XIX century, suggested, many years afterwards, some alteration in the legislation concerning the slaves.—Suggestions to this effect made to the Spanish government by the interested parties.—Scrupulous investigations ordered to be made before these suggestions were acted upon.—New ordinances for the regulation of the slaves, issued on

PAGE.

the 14th of November, 1842.—Extraordinary circumstances demand
some strictness in the Island of Cuba.—Conspiracy of the negroes
against the whites in said Island, plotted and conducted by the
English consul: an official record of the process is inserted to prove
the truth of the assertion.—Excepcional measures then dictated
for the regulation of the slaves—They are not practically applied,
the authorities being swayed by the impulse of humanity that governed the former laws, which after all, prevailed at that time, and
are still in force 65

CHAPTER V.—The reason why the legislation and proceeding of the
Spanish Colonies are taken in this work as the type of the legislation and proceedings concerning the slavery of negroes.—How the
free people of color live in Cuba and Porto Rico, where slavery
exists, and in Santo Domingo where it is abolished.—Domestic
service by hire in said countries, both of slave and free servants.—
Other clases of service public and private.—The slaves on the plantations.—Character of their services, and comparison with the services of the white people in free nations.—Means which negro slaves
have of redeeming themselves from labor in the Spanish possessions.
—Corporeal punishments: its legislation and application.—The
punishment inflicted to the negro slaves and that applied to white
soldiers and sailors in some of the European nations, especially in
England, compared.—Legal means which delinquent slaves have to
escape excessive chatisement.—Trustees for the protection of slaves:
their authority and its application.—Right of the slaves to change
their master for just cause and in accordance with law.—Rules
which, in the Spanish possessions, govern in such cases.—Some
historical considerations on the wrongs to which the beneficent
institution of negro labor has been subjected.................... 85

CHAPTER VI.—The condition of the laboring negroes in America is
not that of slavery, which nomenclature has been erroneously applied to it, and is utterly false.—Exertions of the abolitionists to
destroy negro labor.—Investigation on the origin of this idea.—
There is no truly moral principle practically involved in the prohibition of the redemption of negroes, which is called the slave trade.
—The abolition of slavery such as it has hitherto been effected, is
opposed to the civilization of the negroes, to the prosperity of the
Colonies, and to the interests of the whole world.—Origin of the
abolitionist idea, its propagation and diffusion in official spheres.—
The London Philantliropical Society.—Its agents and its organized
propagation.—First concession made by Spain to England as to the
abolition of slavery: additional articles to the treaty of 5th July
1814.—Spirit of the treaty of September 23, 1817, to abolish the
slave trade.—Its effects are contrary to the moral end with which
it was apparently made.—Treaty of 1835 103

CHAPTER VII.—The system of apprenticeship instituted by the English in their Colonies by way of experiment as a substitute for
slavery.—Character of said system and its negative results.—Considerations on the political ends which suggested such a system.—
Uniform efforts of all the English agents to annihilate the slavery
of negroes in the other Colonies.—This system propagated in France.
—The Colonies are officially consulted as to the freedom of the
slaves.—Three systems are proposed by the French government to
tis Colonies.—Analysis and judgment of said systems.—Replies of
the French Colonies to the consultation of the government.—The
Republic of 1848 decrees the freedom of the slaves.—Operation of
the abolitionists in Spain.—A ship of war manned by negroes is
permanently stationed in the harbor of Havana.—The press is set

PAGE.

to work.—They succeed in obtaining that the Spanish government should consult the Colonies on some points of abolitionism.—Evident tendencies to make the Island of Cuba a State similar to that of Hati.—Charges and defences of the facts stated.—Remarkable letter of Lord Howden to Mr. Corbin: some erroneous statements containing offensive allusions to Spain are rectified.—New steps taken by said minister at Madrid to obtain the unconditional freedom of all the people of cólor in the Island of Cuba.—Lord Palmerston's dispatch to Lord Howden on the same subject.—System of diplomatic and parliamentary recriminations.—To introduce disorder in the colonial possessions of Spain, the right of search on the estates is proposed.—Important considerations on all these matters.—The English recommend the substitution of the negroes by contracted Chinese.—Reply of the United States to said proposition. 133

CHAPTER VIII.—Remarks on the unskillful manner in which the treaties that prohibed the redemption of the negroes were drawn up.—The prohibition of the redemption is opposed to the abolition of slavery: this proposition demonstrated.—The treaties now in force in these matters are also opposed to the liberal tendencies and ideas of progress which may have originated them.—Historic results produced by this prohibition in countries peopled by negroes.—The bloody and already famous scenes in Dahomey.—Disastrous effects of said treaties in the slave holding countries which have emancipated their laborers.—The English Colonies.—The French Colonies. . The Republic of Haiti.—Moral and material state of the Spanish possessions.—In the countries where the institution of slavery exists, the number of slaves has increased since the redemption was prohibited.—The blame which on this account has been laid upon the authorities of those countries might be attributed, for the same cause and with greater reason, to the English cruisers. The blame, however, belongs exclusively to the treaties on this matter now in force 163

CHAPTER IX.—Mutiny of the negroes on board the Ship *Regina Cœlis* and bloody destruction of the whites who composed the crew.—Repugnant demonstrations of joy exhibited in the British parliament on the occasion of that butchery.—Attempts made by the British government on the petition of its Colonies to renew the redemption of negroes under another name.—The same thing attempted by the French government.—Case of the Ship *Charles et Georges* captured by Portuguese cruisers.—International conflict it produced between France and Portugal.—The attitude taken by England in consequence of this conflict.—Imperial ordinance of Napoleon III ordering the suspension of the new form of the redemption of negroes, and announcing his treaty for obtaining Chinese in the English possessions in the East.—Detailed analysis of the regulations by which these laborers are governed in the Island of Cuba.—Their civil condition is the same as that of the negro slaves, and it is even worse in some respects.—Remarkable inconsistency which results between the idea of abolishing the redemption of negroes and stimulating the servitude of the Chinese.—Comments on these inconsistencies to show their true phases to public opinion 195

CHAPTER X.—Calamities which the perverseness of the Abolitionists has occasioned in the world.—Civil war of the United States.—Origin and history of the revolt of the South.—Insurrection at Harper's Ferry.—Death of John Brown.—Excitement and blasphemies which it called forth in the North, and in the slave States.—Fruitless efforts to maintain peace.—Municipal elections.—Parlia-

PAGE

mentary commotions.—The election of Lincoln renders war inevitable.—Proclamations of the Executive abolishing slavery in the rebellious States and respecting it in the others.—The constitutional legality of said proclamations analyzed.—Their negative results towards the re-establisment of the Union.—Remarkable documents as to its contradictory sense.—Aspect taken by the civil war after the issuing of the said proclamations. — Calamities brought down on the people, on the National Treasury, and on the public credit... 216

CHAPTER XI.—Anarchy begins to manifest itself in the Northen States.—Political parties into which the federals are divided, and the principles that each profess.—Brief sketch of their respective political history.—Their characters in the present war.—Dangerous changes produced by the war on the public customs of the country. —Supremacy of the military over the political institutions of the Republic.—Famous outrage of General Burnside against Representative Vallandigham.—Commotion produced by the deed in all the States.—Demonstrations in favor of peace made by the democrats to check the progress of military despotism.—Famous meeting in New York on the 18th of May 1863.—Attitude of the Governor of the State in favor of said meeting.—Demonstrations in opposition by the dominant party.—Means of which the government avails itself to annul the combinations of the partisans of peace.—New treaty with England concerning the negroes.—The invasion of Maryland and Pensylvania by the confederates coincides with all that has been said.—The exasperation of the political parties of the North in presence of the common danger.—Triumphs of the federals in the war.—Republican meeting in opposition to the democrats.—Some emisaries of the London Abolitionists take part in these irritating demonstrations. — The conscription of three hundred thousand men.—Reasons why it was decreed, and manner in which the interested parties explain it.—Riot in New York.— Horrors of anarchy.—Horrible persecution and murder of negroes as a natural result of so many aberrations...................... 245

CHAPTER XII.—The necessity of making peace, and on what basis it should be made.—Obstacles which the question presents on account of the international rights in reference to the negroes.— Various combinations which are announced for the purpose of putting an end to the war.—They are analized and the results are unfavorable.—The peace cannot be solid and lasting unless the existing treaties on the redemption are revised.—With this fundamental improvement the peace would be indestructible between the North and the South.—Project of a treaty to arrive at that object.— The great question whether the two sections should unite or separate politically at the time of making peace.—Authoritative opinions which have been given and still exist in favor of and against both objects or ends.. 209

CHAPTER XIII.—Features which the international treaties should have in order that they may be inviolate.—It is shown that these features do not exist in the treaties which have been made for the prohibition of the redemption.—General summary of all the propositions demonstrated in this work.—Doctrines which result from them, and natural applications indicated by the same.—Project of a general treaty to restore public right in the matter relating to negroes, satisfying true morality, protecting all interests created since the discovery of America and improving civilization in African soil.—Considerations which arise out of the said project of treaty. 293